Dedication

This is Virginia's and Robin's book as much as ours—L. L. and M. C. W.

THE
TRINITY ALPS
a hiking and backpacking guide

Luther Linkhart
with **Michael White**

WILDERNESS PRESS
Berkeley

First Edition July 1983
Second Edition March 1986
Second Printing July 1987
Third Printing August 1990
Fourth Printing November 1991
THIRD EDITION September 1994

Photographs, except for a few that include the authors, are by the authors
Design by Luther Linkhart
Foldout map drawn by Jeffrey P. Schaffer
Cover design by Larry B. Van Dyke

Library of Congress Card Catalog Number 94-27756
International Standard Book Number 0-89997-176-8
Manufactured in the United States of America

Published by Wilderness Press
              2440 Bancroft Way
              Berkeley, CA 94704
              (510) 843-8080

              Write for free catalog

Library of Congress Cataloging-in-Publication Data

Linkhart, Luther.
    The Trinity Alps : a hiking and backpacking guide / Luther
Linkhart with Michael White. — 3rd. ed.
        p.   cm.
    ISBN 0-89997-176-8
    1. Hiking—California—Trinity Alps—Guidebooks. 2. Backpacking—
California—Trinity Alps—Guidebooks. 3. Trinity Alps (Calif.)—
Guidebooks. I. White, Michael.
GV19942.42.C22T755 1994
917.94'21—dc20   94-27756
                                                          CIP

Front cover: Caribou Lake
        Photo © 1994 David Muench

Acknowledgments

Many people were involved in the writing and production of this book. I am deeply indebted to all of them for their help.

My wife, Virginia, walked almost all of the trails with me, cheerfully planning, backpacking, cooking and encouraging in sometimes less than ideal conditions. She also transcribed my trail notes, typed and retyped the manuscript, corrected my spelling, and never lost faith that the book would somehow be completed.

Roger Denney, my long-time trail and fishing companion and professional editor, read the manuscript and improved my style and grammar while leading me gently in the direction of better communication. He, his charming wife Jacqueline, and their daughter Pamela also walked a good many miles of trail with us.

The U.S. Forest Service information persons at Weaverville, Big Bar and Coffee Creek ranger stations, whose names I regrettably neglected to ask, were always cheerfully helpful and informative, as were the wilderness rangers we met on the trails.

Others who walked with us, provided information or were generally helpful include Scott Abrams, Doug Andrews, Lisa Harvey, David Linkhart, Edward Linkhart, Lyda Linkhart, Paul Milburn, and Ruth Murray.

L. Linkhart, December 1985

First and foremost, I thank my lovely wife, Robin, without whom my contribution to this project would have been next to impossible. Her support, encouragement and enthusiasm were invaluable, particularly when she was home and I was alone in the Trinities. She was also a tremendous help in graciously editing my manuscripts.

Special thanks are expressed to our niece, Carmel Snyder, who spent many days watching over our two boys, David and Stephen, while I explored the wilderness.

Link and Virginia have been tremendously helpful in passing on the responsibilities of their creation to me. Their confidence in my ability to carry on with what they have already birthed and nurtured has been quite encouraging. Together they have laid a marvelous foundation by their hard work and diligence. Just getting to know both of them through this process has been a true delight.

Acknowledgment also needs to be made to Thomas Winnett of Wilderness Press for believing in my ability to carry on this project.

M. C. White, December 1993

Table of Contents

Table of Contents

Chapter 1

INTRODUCTION

Pretend for a moment that you are driving north on Interstate 5 south of Redding, California, on a glorious spring day when a north wind has cleared the air in the upper Sacramento Valley so you can see for a hundred miles. As you top a ridge, you and your passengers are enthralled by the frosted beacon of Mount Shasta towering into the sky directly north. Over to the northwest you see an intriguing row of snow-capped peaks beyond the lower ridges close to Redding. Most of your fellow riders are surprised to see snowy mountains over there toward the coast, but a few recognize the Trinity Alps, and regale the group with accounts of marvelous past experiences there. With the possible exception of fish stories, they are probably telling the truth.

For the purposes of this book, the Trinity Alps is an area of approximately 525,000 acres of splendid wilderness and near-wilderness drained by the Trinity, Scott and Salmon rivers in northwest California. Half a million acres, more than 781 square miles, is in the Trinity Alps Wilderness, designated by Congress in the California Wilderness Act of 1984. This magnificent wilderness are includes all of the 234,000 acres previously protected in the Salmon–Trinity Alps Primitive Area plus, obviously, a great deal more.

By comparison with the Sierra Nevada or the Cascades, the Trinity Alps are a small range of mountains in both height and area. Bigger is not necessarily better, however. The Trinity Alps have rushing streams, high waterfalls, gorgeous mountain lakes dimpled with trout rises, glaciated granite peaks, remnant glaciers and cool, deep forests plus some unique features of their own.

What the Trinity Alps don't have, to the extent of other mountain ranges, is crowds of people. Only a few areas in the Alps tend to be crowded at any time. Part of the purpose of this book is to tell you about less-used places that, in some cases, can tolerate more visitors than areas that are currently getting heavier use.

Diamond Lake hangs on a shelf above Stuart Fork canyon

Introduction

The Trinity Alps yield their inner secrets and pleasures only to hikers, backpackers and equestrians. Automobile-bound visitors to Clair Engle Lake and Trinity River resorts see only a little more of the Alps than they would from Interstate 5 on that bright spring day. The general purpose of this book is to inform and inspire hikers, backpackers and equestrians. If we also persuade some occupants of automobiles and motor homes to try a little backcountry exploration, we will be very flattered and pleased.

Natural History

Geology

If you crumple a piece of paper into a ball, then spread it out part way so that it is still crinkled and creased in all directions, you will have an approximate micromodel of the topography of the Trinity Alps. Although the Alps do form a generally east-west divide between the Trinity River drainage to the south and the Scott and Salmon river drainages to the north, the Alps' contorted ridges, canyons and peaks seem to run helter-skelter in all directions.

The Alps are only vaguely related, geologically, to the Coast Ranges to the west, and not at all to the volcanic Cascades beginning with Lassen Peak and Mount Shasta to the east and north. They are, in fact, the southern part of the Klamath Mountains, which include the Marbles and the Siskiyous farther north.

According to plate-tectonics theory, much of the build-up of the Klamath Mountains is the result of ancient seabed deposits, largely volcanic in origin, being scraped off the surface of an oceanic plate as it slid under the edge of the North American plate. In the process, tremendous pressures metamorphosed the deposits into uptilted and distorted strata of slate, quartzite, schist, gneiss, chert and soapstone. Isolated unmetamorphosed sandstones, limestones, mudstones and conglomerates can be attributed to later sedimentation and fallout from eruptions in a nearby volcano chain.

There is no evidence of volcanic lava flows or eruptions within the Klamath Mountains. Granitic magmas did well up at various times, however, and push into the older, overlying rocks. Most of the higher peaks of the Trinity Alps are composed largely of granite. Other igneous rocks, known as mafic and ultramafic, also squeezed up into faults and cracks in the earth's crust. The high iron content of much of this rock accounts for the weathered red and rust colors in a number of peaks and ridges of the Alps.

Further upheavals, lateral movements, and constant erosion over millions of years gave many of the lower ridges and canyons much the same shape as they have today, but the higher peaks and ridges got their final contours from the glaciers that began to form 1.5 million years ago. Although they ran down the canyons only a few miles, the massive glaciers removed cubic miles of rock from the higher areas, ground it up, and deposited it lower down.

The glaciers receded 10–15,000 years ago, leaving behind many small lakes in cirques at the heads of U-shaped valleys with fantastically carved divides between them. Some of the large valleys were dammed by moraines, forming large lakes and marshes that eventually became some of the present meadows. Morris Meadow is an outstanding example.

Continuing erosion distributed glacial till farther down the canyons, and put the finishing touches on the landscape you see today. Elevations range from 900 feet in the lower Trinity River canyon to 9002 feet at the top of Thompson Peak.

Climate

Although the Alps are much wetter than the Sacramento Valley and many other parts of northern California, they are not nearly as wet as some places along the north coast. Precipitation varies greatly in this relatively small area, from as much as 80 inches per year on some of the higher west-facing slopes to less than 20 inches in some of the lower canyons. Most of the precipitation occurs in the winter months, but thunderstorms are not uncommon during the summer.

Vertical strata near Boulder Creek Lakes

Long Canyon shows typical U-shape carved by glaciers

Introduction

Temperature variations are much greater than on the coast, and at higher elevations temperatures are much colder in winter than in the Central Valley. Even Weaverville, at 2000 feet elevation, gets some snow almost every winter. Snowpacks at higher elevations build up to 10–20 feet, and are an important source of water for the Central Valley Project. High-country trails are usually clear of snow by late June, but snow may linger all summer on north slopes in heavy snow years.

Summer daytime temperatures can exceed 90° even at 5–6000-foot elevations. Down in the lower canyons it can get up to 110°. Day-to-night temperature differentials may be as much as 45°.

Plants

An amazing variety of plants grow in the Trinity Alps, most obvious of which are the trees. The forests are marvelously diverse, including more species than any other place we have visited in the United States. They also include some of the largest individuals of some species that we have ever seen. A friend from Idaho, who accompanied us on one of the trips for this book, stopped and stared in absolute disbelief at the first 200-foot sugar pine she had ever seen.

Two unusual conifer species, weeping spruce and foxtail pine, are fairly common in the higher elevations of the Trinity Alps, and rare elsewhere. Shasta red fir grows only north of Redding in California and in southwestern Oregon.

Mixed-evergreen forest along Big French Creek

Very large red firs at 6000 feet on Salmon River Divide

The best way to discuss the forests and other flora of the Trinity Alps is to look at the plant communities that exist there. As in other mountain ranges, plant communities are determined primarily by elevation. However, many other factors, such as soil type, rainfall, wind and north or south exposure also influence where species grow, so dividing lines are never distinct. You will find more intermixing of species between plant communities in the Trinity Alps than in most other mountain ranges. For what they are worth, descriptions of six communities follow.

Mixed-Evergreen Forest—This is the low-elevation community up to approximately 3000 feet. It also includes isolated riparian (streamside) communities that may be found as high as 5–6000 feet. The broadleaf trees included are alders, dogwood, big-leaf maples, black oaks, hazel nuts and Oregon oaks. Evergreens other than conifers are madrones, chinquapins, tanoaks, California live oaks and canyon oaks. Douglas fir is by far the most common conifer in this community, but ponderosa and Jeffrey pines also appear, and sparse stands of Digger pines grow on lower, dry slopes.

Some bushes grow like trees in the lower riparian communities. These include coast, red and blue elderberries, ceanothus, dogwoods, hazelnuts and manzanitas. Thick stands of chaparral extend over dry hillsides. Several varieties of ceanothus and manzanita are the most common bushes. Gooseberries, currants, wild roses and poison oak are also included.

Poison oak, in its many forms ranging from low bushes to tree-climbing vines, is the bane of this plant community, and it extends into the next higher community. It is a violent skin irritant to most people who touch it, and, if you should happen to burn it in a campfire, inhalation of the smoke may cause serious poisoning requiring hospitalization. Its shiny, three-leaves-in-a-bunch foliage is easy to recognize. The Forest Service has published a small, free brochure on poison oak that is very helpful. Ask for it at any ranger station in the area.

Mixed-Conifer Forest—The biggest trees grow here between 3000 and 6000 feet—sugar pines, ponderosa pines, Jeffrey pines, Douglas firs, white firs and incense cedars. Black oaks and alders are here as well as at lower elevations. Vine maples and mountain ash are added. These are the magnificent forests through which you will do most of your hiking.

Shrubs such as azaleas, raspberries, wood roses and coast huckleberries grow in small openings in the forest. Pinemat manzanitas and thimbleberries are common understory plants. Large expanses of brush are not common at this level but, where they do appear, they include huckleberry oaks and other scrub oaks not found at lower elevations.

Red-Fir Forest—Red firs and their subspecies, Shasta red firs, occur almost equally in the Trinity Alps between 5000 and 7000 feet. They often overlap considerably with mixed conifers in the next lower community, especially white firs. Shasta red firs are distinguished by slightly larger, beautiful cones with bracts longer than the scales, giving the cones a silver-flecked appearance.

Western white pines begin to replace their close relatives, the sugar pines, at this level, and the Jeffrey pines take over completely from their relatives, the ponderosas. Mountain junipers are not common in the Trinity Alps, but a few show up in this community. Mountain hemlocks and weeping spruces grow on north-facing slopes and in cirques.

A few groves of cottonwoods line streams in this community. Alders are reduced to bushes, and usually are associated with willows in wet areas. Different varieties of willows grow at all elevations, but are usually shrubs here. Mountain ash and vine maple are also fairly common broadleaf shrubs.

This is the highest community in which there are large stands of trees. Above these elevations trees grow singly or in small clusters.

Some southern exposures at this level are covered with large areas of solid brush, known as mountain chaparral. Ceanothus, manzanita, chokecherry, service berry, tobacco bush, and huckleberry oak are the primary components.

Subalpine Forest—Foxtail pines are at home at elevations of 6500–8000 feet along with a few whitebark pines and mountain mahoganies growing on the most exposed, inhospitable crests. Surprisingly, Jeffrey and western white pines and even occasional incense cedars persist, but in startlingly modified forms. They are stunted and contorted here, pruned by the wind and flattened by the weight of winter snows. The only trees standing reasonably erect on the crests are the closely related foxtail and whitebark pines.

Flattened Jeffrey pine   Weeping-spruce and foxtail-pine fronds

Foxtail pines are sometimes mistaken for firs at first glance. They have short, five-to-the-bundle needles that grow tightly spaced all the way around supple branches that look a little like small, dark green foxtails.

Mountain hemlock grows in protected pockets on north slopes, usually out of the worst winds. Weeping spruces, scattered around the highest lakes and cirques in the wettest and coldest places, also avoid winds.

The only brush in the higher elevations of this community is flattened mats of willows and pinemat manzanita, usually confined to small areas. Mountain chaparral extends into the lower part of the subalpine belt.

Alpine—Only a few true alpine ecosystems exist in the Trinity Alps. They are on or near the summits of the highest peaks, close to 9000 feet elevation. No trees survive at this altitude in the Alps, and only a few shrubs and heaths hug the surface of small pockets of soil between the rocks. The most abundant plants are lichens, but a remarkable number of wildflowers burst into bloom in the very short frost-free period in late summer.

Mountain Meadow—There are meadows in the broadleaf and mixed-evergreen forest community, but true mountain meadows begin in the mixed conifer community, and extend through the subalpine. The obvious plants in mountain meadows are grasses, sedges and wildflowers, but there are also bushes and two species of trees that thrive in or at the edges of the meadows. The trees are lodgepole pines and quaking aspens. Neither is very common in the Trinity Alps, but they are a pleasant surprise when you find them in some of the higher meadows.

Angelica in mountain meadow

Bear grass

Introduction

Wildflowers—More than 100 acres of wildflowers bloom in a solid mass in late July and early August on a northeast-facing slope at the head of Long Canyon. Probably dozens of species are represented, but the most prominent are vivid red paintbrushes, blue and purple lupines, white angelica, and creamy western pasqueflowers that turn into miniature fuzzy white mops when they go to seed.

In a completely different location, under evenly spaced red firs on the south side of the Salmon River divide, the waxy white blossoms of queen's cups and twinflowers shine against the dark background of the forest floor.

The preceding paragraphs give only a small indication of the diversity of the hundreds of species of plants that thrive in the Trinity Alps. To name and describe them all would require more space than is available in this entire book. A great deal of pleasure comes from being able to identify, as well as admire, the many flowers you are sure to see on any summer trip in the Alps. For that purpose we recommend *A Field Guide to Pacific States Wildflowers,* by Theodore F. Niehaus and Charles L. Ripper, published by Houghton Mifflin.

You will be surprised by the number of species you can identify here that are described in that guide as being normally found somewhere else. This is a meeting place for plant species from the Cascades, the Pacific Coast, the Sierra Nevada and the Central Valley of California. In addition, at least one species, the California pitcher plant, found more often in the Trinity Alps than anywhere else, is rare and listed as of special concern in California. Please do not pick any specimens, and be careful not to damage living plants.

Many locations and descriptions of wildflowers are noted in the trips at the points where they occur, but some general descriptions may be in order: The largest displays of flowers are found in mountain meadows. The species vary greatly with the type of meadow and the elevation. You will find California pitcher plants in the wettest, steepest meadows at fairly high elevations, but

California pitcher plant

Washington lily

Moss-covered rock and five-finger ferns

they also grow around the edges of ponds in small openings in the mixed-conifer and red-fir communities. Angelica and yampa bloom in almost all meadows except the very dry ones on flat ridgetops. Those high, dry and often gravelly meadows support pussy paws, cat's ears, sulfur flowers, and cinquefoils. This is only a sample of the marvelous variety of flowers found in the meadows. You will enjoy making you own discoveries and lists.

Streamside locations support a completely different group of wildflowers. Most showy of these are the head-high spikes of larkspurs and monkshoods. Marsh marigolds, buttercups, and Jeffrey's shooting stars bloom beside little rills at higher elevations as soon as the snow melts. Later, and even higher, a dozen or more varieties of monkey flowers display their wide range of colors beside seeps and springs. Edible swamp onions grow right in icy little streams.

A surprising variety of flowers bloom in the deep shade of the mixed-conifer community. Early in the season you will see woodland stars, milkmaids and trilliums. Later, the parasitic flowers, such as coral roots and pinedrops, display their ghostly beauty on leafless forest floors. Mahonia and salal, usually thought of as north Pacific Coast plants, grow under thick stands of Douglas firs. Washington lilies prefer a little more sun in openings in the broadleaf and mixed-evergreen forest, as do gilias, irises, and mints.

The least-often seen flowers are those of the alpine communities, not because they hide, but because few people get up there to see them during their short, supreme effort to bloom and reproduce before the snow comes back. These include phlox, heather, wandering daisy, buttercup, and tiny lupines, coloring small pockets of precious soil among the rocks.

Other Plants—Ferns, mosses, and lichens are abundant in the Trinity Alps. In some lower canyons they approach rainforest proportions, covering rocks and trees alike with a green mantle. In other low elevations gray strands of Spanish moss drape from tree limbs, and staghorn lichens stand out from the trunks.

At boundaries between meadows and forests in the mixed-conifer community, ferns grow head-high, crowding the trails. Acres of brake ferns cover some of the meadows at the red-fir level.

A variety of lichens add their colors to the rocks higher up, and delicate five-finger ferns decorate dripping grottos.

Animals

Warm-Blooded Animals—The most abundant warm-blooded animal in the Trinity Alps is the beef cow. The part of the Alps north and east of Swift Creek is heavily grazed. Fairly heavy use of pack stock in this area puts an added load on the available forage. Although livestock numbers have been reduced overall in recent years, some sections still suffer severely, and a few streams and lakes are heavily polluted. Administration of grazing regulations by the Forest Service is complicated by private land inholdings and split jurisdiction.

Introduction

Another quite common, and wild, large, warm-blooded animal in the Trinity Alps is the black bear. As is common throughout California, the Alps have seen a dramatic increase in the bear population during recent years. You may not see many black bears, since they are quite wary of humans, but be prepared for that possibility. If you don't hang your food properly and clean up your garbage, however, you may hear a bear in the middle of the night, or even meet him face to face as he tears up your gear to get at *his* food. You will see bear tracks, scats (feces) and other signs along most of the trails except the busiest ones. Where you see rotted water-check logs torn out of the tread and ripped apart, it usually isn't a human vandal who was responsible, but a bear looking for grubs in the rotten wood.

Columbian black-tailed deer appreciate the pathways humans have built for them as much as the bears do, so you will see deer signs on all the trails. You will also see does and fawns and, if you're lucky, a buck or two. Every buck has been hunted since he was a year old, so they are justifiably wary. Noises in your campsite at night are much more likely to be made by a deer than a bear. Deer like camp food, especially anything salty, and have been known to chew on sweaty clothes, boots and pack straps. Some old does that have been fed in the past have become terrible pests in the more popular camping areas. Please do no feed them, and above all do not pet them—they can be dangerous, and they are also infested with ticks and lice. Still, a doe and her twin fawns drinking at a fog-shrouded stream at dawn is a most memorable sight. Mountain lions, the deer's only predator besides humans, are very scarce in the Trinity Alps.

The next largest animal in the area is the coyote. The coyote is seldom seen, but is heard fairly often on moonlit nights. Coyote calls, passed back and forth from ridge to ridge, are a thrilling wilderness symbol. Martens, fishers, and long-tailed weasels are also seldom seen, but do frequent the Alps.

Columbian black-tailed doe

Bear and people tracks
on North Fork Coffee Creek trail

Small warm-blooded animals of the rodent order swarm in some parts of the Alps. Mice, chipmunks and ground squirrels prosper where the most humans visit, partly because humans feed them directly, and partly because humans feed them indirectly with remnants of horse feed, horse droppings, and garbage. There is an unfortunate relationship between large rodent populations and large rattlesnake populations—rattlesnakes move in to take advantage of the abundant food supply. We were amazed at the almost total absence of rodents (and rattlesnakes) in parts of the western Trinity Alps where very few people go. Bears, bobcats, weasels, and coyotes may also have something to do with the absence of rodents there.

One rodent that we certainly hope doesn't go away is the cheeky Douglas squirrel (or pine squirrel, or chickaree). The chickaree's strident scolding and frenetic activity in the mixed-conifer and red-fir communities are always a source of amusement to passers-by. The chickaree is never a camp robber, but he may drop a green pine or fir cone uncomfortably close to you as you pass under his tree. Those piles of cone scales and cores under the trees are his.

The much larger California gray squirrel, which lives in the mixed-evergreen forest community, is very shy and seldom seen. Skunks, raccoons, ringtail cats, opossums, and foxes also frequent this level, and rarely move above it.

Oddly, the western states' largest rodent, the porcupine, is rare in the Trinity Alps, although quite common elsewhere in California.

Bats can be seen on any evening, hunting insects over lakes, ponds, and meadows. Their marvelous flight never ceases to amaze.

Birds—Nothing starts the day quite as nicely as birdsong outside your tent. Unless the weather is totally bad, you will never be without that gentle awakener in the Trinity Alps. Vireos, warblers, robins, and finches greet you in the mixed-conifer forest. Of course, you will probably also hear a few raucous jays. In the higher red-fir forest you may hear a mountain bluebird, a golden-crowned kinglet, or a hermit thrush. The distant drumming of a pileated woodpecker isn't all that bad—it's good to know that some creature is that industrious so early.

On the lower trails you are sure to find the dust wallows of California quail, and you may hear a mother quail calling to her chicks to freeze. Even though you have just heard their peeping, you won't be able to find a single chick after they freeze. Their camouflage renders them literally invisible. Blue grouse also have excellent camouflage—you seldom see them in the grass and brush until they explode from under your feet, doubling your heart rate.

Two different university research groups were studying hummingbirds in the Alps while we were walking the trails there. Both groups were working at the subalpine level, where masses of flowers supply hummers with food in midsummer.

Raptors are well-represented at all elevations. Many species of hawks course the ridges, and golden eagles nest in a few places. Even bald eagles have been seen in recent years. A few ospreys nest along the Trinity River, and owls can be heard at night as high as the red-fir forest.

Literally hundreds of avian species are represented in the Trinity Alps. If you want to add to your list, bring your Peterson's *Field Guide to Western Birds* and your field glasses. You are sure to find something new.

Cold-Blooded Animals—Reptiles and amphibians are common in all the Trinity Alps communities except the alpine. Various snakes, such as rubber boas, garter snakes, gopher snakes, king snakes, and various water snakes are fairly common in all the communities up to the subalpine.

Any land mass with as much water in and on it as the Trinity Alps is bound to be home to many amphibians. Red-legged and yellow-legged frogs thrive in the wet meadows and ponds in the mixed-conifer forest community. Higher up you may find tiny green tree frogs. An amazing variety of salamanders live in damp forest areas up to the subalpine level.

The amphibians that get the most attention are the newts and salamanders that live in many of the middle- and lower-elevation lakes. Some of them are 8–10 inches long and bright red, quite startling as they come up to breathe when you are expecting trout.

Insects—Insects infest the Trinity Alps as they do all other earthly paradises. Only a few of them are a problem to humans and, of course, many of them are quite beautiful. Mosquitos can be a considerable annoyance in many areas right after the snow melts. Repellents are helpful during the day, and a screened tent is a godsend at night.

Horseflies and deer flies are irritating later in the summer, but at least they go away at nightfall. Ticks can be a nuisance at low and middle elevations, and can cause infections and Lyme disease. Repellents sprayed on collars, cuffs and pantlegs will help, but the best prevention is daily inspection of your entire body. If discovered soon after it attaches, a tick can be removed by pinching up the skin tightly where the tick is attached and, when the legs begin to wiggle, pulling firmly on the tick's body. If you find an engorged and embedded tick that has been attached for a day or two, you may not be able to get it out in one piece. If so, medical aid is indicated as soon as reasonably possible.

Human History

Three natural resources have influenced the human history of the Trinity Alps almost to the exclusion of everything else. They are, in chronological order, gold, timber and water.

The Natives—Gold meant very little to the Wintu Indians, who lived very well along the Trinity River and its tributaries for hundreds, possibly thousands, of years without even knowing the gold was there. The Wintu had no use for gold, and they certainly had plenty of timber and water for their needs. As a matter of fact, they had just about everything else they needed. Deer and elk were plentiful, providing food and clothing. Each autumn brought salmon and steelhead up the river to be harvested and, in most years, a bountiful crop of acorns. In the summer there were berries and seeds, and small animals to be snared. Bark and rushes roofed their homes, and sedges and willows provided materials for beautifully woven baskets.

The winters were bearable along the river, and the Wintu had no reason to go very high into the mountains at any time except when they went on trading expeditions to the coast or the central valley. What need had a Wintu for gold? Would gold keep a grizzly from attacking? In the end, of course, gold destroyed the Wintu completely. The white men wanted the gold, and the Wintu were in the way.

Gold—Although Jedediah Smith, and possibly other trappers before him, may have visited the Trinity country earlier, it was Major Pierson P. Reading who got the credit for discovering and naming the Trinity River in 1845. The Trinity River got its name by mistake—Major Reading thought the river emptied into the Pacific Ocean at Trinidad Bay, so he named it "Trinity," the English translation of "Trinidad." It was four years later that two miners, looking for a way to the ocean, discovered that the river flows into the Klamath River, not into the ocean at all.

There is conjecture that Major Reading discovered gold at the same time he discovered the Trinity River. That would have been at least three years before John Marshall discovered gold at Sutter's mill. If Major Reading did discover gold on his first trip to the Trinity, he kept very quiet about it. The big rush to the Trinity River didn't start until late 1849 or early 1850.

Introduction

By the end of 1850 the gold rush on the Trinity River and its tributaries was in full swing, and Weaverville had almost as many people as it has today. Trinity Centre (original spelling) had a lot more people than it has today. Even in 1850 several of those people were Chinese. By 1853 close to 2000 Chinese lived and worked in the Weaverville area alone. The Chinese were good for the economy. They worked cheap. If they mined their own claims, they were promptly robbed by renegade whites. Most importantly, they paid four dollars a head per month to the government for the privilege of digging. That went a long way toward supporting the public sector in the 1850s. Whites paid nothing, even though they were also immigrants.

There was even a one-day Chinese tong war in 1854, instigated and promoted by whites. The whites didn't allow the Chinese to use guns (white bystanders might be hit), so the "Hongkongs" and "Cantons" fought it out with knives, spears and hatchets in a field near Weaverville. White "military advisers" on both sides cheered them on and bet on the outcome. The "Cantons" won, but many Chinese on both sides lost—at least ten dead and two or three times that many wounded. There were no casualties among the white "advisers."

More people swarmed over the Trinity Alps (they weren't called Alps then) in the 1850s than have been there at one time since. In less than 10 years most of the available placer gold had been mined, and the Chinese moved on to build a part of the transcontinental railroad across the Sierra Nevada. Only the Weaverville Joss House, museum artifacts, and miles of carefully piled boulders along Trinity Alps streams remain to remind us of the former Chinese community.

The Wintu fared worse than the Chinese. They were simply exterminated, leaving few reminders that they had ever been here.

After the placer gold had been diminished, gold mining became big business. Capital and corporations are required to finance giant dredges, excavate deep shafts and drifts, and build miles of ditches and flumes. This larger-scale mining continued in the Trinity Alps through the 1930s. The most obvious example of large-scale mining is the La Grange Mine, which brought water 29 miles from the lakes at the head of the Stuart Fork in the early 1900s to wash away a big part of Oregon Mountain west of Weaverville, and deposit the remains down Oregon Gulch toward Junction City. You can still see the scars beside Highway 299.

A few individual prospectors and small-scale placer miners have eked out a living in the old way almost to the present. One Mr. Jorstad of Jorstad Cabin on the North Fork Trinity River is an outstanding example. A new breed of gold miner has invaded the Trinity River and the Alps in recent years, however. These miners use gasoline-powered Venturi dredges, wet suits and snorkels to find gold in deep pools that the old-timer placer miners couldn't get at. Existing laws (primarily the 1872 Mining Law) and regulations allow them to work within Trinity Alps Wilderness.

14

Along with the miners of the 1850s came a number of ranchers who homesteaded along the Trinity River, mostly in the area north of Lewiston known as Trinity Meadows, now at the bottom of Clair Engle Lake. Some of their descendants are the cowmen who still take beef cattle to summer pasture in the Trinity Alps.

Mr. and Mrs. Anton Webber, who had traveled extensively in Europe, bought one of these ranches in 1922, and established the Trinity Alps Resort on the Stuart Fork. The Webbers are credited with naming the mountains the Trinity Alps because they resembled the Austrian Alps the Webbers admired so much in Europe.

Timber—The miners and early settlers, although certainly profligate in their use, hardly made a dent in the vast supply of timber in the Trinity Alps. With the coming of railroads in the late 1800s, however, the cutting began in earnest, and logging and sawmilling soon eclipsed mining as the main industry of the Trinity area.

Later improvement of roads and mechanization of logging increased the rate of cutting dramatically, and pushed the cuts to the boundary of the former Salmon–Trinity Alps Primitive Area in many places. In spite of intense pressure on the Forest Service and Congress by lumber companies and other timber interests, however, we now have a magnificent Trinity Alps Wilderness. Checkerboard ownership of some of the land within the wilderness area by timber companies will have to be resolved by land trades and buy-outs. Checker- boarding came about through grants by the federal government in the 1800s of alternate sections of land to the Central Pacific Railroad (now the Santa Fe/Southern Pacific) as inducement to build the transcontinental railroad. Some alternate sections were also granted to state universities and local school districts, and most of these sections also ended up in private ownership.

Water—Many acrimonious, and sometimes fatal, arguments took place among the early miners about water rights, but those arguments were over nothing compared to what happened when the Central Valley Project was voted into existence at the insistence of Central Valley and southern California water users. The CVP steamrollered Trinity County residents and what few conservationists there were in those days, and went about diverting the Trinity River to the Central Valley and southern California.

Trinity, Lewiston and Whiskeytown dams were completed in the early 1960s, drowning Trinity Meadows, among other things, and destroying one of the finest salmon and steelhead fisheries left in California. An effort is still being made to propagate salmon and steelhead at the hatchery below Lewiston Dam, but for all intents and purposes the salmon are now gone, and the steelhead are rapidly diminishing. In place of beautiful Trinity Meadows and a chance to fish for salmon and steelhead we now have the opportunity to water-ski on red-dirt-rimmed Clair Engle Lake.

Recreation—Except for occasional horse-mounted hunting and fishing expeditions, recreational use of the Trinity Alps got started with better roads in the 1920s, and a number of dude ranches and resorts soon flourished around Trinity Meadows, Trinity Center and Coffee Creek. Horses still carried most of the visitors to the backcountry until the late 1950s, when much improved backpacking equipment and lighter, better backpack foods generated a whole new group of wilderness explorers. Backpackers far outnumber horse riders in the Trinity Alps today.

Chapter 2

ACCESS, FACILITIES AND SUPPLIES

Highways, Cities and Towns

Redding on Interstate 5 and Eureka on coastal Highway 101 are the closest cities of any size to the Trinity Alps. Weaverville, point of departure for most of the Trinity Alps trailheads, is a town of 1500 people 47 miles west of Redding and 108 miles east of Eureka on State Highway 299.

Redding is a little over 200 miles north of the San Francisco Bay Area, 160 miles from Sacramento and 545 miles from Los Angeles. Eureka is 295 miles north of San Francisco and 479 miles south of Portland, Oregon. If you are coming south from Oregon on Interstate 5, you should turn off at Yreka, California, and follow State Highway 3 through Callahan to Weaverville, or turn off Interstate 5 at Gazelle, north of Weed, and take Forest Road 17 across to Callahan.

Amtrak and major bus lines stop in Redding, and a local Redding-Eureka bus line stops at Weaverville, Junction City, and other points on Highway 299, but hitchhiking would be the only way to the trailheads. Redding and Eureka have airports with a few commercial flights, and you can rent an automobile in either city. Light airplanes can land at Weaverville and Trinity Center, but no rental vehicles are available. Unfortunately, most visitors must drive their own vehicles to the Trinity Alps.

If you want to stay overnight at Redding on the way to the Trinity Alps, there are plenty of motels and a few good commercial campgrounds. Two public campgrounds are at Whiskeytown Lake, 8 miles west of Redding on Highway 299, but they are often full in midsummer. Stores in Redding offer almost anything you might need at the last minute, with the possible exception of gourmet pack food items. Eureka and Arcata have even more stores, motels, and commercial campgrounds than Redding.

Access, Facilities and Supplies

Weaverville has motels, a hotel, grocery stores, and, as of our latest visit, a sporting-goods store that stocks some pack food as well as fishing gear and flies. The U.S. Forest Service has a district headquarters at Weaverville. It is the best place to get your wilderness permit and the latest trail and weather information. A self-service wilderness-permit station allows you to fill out your own permit when the office is closed. It is on the left as you go out of town on Highway 299 toward Eureka.

Historic buildings dating from gold rush days line the main street of Weaverville. Exterior spiral staircases leading from arcaded sidewalks to the second stories of two old buildings add a quaint touch. The Trinity County courthouse in the center of town is a fine old brick building more than 100 years old. If you have time, the Weaverville Joss House State Historical Park and the J. J. Jackson Memorial Museum, close together on Highway 299, are well worth visiting.

An excellent Bureau of Land Management (BLM) fee campground is a mile down the Trinity River from the Highway 299 bridge at Douglas City 6 miles south of Weaverville. Douglas City is a filling station, motel, and tavern near where Major Reading is supposed to have first seen the Trinity River. You have to drive through the town, off Highway 299, to get to the campground. A rest stop and information booth a mile north on Highway 299 is very convenient.

Junction City, at the confluence of Canyon Creek and Trinity River 8 miles west of Weaverville on Highway 299, is the oldest settlement along the river and the only town with a full-fledged grocery store between Weaverville and west Trinity Alps trailheads. Another excellent BLM fee campground is 1.5 miles down the river from Junction City, and you can get a wilderness permit from a Forest Service work center at the east end of town. Many river resorts, RV camps, taverns, and fishing-tackle shops are strung along the Trinity River west of Junction City. Big Bar ranger station is 16 miles west on Highway 299.

Trinity Center is the only town on the shoreline of Clair Engle Lake, near the eastern part of the Trinity Alps. It is 30 miles north of Weaverville on State Highway 3. It is easy to end up in Wyntoon resort instead of Trinity Center if you miss the turnoff toward the lake just south of the Swift Creek bridge. The present town is not the original "Trinity Centre" of gold rush times at all. The only old building in town is the Odd Fellow hall, which was moved from the original site, now at the bottom of Clair Engle Lake. Trinity Center has the only airstrip close to the Trinity Alps, a motel, grocery store, and two or three fast-food outlets. The Scott Museum is an interesting collection of pioneer memorabilia.

A shortcut from Highway 299 on county roads through the old town of Lewiston will get you to Clair Engle Lake and Trinity Center a little quicker than going through Weaverville. Be careful to turn left toward Highway 3 after you cross the Trinity River below Lewiston Dam unless you want to see Lewiston Lake, Trinity Dam and a lot of red-dirt hills before you get to Highway 3. Lewiston has grocery and sporting-goods stores and a number of

RV camps along the river below town. Steelhead, usually swimming in the pool under the old Trinity River bridge, are worth stopping to look at.

The Coffee Creek road junction with Highway 3 is 40 miles north of Weaverville. Less than a quarter mile west of Highway 3 on it, a right turn leads to the complex that includes a grocery, a filling station, and a Laundromat. The Carrville Inn on the old Carrville road north of Coffee Creek is a most pleasant bed-and-breakfast resort.

Callahan is on Highway 3 north of Scott Summit. It is 65 miles from Weaverville, but only 30 miles by paved Forest Road 17 from Gazelle on Interstate 5 north of Weed. Even if you are coming up from the south, it is faster to go by way of Gazelle If you are coming from Oregon, the best route is Highway 3 from Yreka. Callahan has an old-time general store with a gas pump in front, and that is about all.

Car-Camping and Other Recreation Facilities

In addition to the campgrounds mentioned in the preceding section on highways, cities and towns, the best car-camping campgrounds close to the Trinity Alps are in "the Trinity Unit of the Whiskeytown-Shasta-Trinity-National Recreation Area" around Clair Engle and Lewiston lakes. That is a terrible mouthful of title, but officially that's what it is. You should be able to pick up a folder for the Trinity Unit (Clair Engle and Lewiston lakes) from any ranger station, Forest Service information office, or tourist information facility from Redding out to Big Bar. At least 15 car-camping campgrounds are shown within the Recreation Area on the map in the folder, but not all of them are open at all times. All these campgrounds charge fees.

Of course, you can do more than camp in the Recreation Area. You can picnic and swim at a number of locations around Clair Engle Lake. A nice little

Visitors tour Weaverville
Joss House

Sidewalk stair,
Weaverville

Congregational
Church, Lewiston

swimming area with dressing rooms and picnic tables is north of the Stuart Fork where Highway 3 crosses Stoney Creek above the lake. If you have a boat, you can fish and water-ski on the lakes. You can also rent a boat at any of four commercial marinas.

National Forest campgrounds outside of the Recreation Area on the south side of the Trinity Alps are not as developed or as well-maintained as the Recreation Area campgrounds. With the exceptions of Eagle Creek, Horse Flat and Scott Mountain, they are also apt to be badly overcrowded.

In the Klamath National Forest on the north side of the Trinity Alps, several good National Forest campgrounds are along Forest Highway 93 between Callahan and Forks of Salmon.

Resort and Pack Stations

A general overview of resorts and horse packers in the Trinity Alps follows. However, ownerships, locations and policies change frequently, so we recommend the Shasta-Cascade Wonderland Association as a source of current and detailed information. Shasta-Cascade W. A. maintains a tourist information center at 14250 Holiday Road, Redding, CA 96003. Their telephone number is (916) 275-5555.

Two guest facilities, Josephine Lake Lodge (formerly Carter's Resort) and Camp Unalayee, are on inholdings within Trinity Alps Wilderness. The lodge is a full-service resort 3 miles south of the Big Flat trailhead and campground. Camp Unalayee is an independent, nonprofit organization stressing wilderness skills, environmental education, and cooperative, multicultural living situations.

Other resorts that are within the Trinity Alps, but not in the Wilderness, are Mountain Meadow Ranch and Coffee Creek Ranch, both on or near the Coffee Creek road, and Trinity Alps Resort on the Stuart Fork.

Swimming at Whiskeytown Lake

Pack trip in Long Canyon

Wyntoon, Estrellita, Cedar Stock and Pinewood cove are lake-oriented resorts on the west shore of Clair Engle Lake. Wyntoon has an excellent grocery and liquor store on Highway 3. All four have cabins, stores, commercial campgrounds, and marinas. We found one resort in operation on the north side of the Trinity Alps, located up the Crawford Creek road from Cecilville.

A large number of resorts, RV parks, and commercial campgrounds are along the Trinity River from Lewiston Lake down to Willow Creek. Shasta-Cascade W. A. is the best source of detailed information.

A number of outfitters held long-term and annual permits to provide packing and guide services in the Trinity Alps Wilderness as of the summer of 1993. Of these, most provide horse trips and two use llamas. Some of the resorts provide wilderness excursions as part of their packages and at least two groups will guide clients into the Alps for fishing purposes. Once again, for detailed and current information, contact Shasta-Cascade Wonderland Association, and the Forest Service in Weaverville (916-623-2121).

Chapter 3

THE WILDERNESS AND HOW TO USE THIS BOOK

The purpose of this book is to inform people generally about the Trinity Alps, and to inform backpackers, hikers, and equestrians in some detail about 425 miles of essentially wilderness trails in 32 backcountry trips into the Alps. We, the authors and publisher, do not intend that you should walk or ride the trails with your nose in the book to find your way. You would miss some very wonderful scenery that way. Besides, we don't carry other authors' complete guides when we backpack in other places, so we don't flatter ourselves that you will carry the full weight of this one either. You have our permission to photocopy the pages for the trip you are planning.

We assume that you can find your way reasonably well in the backcountry with the aid of topographic maps and compass, so we don't go into minute details about the trails. We do point out where the trails are different from what's on the topo maps, and give more detail in places where the trails are difficult to follow. If you would like to know more about using map and compass, we recommend Thomas Winnett's *Backpacking Basics,* also published by Wilderness Press, Berkeley.

A lot of the information in the trip descriptions is intended to help you plan and anticipate the pleasures of a particular trip, and to decide which trip you want to take and when to go. If you walk or ride all of the trips eventually, you won't regret it. We, the authors and their wives, enjoyed them all (a total of approximately 650 miles, including round trips, backtracks and misdirections), and hope we can transmit some of that enjoyment to you.

Where to Go and When

Most of the trails in the Trinity Alps are open by late June in all but very heavy snow years, and remain so until sometime in October and occasionally early November. If you prefer not to be in the backcountry during hunting season, avoid trips during the last week of September and the first two weeks of

October. Bow hunting usually precedes the regular deer-hunting season, and hunting for black bear comes later in the fall. Check with the Department of Fish and Game about the actual dates of each season, as it may vary from year to year and district to district. Personally, we have hiked in the Trinity Alps during hunting season without any problem whatsoever. The number of actual hunters you may be exposed to seems to diminish with the amount of distance you're willing to put between yourself and the nearest road. Any that you meet way back in the wilderness are typically competent and respectful backcountry users. Fall in many ways is one of the nicest seasons in the Trinity Alps and should be enjoyed by all.

No downhill ski areas are currently operating in the Trinity Alps, and there are no designated or groomed cross-country ski trails. It is possible to cross-country ski the Scott Mountain divide and the Marshy Lakes road from Scott Mountain Summit. Otherwise, walking several wet, lower miles to get to

Backpackers on the Four Lakes Loop trail above Luella Lake

the snow tends to discourage cross-country ski exploring. Much of the backcountry is also very avalanche-prone.

At the beginning of each trip description you will find a "Season" heading, which may or may not agree with the general season noted above. There are usually good reasons for the discrepancy. Some passes and north slopes are open earlier or later than others. Some streams cannot be forded earlier in normal years than the times listed. However, no two years are alike, and you should use your own good judgement, aided by all the current information you can get, to decide when and where to go.

The headings at the beginning of each trip description do not include a classification of how easy or difficult the trip is. Instead, we think you should look at the elevation-change figures, the mileage, the topo maps and some of the trail descriptions, and decide for yourself. After all, what is difficult for one may be very easy for another. The difficulty of a trip also depends greatly on the weather, your physical condition, and what you expect to find. The only factor that we can do anything about is what you expect to find. Keep in mind that the elevation-change figures are down as well as up.

For many of the same reasons, the number of days we have listed for each trip is very subjective. We do believe that the smaller number of days we have listed for each trip is the minimum you should consider taking if you want to enjoy the trip. The higher number obviously includes a layover day or two. You won't find any first-day, second-day, third-day schedules in the trip descriptions—we think you should set your own pace. We do tell you where campsites are, so you can plan where to camp.

Many miles of trails in the northwest part of Trinity Alps Wilderness are not covered in this book. During the 1970s and early 1980s, a number of marijuana growers virtually took over an area including East Fork New River, Pony Creek, Slide Creek, Eagle Creek and Mary Blaine Meadow. During this period the U.S. Forest Service did not patrol or maintain any of these trails, and advised recreational hikers and riders not to use the trails. Two guard stations were burned down, shots were fired at or near Forest Service personnel, and vehicles were vandalized and burned at trailheads. The district ranger at Big Bar told us in 1982, "Large areas in my district are not under our control."

Beginning in 1983, and continuing through 1984 and 1985, a major law-enforcement and clean-up effort was carried out in the area by armed forest rangers, state and federal narcotics agents, and Trinity County deputy sheriffs. Marijuana plantations were destroyed, illegal structures torn down, and large amounts of trash packed out. Maintenance crews worked on some of the trails again.

In the summer of 1987 we were told by the present Big Bar district ranger that not only are the trails safe and adequately patrolled, but he would like very much to have a great deal more recreational use in the area. We suggest, however, that you check at the Big Bar ranger station or the Denny guard station before using any trails in the west part of the Wilderness.

Marijuana growing may be attempted in any remote area where an adequate supply of water is available. Be alert on lightly traveled trails for evident of illegal growing, such as plastic pipe, irrigation ditches, semipermanent habitations, fertilizer bags, insecticide containers and cultivated soil. If you should find such evidence, immediately turn around, go back the way you came, and report what you saw to authorities as soon as possible. Do not attempt to confront growers. Some may be armed and dangerous.

Fishing

Fishing is generally good in the Trinity Alps. Sometimes it's even terrific! Almost all the lakes have been stocked with trout at some time, and some are still stocked regularly. The only lakes without trout are a few that are just too remote and too small, and some high lakes that are so shallow that they freeze solid in the winter, killing the fish. Most of the trout in the lakes are eastern brooks because this species can reproduce without running water. However, a few lakes have good populations of rainbow trout that are spawning successfully in inlet and outlet streams. Some lakes also contain large rainbow and brown trout that were stocked a few years ago. Upper Canyon Creek Lake, for example, has a good population of all three varieties in large sizes.

Fishing in streams that empty directly into the Trinity River below Lewiston Dam, and all the tributaries of those streams, is influenced by steelhead and salmon runs. You will see a few adult steelhead resting in the deep pools of these streams during the summer. They are making their spawning run. If you are lucky, you may also see a salmon or two, but they are becoming very scarce. It is legal to catch adult steelhead with a single hook in the Trinity River tributaries, but you are not apt to do so during the summer months. It is illegal to catch salmon in the tributaries by any means.

Trout caught at Boulder Lake end up in the pan for breakfast

The small trout (6 inches and under) that you can catch quite easily in the Trinity River tributaries are almost all young steelhead that have not yet made their pilgrimage to the ocean. It is legal to catch them, but please don't be greedy and take a lot of them. Native, landlocked rainbow trout normally do not live in streams where steelhead and salmon run and spawn. You will find native rainbows in the upper reaches of some of the tributaries above where the steelhead and salmon run. Falls block Canyon Creek to steelhead and salmon within 3 or 4 miles of its mouth, so you will find native rainbow trout in most of its length.

South Fork Salmon River, the only stream on the north side of the Alps big enough to be worth fishing, also has steelhead and salmon runs.

Of course, all streams that empty into Clair Engle Lake or the Trinity River above the lake no longer have steelhead or salmon runs. All these streams that are of any size have at least some native rainbow trout in them, and some of the higher tributaries have eastern brook trout. The lower, more easily reached stretches of these streams are badly overfished. Stuart Fork, Swift Creek and Coffee Creek are particularly hard-hit.

A few streams and lakes have been stocked with golden trout. They are noted in the trip descriptions. All the trip descriptions contain fishing information. Almost all of the information is based on the personal experience of the authors, and is biased toward dry fly fishing, but that certainly doesn't mean that you can't catch trout by some other legal means. In fact, you may very well catch fish where the authors didn't. A valid California fishing license and compliance with California fishing regulations are, of course, required. Good luck!

The Trailheads

All of the trailheads, with the possible exception of Tangle Blue Creek, can be reached in a modern sedan, but the sedan may be very dusty or muddy by the time you get there. Getting to some of the trailheads requires driving 15 miles or more of dirt and gravel roads.

We have tried to make the trailhead directions in the trips as explicit as possible without belaboring them too far. Unfortunately, new logging roads may be added along the trailhead routes, so it is a good idea to check at a ranger station to ensure that our directions are still correct. Increased logging activity, particularly on the west side of the Alps, requires that for your own safety you need to be watchful of logging trucks barreling along the access roads. You should allow more time than you think is necessary to get to most of the trailheads. Highway 299, Highway 3 and Forest Highway 93 are slow roads before you even get to the dirt and gravel roads.

Road and trailhead signs have a habit of disappearing in the Trinity Alps so, in case things don't look right, you should carefully check the mileage figures and descriptions of the trailheads given in the trips.

Safety of your vehicle at the trailheads is no more a problem in the Trinity Alps than it is at trailheads anywhere else in California, or other western states for that matter. You should be aware, however, that break-ins and vandalism are a possibility. Don't leave valuables in your vehicle. Strangely, the Alps is the only place we have had repeated incidents of mice getting into our vehicle while it was parked at trailheads. The little pests love toilet paper and plastic bags.

Precautions and Equipment

The Trinity Alps pose no special problems or threats to backcountry travelers that you might not encounter in any other wilderness or semiwilderness in the western states. Some precautions and pretrip planning can certainly save you some discomfort and concern, however. It is possible to get into trouble if you are foolish, or if you panic. A sad incident occurred in the Alps in the very hot, dry summer of 1981. According to an official who had contact with the group, a youth group led by two adults started up the notoriously steep, exposed trail from Portuguese Camp to the Sawtooth Ridge crest late on a hot morning. Two-thirds of the way up, one boy became sick with "flu-like" symptoms, and was unable to walk any farther. His companions, not in much better shape, all went on over the ridge to look for help, leaving the sick boy on the trail alone in the sun. When they finally found help, and got back to him, the boy was dead.

Apparently no one big mistake led to the boy's death, just a series of poor decisions and lack of precautions. The group should not have attempted that trail in the middle of the day without carrying a lot of water. Basic first-aid training should have taught them to recognize the symptoms of heat exhaustion, and to rig some kind of shade for the stricken boy, loosen his clothes, lower his head, fan him, and above all stay with him. Only two people needed to go for help. The rest of the group should have at least tried to carry the sick boy to shade and water.

The most important precaution all backcountry travelers should take is to never travel alone. If you should get sick or have an accident, help could be a long time coming in some parts of the Trinity Alps.

Altitude—A cursory examination of a few topographic maps will show you that altitude sickness should not be much of a problem in the Trinity Alps. Very few of the trips go above 7500 feet on the trails. Many of the trailheads are below 3000 feet, so your first day on the trail is certainly not likely to be affected by altitude. Any increase in altitude does aggravate distress caused by heat and dehydration, so take it easy, and drink a lot of water, especially on that first day.

Hypothermia—It is very unlikely that you will ever encounter subfreezing temperatures in the Trinity Alps during the summer months, but that doesn't eliminate the possibility of your suffering from hypothermia. Wet clothes and wind chill can cause hypothermia at temperatures well above freezing. Hypothermia is simply lowering of body temperature caused by loss of heat through the skin faster than the body is producing heat. A drop of one degree in body temperature can cause violent shivering, slurred speech, and loss of judgment. A two-degree drop brings loss of coordination, loss of memory, and further loss of judgment and initiative. If your body temperature falls three degrees, you will be unable to walk, will suffer debilitating lassitude, and eventually will die if you do not get help.

The insidious thing about hypothermia is that the victim does not realize what is happening to him, because of the lack of judgment brought on by the first stages. If wet and cold conditions are encountered, it is vitally important that every member of a group watch every other member for signs of hypothermia. At the first signs of hypothermia in anyone, the group as a whole should seek shelter, build a fire if possible, and do everything they can to get warm and dry.

If a person reaches the second or third stage of hypothermia, he must be helped. To abandon anyone in this condition amounts to an almost certain death sentence. The victim should be gotten to shelter, stripped, and put in a dry sleeping bag with another, unaffected person, also stripped. Skin-to-skin transfer of heat is the best cure. Warm, *nonalcoholic* drinks will also help. Adequate clothing and good tents will prevent hypothermia. Wool clothing provides excellent insulation when wet. Cotton jeans are the absolute worst.

The Sun—Heat exhaustion and sunstroke are not uncommon afflictions in the Trinity Alps. These conditions are brought on when body heat is not being dispersed fast enough through the skin, the exact opposite of hypothermia. Symptoms of heat exhaustion are flushed skin, rapid breathing to the point of hyperventilation, and general debility. Symptoms of sunstroke are pale, but hot, skin and fainting. Treatment for both conditions involves getting the victim out of the sun and cooling him off. Sponging as much skin area as possible with cool water is good for both conditions. In addition, the sunstroke victim should be treated for fainting by putting his head lower than the rest of his body. Never give an unconscious or semiconscious person anything to drink.

Heat exhaustion, sunstroke and dehydration can be prevented by traveling in early morning and late afternoon on hot days instead of during midday hours. Drinking plenty of water is also essential. The trip descriptions warn you of sections of trails without water. Take heed, and carry an ample supply. Wearing a hat will reduce risk of sunstroke.

Risk of serious sunburn increases with longer exposure and higher altitude. Use sun-block lotions or creams.

People with sun-sensitive eyes obviously should wear sunglasses.

Lightning—Occasional thunderstorms rumble through the Trinity Alps during the summer months. You need only look around when you cross one of the many high crests to understand why you should not be up there during a thunderstorm. Those trees weren't split, shattered and seared by Paul Bunyan.

The safest place to be in a thunderstorm is in the middle of a wide valley in an extensive stand of short trees. In addition, you should be at least 100 feet from your pack or any other metal object. Next safest place is under a *solid* rock overhang. Avoid tall, isolated trees and high, open areas.

Report all forest fires you see to the Forest Service as soon as you can. Do not try to put out fires of any size without help.

Drinking Water—We did not suffer any ill effects from drinking stream or lake water in the Trinity Alps. However, we did filter, boil or chemically purify most of it before we drank it. Only springs issuing from near the tops of ridges or peaks can be considered safe to drink. You only have to walk upstream a few times from where you just drank and find cattle-trampled muck or human debris to realize you can't be too careful. The best rule is, don't drink any unfiltered water.

Giardiasis, a severe intestinal disorder caused by the organism *Giardia lamblia* in drinking water, is common enough in the Alps to cause concern. In addition, high coliform counts are fairly common in the Alps' waters, so be warned. Wilderness rangers do check lakes and streams from time to time, and the Forest Service can warn you of waters that are particularly suspect.

Dangerous Animals—This subject is covered to some extent in the natural-history section above. In brief, you should not feed or pet any wild animals. That includes feeding them inadvertently by leaving your food where they can get at it. Bear-bagging is necessary in any campsite in the Trinity Alps. Hang your food bag high and well away from the trunk of the tree. Mice and other rodents are as much a problem as bears.

Bears are actually scarce now along the more heavily traveled trails, but deer (usually does) have become accustomed to people, and are pests in some campsites. Please don't feed them.

Rattlesnakes and their relationship with rodents are also discussed in the natural-history section. You might like to know that the most likely place to find a rattlesnake is near or under the end of a foot-log across a stream. Rodents cross on the foot-logs too, and the snake waits there for his dinner to come to him. The only rattlesnake-bite incident we heard of while we were in the Alps involved a man pulling a rattlesnake off his dog. You may also come out a loser if you try to separate the participants in a dog-bear encounter. Rattlesnakes and bears will both avoid you if they can. Please don't kill rattlesnakes just because you see them. They are an important part of the environment, and were here long before you were.

Treatment of rattlesnake bites is so controversial at this point that we hesitate to recommend any treatment. We are convinced that a person in good condition can survive a rattlesnake bite without any immediate treatment if he keeps calm. Rattlesnakes do not always inject venom when they strike. Of course, the victim of a rattlesnake bite should be taken to a hospital as soon as possible. The victim should not walk out on his own. He should ride or be carried. Get help. Some restriction of blood circulation between the bite and the heart will slow down spread of the snake venom. Do not apply a tight tourniquet.

Insects—Insect pests are covered rather thoroughly in the natural-history section above except that one of California's 49 species of ticks may carry Lyme disease. A folder about Lyme disease is available at all ranger stations.

Stream Crossings—A number of stream crossings in the Trinity Alps that might otherwise be dangerous early in the summer are bridged. Some that are not bridged are specifically pointed out in the trip descriptions. A few streams that do not have bridges, and that you should be generally wary of during high water, are Virgin Creek, North Fork Trinity River, Grizzly Creek, Rattlesnake Creek, Canyon Creek and Stuart Fork.

Thomas Winnett's book, *Backpacking Basics,* has an excellent section on roped stream-crossing technique. In order to rope safely across a stream of any size, you need 150 feet of light climbing rope.

Maps

The map inside the back cover of this book gives you a general idea of where things are in the Trinity Alps and how to get to them. All of the trails in the 32 trips are shown as accurately as we can at this small scale. The trailheads and the roads leading to them are included, so you can use the map to get to the trailheads if the roads don't change too much. A few connecting and extending trails, not included in the trips, are on the map to help you plan different or longer trips.

Familiarity with and experience in "orienteering" with topographic maps and compass is absolutely essential for off-trail travel in the backcountry, and is highly desirable for on-trail travel. Many conservation and hiking organizations give classes in orienteering, as do some junior colleges and adult schools. A number of books, including Thomas Winnett's *Backpacking Basics,* also cover the subject well.

The "Topo Maps" listed at the beginning of each trip are U.S. Geological Survey topographic maps. They come in two different scales. Older 1:62,500-scale quadrangles covering 15′ of latitude have been replaced by 1:24,000-scale quadrangles covering 7.5′. Some of the newer 7.5′ quadrangle maps are referred to as provisional, meaning they haven't been completely processed into their final form but are certainly more accurate than the older 15′ maps. Twenty 7.5′ quadrangles cover the backcountry area described in this book, and the map in the back shows the location and name of each one.

Some of the USGS quadrangles are sold at the Shasta-Trinity National Forest Information office in Redding, and at the Weaverville, Big Bar and Coffee Creek ranger stations. Many sporting-goods and recreational-equipment stores also carry the maps, or you can buy them over the counter at the following USGS locations:

7638 Federal Building   345 Middlefield Road
300 North Los Angeles Street Menlo Park, California
Los Angeles, California

USGS quadrangles can be ordered by mail from:

Branch of Distribution	The Map Center
U.S. Geological Survey	2440 Bancroft Way
Federal Center	Berkeley, California 94704
Denver, Colorado 80225	(carries the maps for this book)

The U.S. Forest Service published a topographic recreation map of the entire Trinity Alps Wilderness in 1985. This map is available at all the ranger stations and recreation-area visitor centers in the area. The new map contains a lot of information in one piece, and is very useful for planning trips and finding trailheads. Because of its small scale and a few inaccuracies, however, it should not be depended upon for topographic or trail details.

The Shasta-Trinity National Forest and Klamath National Forest maps, also published by the Forest Service, are of little use as trail maps due to their small scale and lack of topographic detail.

Trail Signs and Marks

You should be aware of a couple of peculiarities about the newer signs in the Trinity Alps. The first is that no distances are shown in either kilometers or miles. The other is that trail junctions are shown as destinations. Only the trail listed at the top of the sign with a line under it is the trail at the junction where you are. The trails listed under the line are at junctions somewhere in the directions the arrows point, not where you are. It can be confusing. To add to the confusion, signs have been removed from trail junctions in some parts of the Alps, requiring you to check distances and landmarks carefully.

Some trailhead signs and all the remaining older Forest Service trail signs show distances in miles. Most lakes have signs showing the name of the lake and the elevation. Some trails are marked with pieces of old auto license plates nailed to trees 8–10 feet above the ground. Most other trails are marked with conventional blazes at eye level on trees beside the tread. Where there are no trees in meadows and on bare rock, the route is often marked with "ducks" and rock cairns. A duck is two or three rocks obviously stacked by human hands. A cairn is a bigger pile of rocks, usually pyramidal in shape.

You will find an occasional yellow-and-black location marker nailed to a tree along some trails. The numbers in the squares of a grid on the marker correspond to the section numbers on the USGS topo map for the area. A nail driven into the grid shows you the location of the marker you're looking at, which you can then transpose to the topo map.

Descriptive Terms

Trails—The trip descriptions give information about the composition and condition of the trail tread and whether or not the trail has been relocated from the route shown on the topo maps. Steepness of ascent and descent is defined approximately by the following terms:

level	0 to 2% grade	moderately steep	8% to 12% grade
gradual	2% to 5% grade	steep	12% to 20% grade
moderate	5% to 8% grade	very steep	more than 20% grade

We also try to give you an idea of the amount and type of traffic you might expect to find on a particular section of trail.

Campsites—Availability of drinking water and firewood is noted in the campsite descriptions. Rating of campsites from poor to excellent is based on scenery, unique natural features in the vicinity, privacy, proximity to fishing, swimming and side trips, protection from the elements, and how badly the site has been used. There are no developed public campsites in Trinity Alps Wilderness.

Care of the Wilderness

Trinity Alps Wilderness is new. It was designated by the U.S. Congress as a part of the California Wilderness Act, Public Law 98-425, which received final action by the Senate on September 28, 1984. This act designated a wilderness area of approximately 500,000 acres with boundaries very close to what a number of conservation organizations and the board of supervisors of Trinity County had been lobbying for for years. It is a triumph for wilderness proponents and nonmechanized recreationists.

The Act also requires that private lands within the designated wilderness be exchanged or eventually bought out. Until such exchanges or buy-outs are implemented, these private inholdings are to be nominally managed as wilderness.

Owners of mining claims within the designated wilderness may continue exploration and mining for at least 10 years, and must be given reasonable access to their claims. No new claims may be filed without an act of congress. The Forest Service must validate all existing claims within a reasonable time. It is expected that the Wilderness Operation Plan will establish stricter environmental controls on mining than have been in effect in the past.

What this marvelous wilderness area looks like in the future will depend on how we treat it today. The Trinity Alps have not yet seen the heavy recreational use that is common in some areas of the Sierra Nevada. Far more people were in the Alps 130 years ago than are here now, and preservation of wilderness was not on those miners' minds at all. The Alps recovered quite well from the mining debacle, but people were scarce in the Alps for 100 years or so. Recreational use of the Trinity Alps is certain to increase in the future, and it is up to us to ensure that our grandchildren can enjoy at least some of the same wilderness experiences that we enjoy today.

We can do several things to help preserve the miracle of wilderness for future generations, or even for ourselves next year: We can pack out all of our trash, and other people's trash as well. That includes *complete* foil packages. Aluminum foil really does not burn completely; it always leaves scraps that people do not pick out of the ashes. We can make small fires instead of big ones, never leave fires untended, and put them dead out before we leave them. We can wash our dishes and bathe ourselves well away from lakes and streams, and dispose of waste water where it will not drain into the water supply. We can camp in inconspicuous sites and make a concerted effort to remove all traces of our stay. Above all, we can think about how we would like to find the wilderness, and do everything we can to keep it that way for those who come later.

Campfires and Fire Rings—We like to have a fire in our campsite; most everyone does. It is a marvelous, cheery accessory to the wilderness experience. Things have come to the point, however, that we should question whether we really need that fire, or at least how big it should be and how long we should keep it burning. Shouldn't the people who come next year, or 10 years from now, have a chance to have a small fire too? Only a finite amount of dead wood is available, and we certainly don't want to destroy the standing trees that are an integral part of our wilderness.

As for fire rings, we certainly would be much better off without them, especially the high, built-up variety. Fire rings are eyesores. They collect trash that is difficult to dig from between the rocks. They make it much more difficult to thoroughly extinguish fires—coals continue to smolder in the chinks between the rocks. A fire ring will support a grate sometimes, but so will two rocks, and your pot will heat faster if it is set directly in the fire, or on coals pulled out of the fire. Besides, it's really much easier to cook on a mineral-fueled stove. In some places in the Trinity Alps you will have to—there isn't any firewood now.

We find that a fire burns very well on a flat, cleared surface without any rocks at all. Then it can be thoroughly drowned, and the wet ashes scattered.

Tools—You really need only two tools on a wilderness trip. The most important one is called a shovel. It need not be big, cumbersome or heavy, but it should have a sturdy, steel blade and a well-attached, short, strong handle. It serves three important wilderness purposes—to scrape a place for a fire, to put the fire completely out, and to dig a hole to dispose of human waste. Nothing else does any one of those things nearly as well. A fire can be put completely out only by drowning and stirring, and drowning and stirring again. Covering a fire with dirt seldom puts it out. We have found literally dozens of fires burning in empty campsites under piles of dirt.

Human waste should be disposed of in a 6–8-inch-deep hole in mineral soil at least 200 feet from campsites and water. If you must dig in grass, remove a piece of sod intact, and replace it intact. You can do that only with a shovel. A stick or plastic trowel won't do it. Please do not bury garbage—it will only be dug up again by animals. Food scraps should be burned or spread on top of the ground well away from campsites and trails.

Modern backpacker's tents do not require ditching, nor do you need to dig out a large level place on which to pitch your tent. Those scars stay for a long time. We encourage you to use your shovel instead to take apart and scatter fire rings.

The second important tool is a good pocket knife. It's very difficult to clean fish without one. It has other uses too.

We carry a third tool, indispensable for repairing backpacks and fishing equipment—a small pair of needle-nosed pliers with a side cutter. You can find old bailing wire in a lot of campsites in the Trinity Alps, but you might also want to carry a small coil of 18-gauge malleable steel wire.

Wilderness Patrol—We wish there were more of them. They are some of the hardest working, most dedicated people we have ever met, but there just aren't enough wilderness rangers to do all the things they need to do. Most of the small force in the Trinity Alps are volunteers.

When you meet a wilderness ranger, he or she will be carrying a radio, first-aid kit, axe, shovel and one or two plastic trash bags, empty or full depending on how many slobs have been in the area recently. You can assist the rangers greatly by carrying out your own garbage. They have plenty to do in directing and educating people, maintaining trails, and conducting rescue missions when necessary. The rangers can and do issue citations to flagrant violators of Forest Service regulations.

Regulations and Trail Courtesy

Regulations—Although regulations may change, a wilderness permit was required in 1994 to enter Trinity Alps Wilderness. Backpacking and backcountry camping on National Forest land outside of the wilderness and not in established campgrounds requires a campfire permit. If a wilderness permit is not required, you should still inform a ranger station of where you intend to go, and inquire about conditions in the area. You can also telephone to find out when the stations are open and for other information. Permits and information can be had in person or by mail from the following locations:

U.S. Forest Service
2400 Washington Avenue
Redding, CA 96001
Telephone (916) 246-5222

Weaverville Ranger District
P.O. Box 1190
Weaverville, CA 96093
Telephone (916) 623-2121

U.S. Forest Service
Coffee Creek Station
Star Route 2, Box 3640
Trinity Center, CA 96091
Telephone (916) 266-3211

Big Bar Ranger District
Star Route 1, Box 10
Big Bar, CA 96010
Telephone (916) 623-6106

Wilderness permits can also be had at the Callahan ranger station and the Cecilville guard station in the Klamath National Forest, the Forest Service work center at Junction City, and the guard station at Denny. Personnel are not always available at these latter locations, however. You can write your own permit at self-service stations at Weaverville, Coffee Creek and Big Bar.

Campsites should be at least 150 feet from streams and lakes where possible. Only dead wood on the ground may be used for firewood. No living foliage or upright trees may be cut for any purpose. No motorized equipment may be used in Trinity Alps Wilderness or on posted trails, except specifically authorized mining dredges. Smoking is prohibited while walking or riding on trails.

Forage and tie regulations for saddle and pack animals are available at the ranger stations.

Trail Courtesy—Consideration of your fellow hikers and riders dictates that you not cut across switchbacks, especially in the downhill direction. In addition to erosion damage brought on by cross-cutting, there is definite danger of dislodging rocks to roll down on people below.

Hikers and backpackers should get off the trail and stand or sit quietly when meeting or being overtaken by saddle and pack animals. This is not to show deference to a higher social order; rather, horses may shy when crowded or frightened by unexpected noises or movements. Hikers as well as riders might be injured. Saddle and pack animals have the right of way because they cannot be easily maneuvered off the trail.

Chewing-gum and candy wrappers are the most prevalent eyesores along the trails. Please pick them up when you see them.

Trip 1

East Weaver and Rush Creek Lakes

Trip Type: Round trip of 2 to 4 days

Distance: 4 miles to Rush Creek Lakes including climbing Monument Peak; 7.5 miles round trip

Elevation Change: 3720 feet one way including Monument Peak, average 930 feet per mile

Season: Early July to mid-October

Topo Map: *Rush Creek Lakes* (provisional 1982) 7.5′ quadrangle

Even the drive to the trailhead is awe-inspiring. In the 9 miles from Weaverville you climb 5000 feet. The last 1.7 miles are one-lane and hung rather precariously on the side of Weaver Bally Mountain. As long as you've come this far, you might as well drive another 1.4 miles out to Weaver Bally lookout and say hello to the person on duty in the tower. No one in Weaverville can do anything without the lookout knowing about it. You look right down Weaverville's chimneys from here, and have a lofty view of several hundred square miles of forests, mountains and canyons as well.

This trip offers a bonus opportunity to walk to the top of Monument Peak and enjoy a breathtaking 360° panorama that includes *all* of the Trinity Alps. West of Monument Peak you will see the recovering burned area left by the 1987 fire that ran up Bear Gulch to the divide below the peak.

East Weaver Lake is a pleasant place to have lunch along the way, and under other circumstances might be your destination, but it is just completely outclassed by its neighbors, the Rush Creek Lakes. They are pristine little jewels, strung down a rugged canyon from a magnificent, pinnacled cirque under the shoulder of aptly named Monument Peak.

As you rest atop the narrow crest above the Rush Creek cirque, and look across at 4–5 miles of the brutally steep, dry trail snaking up the ridge from Kinney Camp to Rush Creek Lakes, you feel very proud of yourself for having gotten here so easily. Of course, you still have to get down the almost vertical wall of the cirque and back up again, but it's worth it. Just look at those lakes!

Starting Point

To get on the Weaver Bally road, Forest Road 33N38, you drive out of Weaverville on Highway 299 as if you were going west to Eureka. Pass the Forest Service offices on the left, then turn right just past a large complex of Sheriff's facilities above the highway on the right. The paved road turns right again one block from the highway; unpaved Forest Road 33N38 goes straight ahead, north. The road is rough, but passable to almost any vehicle if it hasn't rained recently. The surface improves beyond the first mile as you start to climb seriously in Munger Gulch.

You have a good opportunity to observe the changes of flora as you climb from 2000-foot elevation at Weaverville to over 7000 feet at the top of the mountain. You start in ceanothus brush with some ponderosa pines, incense cedars and Douglas firs. Big-leaf maples, madrones, live oaks and canyon oaks grow in Munger Gulch. Above the gulch you first see black oaks, then white firs and sugar pines. Nearer the top of the ridge are heavy stands of huckleberry oak and ceanothus brush, with some manzanita. The trees change to Jeffrey pines, lodgepole pines, western white pines and Shasta red firs near the crest.

The road switchbacks to the top of a spur ridge and, at 7.5 miles from Highway 299, dips down to Low Gap, marked by a sign in an open forest of white firs. A number of side roads branch off Forest Road 33N38 on the way up, but you won't have any trouble telling which is the main road—just keep going

Weaver Bally lookout has a lofty view of forests, mountains and canyons

uphill. After keeping left at a fork in Low Gap, you soon climb very steeply on a rough, one-lane track with a few turnouts along the side of a huge, brush-covered ridge. The next mile or so could be difficult for some sedans. At 8.8 miles from the highway, a pipe trickles icy water from a boxed spring on the uphill (north) side of the road. The East Weaver Lake trailhead is .2 mile beyond this spring, but you probably won't see it unless a new sign has been put up. You have to drive another half mile to the top of the ridge to turn around anyway, and from there you can see the trail on the side of the hill above the road and locate the trailhead.

The closest place to park is a wide spot in the road .3 mile above the trailhead. Before you drive back down from the top of the ridge, you will probably want to drive another mile out to the end of the ridge and the view from the Forest Service lookout there.

Description

The beginning of the East Weaver Lake trail from the Weaver Bally road is hard to find. As you walk down the road from your parking place, you can see the trail above the road, but it's still a steep scramble up the bank to get to it. Once on the trail, good tread rises at a moderate-to-moderately-steep rate northeast across the side of the ridge in heavy brush. At the crest of the ridge, .4 mile from the trailhead, you turn back sharply west and drop down to contour around a basin at the head of East Weaver Creek. Good trail descends gradually through groves of red fir to a point almost directly west of little East Weaver Lake, nestled in a fold of rock on the floor of the basin.

You descend the steep side of the basin on rough, zigzagging tread to a ledge over the west shore of the mossy 1-acre lake. Heavy cattle grazing in the basin should discourage you from drinking the water from East Weaver Lake without purifying it. Inlet and outlet streams dry up during the summer. A fair campsite is near the trail above the lower end of the lake; a poor site in a little meadow too close to the upper end to the lake should not be used. The lake supports a small population of eastern book trout that aren't too hard to catch.

You may be tempted on the way down to try a shortcut across the side of the basin to the saddle north of East Weaver Lake, where the Bear Gulch trail crosses the ridge. Don't try it! Very thick, tall brush makes the steep hillside almost impassable. The better course is to continue on the trail down the side of the canyon below East Weaver Lake .3 mile to the junction with the Bear Gulch trail. From this junction it is a moderately steep climb on fair trail through meadows, patches of brush and open forest to the top of the ridge, 1.8 miles from the trailhead.

As you reach the crest of the saddle above Bear Gulch, you come into direct contact with the recovering damage caused by the 1987 fire. The crest of the ridge was the fire line to stop the fire from running on over into East Weaver Creek. In spite of the burned and felled trees in the foreground, the views up to the head of Canyon Creek on the west side and back down East Weaver Creek to the east are still spectacular. Your route from the point where the Bear Gulch trail drops over the west side of the ridge is obvious. Head north along the crest toward a gap just east of the highest point of Monument Peak, which dominates the horizon. Along the 1987 fire trail farther up the ridge, you walk through the remains of what was a magnificent climax forest of red firs. Some of the downed trees were burned, but most were felled by fire crews to form a fire break. As the climb gets steeper, the fire trail becomes less evident, but the way is clear toward the low point in the ridge east of Monument Peak. A final quarter mile of very steep climbing brings you to a narrow crest overlooking the beautiful cirque at the head of Rush Creek.

Rush Creek runs out the open north side of this deep cirque through meadows and over rock ledges to connect the string of little lakes and ponds called the Rush Creek Lakes—eight of them in all. A row of slanted pinnacles tops the east wall above the largest Rush Creek lake, out of sight from here behind tall firs and rock outcrops. The west wall leads up to crags below the pyramidal tip of Monument Peak.

To get to the top of Monument Peak, you climb west over broken blocks of metamorphosed rock. As you climb higher, Upper Rush Creek Lake comes into view on the floor of the cirque below. Although the elevation is only 7771 feet, the top of Monument Peak offers unrestricted views of all the higher Trinity Alps to the north, and overlooks the vast canyons of Canyon Creek and the North Fork Trinity drainage farther west. To the east you look past Clair Engle Lake and the Trinity Divide to Mount Shasta and southeast to Lassen Peak on the distant horizon.

Getting to the floor of the cirque and to Upper Rush Creek Lake involves scrambling down some very steep slopes of loose dirt, rock and talus, and of course, you will have to climb back up again unless you go on down the Kinney Camp trail. Your route down from the crest first leads west, then north and finally east along a ledge to the bottom of the cirque. Occasional ducks and traces of use trail mark the way. The deep, almost round, 2-acre upper lake lies under the nearly vertical east wall of the cirque. Direct sun reaches the water for only a short time even in midsummer, and snow may linger until August. This tends to discourage swimming. The shoreline is rough and brushy, but if you can find a place to fish, a good catch of eastern brook trout is almost assured.

The smaller, shallower lower lakes are warm enough for swimming in late summer. However, no obvious trail connects the string of lakes, and you must find your way over rough terrain to see them all.

Trip 2

Stuart Fork to Emerald, Sapphire and Mirror Lakes

Trip Type: Round trip of 4 to 7 days

Distance: 14.5 miles one way to Sapphire Lake

Elevation Change: 4240 feet, average 292 feet per mile

Season: Mid-June to mid-October

Topo Maps: *Rush Creek Lakes, Siligo Peak,* and *Mount Hilton* (all provisional 1982), *Caribou Lake* (provisional 1986) and *Thompson Peak* 1979 7.5′ quadrangles

Set in a matrix of gleaming, glaciated granite at the head of rushing Stuart Fork, Emerald, Sapphire and Mirror lakes are the crown jewels of the Trinity Alps. The long canyon of Stuart Fork and the three subalpine lakes at its head are still breathtakingly beautiful in spite of a long history of use and abuse by mankind. The walk to them is delightful, although not exactly a pristine wilderness experience.

Don't expect solitude—Stuart Fork is one of the most heavily used trails in the Trinity Alps. However, you won't feel crowded unless you insist on camping at Emerald or Sapphire Lake. Farther down the valley, Portuguese Camp, Morris Meadow, Oak Flat and other campsites can accommodate large numbers of campers.

Stuart Fork valley offers a cross section of much of the natural history of the Alps. Below Oak Flat the river has cut through jumbled sedimentary and metasedimentary rock strata and glacial till. Dense mixed forest covers the sides of this lower valley, and the river flows swiftly through a rocky channel with occasional wide gravel bars studded with cottonwoods and big-leaf maples. Several thousand years ago, receding glaciers left extensive terminal moraines above Oak Flat, damming a large lake that eventually filled in and dried out to

Old Pelton waterwheel, air compressor and tank above Emerald Lake

become the present Morris Meadow. At the head of the valley the three lakes shimmer in their solid rock basins much as the glaciers left them. Men, horses and mules labored prodigiously back in the 1890s to build dams at Emerald and Sapphire lakes and divert the water through an elaborate system of ditches, flumes and siphons to the La Grange Mine on Oregon Mountain, 29 miles southwest. Not much evidence of this monumental effort is left along the Stuart Fork today, but at Oregon Mountain the results are very evident where a large piece of the mountain was washed down Oregon Gulch to Junction City and beyond.

Groves of red fir begin to appear in the canyon above Morris Meadow, and you will see sparse weeping spruces, mountain hemlocks and whitebark pines clinging to the walls of the giant granite cirque at the head of the canyon. This subalpine terrain also supports thick mats of ceanothus and huckleberry oak as well as willows and alders in the wetter areas.

Flowers and wildlife are abundant along the trail throughout the summer, especially in and around Morris Meadow. Fishing is good in the Stuart Fork for rainbow trout to 10 inches and fair for small eastern brook trout in Emerald and Sapphire lakes. Mirror Lake has both rainbows and brooks to 10 or 12 inches. Morris Meadow is a popular center for deer hunting in the fall.

One of the nicest things about this trip is that it starts in cool forest below 3000 feet, and the first day or two are an easy amble before you come to the steeper part of the trail above Morris Meadow.

If you don't like retracing your steps all the way, you can make a strenuous through-trip to Big Flat at the end of the Coffee Creek road by way of Sawtooth Ridge and Caribou Basin or up Willow Creek and over the very steep divide near Tri-Forest Peak. The trip through Caribou Basin, including Emerald and Sapphire lakes, will total almost 30 miles. The route up Willow Creek is 2 or 3 miles shorter. An even longer loop trip will take you up Deer Creek, around the Four Lakes Loop and back to the Trinity Alps Resort by way of Siligo Meadow, Van Matre Meadows, Stonewall Pass and Red Mountain Meadows for a total of 44 miles. Other alternatives, requiring a car-shuttle, are to go out from Deer Creek to the Long Canyon trailhead or over the divide to Granite Lake and out to the Swift Creek trailhead.

Starting Point

Approximately 13 miles north of Weaverville, Highway 3 turns northwest out of the lower end of Slate Creek canyon and runs above the shoreline of Clair Engle Lake past Tan Bark picnic area and a Forest Service information center, then crosses a bridge over the Stuart Fork arm of the lake. At the north end of the bridge the Trinity Alps Resort road turns west from the highway. Keep left on this paved road past a side road, and, at .5 mile, you will be in the center of Trinity Alps Resort. The store here is a good place to pick up last-minute supplies, and good meals are available in the dining room.

Beyond a row of cabins by the river the road changes to dirt and gravel and turns up through the resort's stable and corrals. This looks like a private road, but isn't. Drive carefully through the resort, however, and be alert for children and animals crossing the road. A quarter mile beyond the corrals you will see the Trinity Alps Creek trailhead on your right with room for one or two cars to park. Just past Bridge Camp campground, 3.5 miles from Highway 3, a locked gate blocks the road and a large parking area is on your left. This is the Stuart Fork trailhead.

Bridge Camp is a no-fee campground, but is cramped and dusty. The fee campgrounds around Clair Engle Lake offer a better choice.

Description

The first mile of the Stuart Fork trail is on roads across private land. Forest Service signs ask you to respect private property rights and to stay on the roads. At a fork just beyond the gate, the road to the left leads to a mining camp beside the Stuart Fork. Your road to the right has a trail sign listing "BOULDER CREEK TRAIL—5, DEER CREEK TRAIL—8, CARIBOU TRAIL—12" and "SAPPHIRE LAKE—14" as destinations. From here to the wilderness boundary the right direction at all junctions is marked by metal stakes with white reflectors in the form of trail blazes.

The road ends at the wilderness boundary just beyond an occupied cabin at Cherry Flat, and you continue on well-defined trail 200 yards to a crossing of Sunday Creek, first water on the trail. Above Sunday Creek the trail leaves the partly cut-over land it has traversed since the trailhead and climbs away from the river into dense forest of predominantly Douglas fir with occasional incense cedars, ponderosa pines and sugar pines.

This relatively new section of trail drops down into a flat beside the Stuart Fork, 1.5 miles from the trailhead, and rejoins the old trail shown on the *Trinity Dam* topo map. Beyond the flat you climb moderately up the side of the

Deep Creek Falls   **Evening in Morris Meadow**

canyon, down to another flat with excellent campsites, then up and down again to a crossing of Little Deep Creek close to its confluence with the river. You pass another excellent campsite here between the trail and the river, then climb over a mound of glacial till, the first we've seen on the way up the valley, and come to a steel girder bridge over Deep Creek. This bridge was washed out by high water in 1983 and replaced in 1985.

After climbing moderately over another small hump above Deep Creek, you descend to yet another flat where a spring runs across the trail and a number of fine campsites lie between the trail and the river. You are far enough from the trailhead here (4 miles) that fishing will probably be good in the Stuart Fork. By August the water may be warm enough to swim, too.

Another gentle ascent leads to the lower end of Oak Flat, a wide, gently sloping shelf, 200–300 yards away from the river, heavily forested with very large Douglas firs, ponderosa pines and black oaks. At about 1 mile from Deep Creek you will find a fine spring flowing across the trail. About 150 yards beyond the spring the Boulder Creek/Alpine Lake trail branches west to drop over a high bank to a forested flat and a large gravel bar beside the river. Many excellent campsites, with an adequate supply of firewood, are on the flat and the bar, above and below the unbridged trail crossing. This crossing is dangerous in high-water conditions. Fishing for pan-sized rainbows was excellent when we stopped there.

Back on the Stuart Fork trail, you traverse another .5 mile of dense forest north of the Boulder Creek/Alpine Lake junction before coming out in more open terrain on the east side of the canyon above the river. The trail runs along the embankment of the old La Grange Ditch here, the first place we've seen much evidence of the mining efforts along the Stuart Fork. From this vantage point we also get our first look at the high Alps at the head of the valley. Another group of first-rate campsites is in a flat between the ditch and the river.

The trail soon climbs away from the ditch on the brushy east slope, then levels off before dropping down through some terminal moraines to cross Salt Creek. Salt Creek is a swift-running little stream—clear, cold and lined with ferns and wildflowers. Above the south bank the remains of a log cabin are slowly mouldering back into the soil. Some fair-to-poor campsites are nearby. Just north of Salt Creek you climb around a shoulder of rock, then ascend a series of new switchbacks .3 mile east up a draw before turning north again over and around more moraines.

A half mile from Salt Creek, and 7.5 miles from the trailhead, you come to a steel truss bridge across the steep-walled, narrow canyon that Deer Creek has cut into the dark sedimentary rock. A pack stock bypass trail leads to a ford above a waterfall plunging into the deep pool under the bridge. The bypass also provides access to the creek for drinking water, but you will be grateful for the bridge if the water is high at all—Deer Creek is a good-sized stream.

A short, steep climb takes you up the north bank of Deer Creek and east into the piled-up moraines south of Morris Meadow. Half a mile north of Deer Creek through the moraine ridges, Cold Spring flows copiously across the trail and a small clearing offers a few excellent campsites. You continue to climb moderately to moderately steeply another .5 mile to the south fork of a **Y** beginning the Deer Creek/Four Lakes trail east. A level stroll of .3 mile through open forest and patches of meadow leads to the trail junction at the north side of the **Y**. Just beyond this junction you walk out into the wide lower end of big, lush Morris Meadow, 8.7 miles from the trailhead.

A midsummer evening at Morris Meadow can be truly memorable—offering an exquisite tableau of deer grazing in waist-high grass, backlit by the setting sun reflected off the multicolored backdrop of Sawtooth Ridge rising 2000 feet above the forest fringe at the north end of the meadow. The main part of the meadow is roughly a mile long by a quarter-mile wide, covering the flat floor of the glacier-carved upper Stuart Fork valley. On the west side tilted, glistening slabs of granite sweep up to remnant snowfields under the 8886-foot peak of Sawtooth Mountain. To the east, Sawtooth Ridge tapers off into a massive forested ridge separating this valley from the Willow Creek and Deer Creek drainages. Stuart Fork, hidden in a tangle of willows, alders and incense cedars, meanders down the west side of the valley.

White-flowering yampa dots the green expanse of grass in August, and pale bog orchids hide amongst the sedges in marshy areas. Earlier in the summer there are wide expanses of lupine and Indian paintbrush.

Many excellent campsites are hidden in patches of forest interspersed with small meadows at the south end of Morris Meadow. A semideveloped horse packers' camp is in a grove of incense cedars that juts into the west side of the meadow, and more campsites are in the forest at the north end. Please don't camp in the meadow itself; plenty of established sites are available. Freeloading deer, too often successful, are a problem in Morris Meadow, as are chipmunks and ground squirrels. No bears were evident when we were here last, but bears have been here in the past and probably will be again—hang all food! Water from the Stuart Fork should be purified. Continual heavy use makes its purity suspect.

Before continuing on up the valley to Emerald and Sapphire lakes, you should consider carefully whether you want to carry your packs up there or use Morris Meadow, or one of the other camps as far up as Portuguese Camp, as a base and make day trips to the high lakes. It is 5 miles from the south end of Morris Meadow to Emerald Lake; not much more than a 2-hour trip with daypacks. Campsites at Emerald and Sapphire lakes are fair at best, and will accommodate no more than 20 people, total, without serious overcrowding. To be safe, you should purify water from the lakes for drinking, and if people continue to camp there, water quality can only get worse. Firewood is nonexistent and only one small site at Emerald has any trees in which you can hang food, so bears can be a serious problem.

It is possible to camp at Mirror Lake, and if you plan to rock-climb or explore the upper cirque, it is the only logical place to camp. Mirror Lake is not often crowded, but it is a good idea to check when you pick up your wilderness permit to see if any other parties plan to be there. More than two small parties at Mirror Lake would be very crowded. Again there is no firewood, so be sure to take your stove. Only persons in good physical condition and experienced in cross-country travel should attempt the difficult hike to Mirror Lake with packs.

You can follow any of a labyrinth of trails through Morris Meadow to the north end, where you should work up toward the east side and look for a large double-trunked ponderosa pine. The main trail runs north past this tree and into the open red fir forest beyond. A quarter mile through grass and ferns on the floor of beautiful mature forest brings you to a few good campsites close to the now much smaller Stuart Fork. Some heavy timbers are still stacked here from the days when mule trains carried them up to the construction sites at the lakes. The timbers are historically valuable; please don't burn them.

The trail next leads moderately steeply up the east side of a narrower canyon through patches of forest, waist-high ferns and open, brushy slopes. To this point, the trail tread has been in excellent condition, but it gets rougher now, and is washed out in places. Two miles from Morris Meadow, as the canyon is turning west, a marvelous cold spring gushes across the trail. The hillside is very moist for some distance on both sides of the spring and we tunnel through thickets of alders and big-leaf maples. In small openings masses of flowers—larkspur, monkshood, leopard lily, bog orchid and fireweed—crowd the trail. Another .5 mile brings us into an area of small meadows and willow flats, bisected by the small river, where a few good campsites nestle in groves of quaking aspen and fir. At the head of this wide spot in the canyon, Portuguese Camp, with room for 10–15 people in several excellent sites, is sheltered in a grove of large red firs.

Side Trip to Sawtooth Ridge/Caribou Trail

A fairly new sign at Portuguese Camp reads "STUART FORK TR. 9W20, CARIBOU TRAIL, DEER CREEK TR."—no mention of Emerald or Sapphire Lake. The Caribou trail junction is 300 yards west, up the rocky Stuart Fork trail in the middle of a thick patch of brush. A sign of the same vintage as the one at Portuguese Camp marks the junction.

Opinions vary about how many switchbacks are on the 2200-foot climb up the very steep south face of Sawtooth Ridge, but the consensus seems to be somewhere between 89 and 98. Once you have found the junction and decided for sure that you want to make the trip to Caribou, you will have no trouble following the track up the ridge; there is simply no other place you can walk through the heavy brush and up the open metamorphosed rock above. It is 3.6 miles from this junction to Big Caribou Lake. With packs it will take you a minimum of four hours to walk that distance, including some time at the crest for absorbing and photographing the incredible views. Carry water, and start early in the morning; the south slope can get brutally hot by noon in midsummer. A young person died on this hill in 1982, presumably of heat prostration and complications. Horses are not allowed on this section of the trail.

From the crest of the ridge you can see Big Caribou Lake and all of the trail down the north side to it. Directions for finding the trail from Big Caribou Lake headed south are in Trip 13, as is the description (in reverse) of the 9 miles of trail out to Big Flat trailhead.

A half mile above Portuguese Camp the Stuart Fork trail passes a few fair campsites and comes close to the tiny river for the last time before climbing up the north side of the canyon on its way to Emerald Lake. Turning west again across the slope, you climb moderately to steeply on open, rocky slopes and through belts of brush and red firs, headed for the north side of the massive rock dike at the lower end of Emerald Lake. The outlet creek that will be the Stuart Fork cascades over ledges below to the south. Halfway along a level stretch of trail, surrounded by lush foliage and wildflowers, another fine spring tumbles down a ledge and across the trail.

As you climb the final quarter mile of rough, steep trail to the top of the dike, the rock under foot changes from metamorphic to granite. The canyon walls on both sides of Emerald Lake are also granite, showing a sharp line of demarcation where the red, metamorphic strata of Sawtooth Ridge begin. The trail passes a terribly over-used campsite in a small grove of firs at the north end of the rock dike, then dips down almost to the lake before climbing again to run above the north shore on its way to Sapphire Lake. Horses and pack stock are discouraged above Portuguese Camp since there is no forage and no tie area at Emerald Lake. The trail to Sapphire Lake is generally considered impassable to horses.

Emerald Lake is an outstandingly beautiful, 21-acre lake filling a bowl gouged out of solid granite by the same glaciers that were born in the giant cirque above and that carved out the 2000-foot deep canyon. A dam of cut and fitted granite blocks was built in the 1890s to fill the notch worn by the outlet stream at the south end of the natural granite dike at the east end of the lake. This dam raised the level of the lake more than 20 feet to store water to be run down the ditch to the La Grange Mine. The dam is broached now, and the lake has returned to its former level, but the rest of the dam remains as a monument to the prodigal efforts men will exert to get gold out of the ground.

Emerald Lake is normally warm enough for good swimming by the first of August. The shelving rocks and sandy slope at the northeast corner of the lake provide easy access to the water and a convenient place to sun-bathe and admire the scenery. Unfortunately, some people choose to camp here to the discomfiture of others and, eventually, of themselves. It would be hard to imagine a worse place to camp. Fishing is not spectacular in the lake, but some small brook trout will usually rise to flies toward evening. Best place to fish is near the inlet at the southwest end of the lake.

The trail to Sapphire Lake contours around the north shore of Emerald Lake, turning southwest through brush and across a talus slope about 100 yards above the water. As you approach the connecting stream between the two lakes, the trail turns to snake up west over steep granite shelves. Beyond a shoulder of rock you will see rusting remains of machinery on the rock face below between the trail and the cascading creek. There is an air compressor, a tank and a winch, dating from the turn of the century, and the high-pressure Pelton waterwheel that provided power. It must have been quite a sight when it was operating, with water flying everywhere; there doesn't seem to have been any housing at all around the wheel. The nozzle and a few of the cups from the rim of the wheel are still there.

Near the top of this second granite dike pieces of penstock and compressed air pipe are scattered about. The remains of two derricks, which must have been driven by compressed air engines, sit among jumbled piles of granite blocks intended for use in a dam across the outlet of Sapphire Lake. A shelter has been built of some of the timbers the miners hauled up here. All these things are historical objects and are protected as such. Please leave them in place for future visitors to see.

Sapphire Lake is twice as big as Emerald Lake, and is reported to be more than 200 feet deep, deepest lake in the Trinity Alps. From the dike at the east end of the lake, three sides of a giant granite cirque with remnant snowfields spread before your eyes. Almost directly west a higher shelf hides Mirror Lake, hanging under the sheer upper ramparts. Thick brush and scrub willows cover some of the lower slopes near the lake, but trees are scarce. Only a few stunted weeping spruces, mountain hemlocks, red firs and whitebark pines manage to grow in cracks and pockets in the rocks.

Fishing is no better in Sapphire Lake than in Emerald Lake, and only the most hardy will find the water warm enough for swimming, but Sapphire is a spectacularly beautiful lake—a jewel, as its name implies. A few very poor campsites have been scraped out in the rocks at the outlet end of the lake. There is no firewood and no place to hang food.

Off-Trail to Mirror Lake

To get to Mirror Lake, you must first get to the west end of Sapphire Lake. A rough trail has been blasted and picked out of a cliff face on the north side of the lake for the first 200 yards. Beyond the cliff the trail disintegrates into several tracks across a seep and up into heavy brush. At this point you may begin to wonder whether you would have been better off to climb over the tumbled granite blocks on the south side of the lake. Either way is difficult, but most people choose the north shore—some of those rocks along the south shore are as big as two-story houses.

On the north side work your way up to a shelf 100 feet or more above the water and push through the brush almost directly west. Other people have been here so you will probably find some traces of a use trail. At a little less than a half mile the brush thins somewhat in a slide area 300–400 yards from the lake and some ducks point north toward a pair of sheer-faced granite knobs. You can get up this way, crossing below a waterfall on Mirror Lake's outlet, then scrambling around an outcrop and up a tilted ledge and a chimney to the lip of the shelf. However, a safer, though longer, route is to continue west to the north edge of the giant talus slope at the head of Sapphire Lake and boulder-hop up to the far end of the shelf on which Mirror Lake sits. Either way is very strenuous, but your first glimpse of exquisite Mirror Lake beyond the ridges of glaciated granite on the shelf will make the climb worthwhile.

For thousands of years, slowly moving ice ground and gouged at this resistant granite shelf to leave behind the polished mounds and ridges and the 12–15 acre lake with its convoluted shoreline and four small rock islands. Mirror Lake lives up to its name; soaring walls of granite on three sides, punctuated with dwarfed weeping spruce and hemlock, and a perpetual snowfield above the west shore are beautifully reflected in the usually placid water. From the open east edge of the shelf a sensational panorama includes all of the upper Stuart Fork canyon. Emerald and Sapphire lakes shimmer far below, and sheer canyon walls climax in Sawtooth Ridge to the north and Sawtooth Mountain to the south. Sunrises seen from this high perch are truly inspiring.

A few unprotected, fair campsites are in the hollows of rock southeast of the lake. Although more trees seem to survive up here than down at Sapphire Lake, firewood is very scarce and you should cook on a stove. Shallow areas of the lake may be warm enough for swimming on mid-August afternoons, and 10-inch rainbow trout cruise the drop-offs at sundown looking for something to eat. The walls of the upper cirque offer challenges for experienced rock climbers.

The heavy use that prevails around the two lower lakes has not yet reached Mirror Lake and you will find it, and its surroundings, almost pristine. Please tread lightly and leave nothing that will remind others that you have been here.

Mirror Lake

Trip 3

Stuart Fork to Alpine Lake

Trip Type: Round trip of 2 to 4 days

Distance: 8.7 miles one way from Stuart Fork trailhead (3.6 miles one way from Oak Flat junction)

Elevation Change: 3800 feet one way from trailhead, 2780 from Oak Flat, average 437/772 feet per mile respectively

Season: Mid-July to late September

Topo Maps: *Rush Creek Lakes* and *Siligo Peak* (both provisional 1982) 7.5′ quadrangles

Although the elevation is only 6112 feet, Alpine Lake does have many of the characteristics suggested by its name. This picturesque lake fills the bottom of a slot carved by glaciers on the east side of the ridge north of Little Granite Peak and west of the lower Stuart Fork valley. Little sun reaches the bottom of the steep-walled basin and some snow may linger around the lake until the end of July, resulting in an ecosystem that might be expected at higher altitudes.

Along with the spectacular vertical scenery around the lake, the main attractions are the abundant marsh-oriented wildflowers in the verdant little valley just below the lake and the opportunity to explore, off-trail, the high ridge leading north to secluded Smith and Morris Lakes and rugged Sawtooth Mountain.

Since the Forest Service improved the trail in the late 1970s, adding a mile of longer switchbacks, Alpine Lake has become a higher use area. Firewood is scarce, the three small campsites at the lake are often full, and the mouse and chipmunk population has exploded. Fishing is only fair for small eastern brook trout in the lake itself and in pools in the creek below the lake. The view from the top of the trail back down the Stuart Fork valley to Clair Engle Lake is still spectacular.

The 2600-foot climb from Oak Flat to the lake is arduous, and must have been a horror before the new switchbacks were added. Some very steep and rocky pitches block access to horses and pack stock. If carrying a pack, you should plan on a 4-hour climb from Oak Flat and get an early start; the last 2 miles up the hill are through heavy brush, steep and in full sun. Water is available only once, 1.75 mile from the Oak Flat junction, until the outlet stream is crossed just below the lake.

Starting Point

To reach the Alpine Lake trail junction in Oak Flat, walk 5.1 miles up the Stuart Fork trail from the trailhead at Bridge Camp, 2 miles north of Trinity Alps resort. Directions to the trailhead and the description of the Stuart Fork trail to the junction are in Trip 2.

Description

Two hundred yards west of the Stuart Fork trail junction, the Alpine Lake/Boulder Creek trail drops over a steep bank to a shaded flat and a large, open gravel bar beside the river. A number of excellent campsites are on the flat and in clumps of cottonwoods and firs on the gravel bar. Driftwood on the bar offers an adequate supply of firewood for a long time into the future if we are all conservative in our use. Fishing is better here in the Stuart Fork than at Alpine Lake, unless the water is high, in which case you are not going to be able to make the ford and reach the trail to Alpine Lake on the other side anyway.

If the river is very low, you may be able to boulder-hop across near the remains of an old diversion dam, but more likely you will have to wade. Up on

Waterfall on the way to Alpine Lake

Alpine Lake

the west bank of the Stuart Fork the trail runs south, climbing slightly, almost to Boulder Creek, then turns back to climb more steeply a little west of north before turning west into the north side of Boulder Creek canyon. You soon climb higher up the side of the canyon in thick, mixed forest, through a significant number of deadfalls, and start a series of moderately steep zigzags up the nose of a ridge away from Boulder Creek. As the climb eases in more open forest, 1 mile from the Stuart Fork crossing, a large, dead ponderosa pine snag, along with a small cairn, marks the somewhat inconspicuous junction of the Alpine Lake trail turning steeply north. A sign on the snag states "STUART FORK TRAIL" back the way you came, and a smaller sign on a fir on the opposite side of the trail says "CANYON CREEK," pointing up the continuation of the Boulder Creek trail over the crest to the west and down Bear Creek to Canyon Creek.

After a short, steep start north up the Alpine Lake trail through a field of granite boulders, you begin a series of long switchbacks, climbing moderately in heavy brush well east of the outlet creek from the lake. Three-quarters mile from the trail junction a switchback extends almost to the little creek and to a good, but small, campsite tucked under a large Jeffrey pine. A short, steep scramble down to the stream will allow you to cool your fevered brow in clear, cold water and to refill your water bottles. As usual, treat the water before you drink it.

You continue up the next set of switchbacks over broken granite covered with a mat of huckleberry oak, manzanita, ceanothus and scrubby Oregon oak. A half mile from the water stop, you climb very steeply onto some granite knobs where you can hear, but not see, a waterfall. Another .3 mile through brush and over rocks brings you to the foot of the ledge over which the little creek is falling, 50 yards from the trail and almost impossible to reach. Some very steep zigzags up through rocks at the east end of the ledge lead to the top of a knob, where you can see into the cirque above Alpine Lake.

An almost level traverse across the top of the canyon takes you west through some tiny, flowery meadows to a crossing of the outlet creek just below a cascade over a rock dike. Instead of climbing directly up the faint track beside the cascade, you should look for the trail along the base of the dike and walk 50 yards south before switchbacking over the top. Beyond the dike you are at the lower end of a beautiful green valley a little less than one-quarter mile long and half as wide. The creek meanders in a wide, still channel through lush, marshy grass and sedges, dotted with wildflowers. Little brook trout flick a series of interlocking rings that fracture the reflections of a few huge granite boulders deposited by ancient glaciers.

The trail runs up the south side of the valley for almost 300 yards, then turns and crosses the creek to continue through the grass on the north side and over a low moraine to the lower end of the lake. Be sure to cross the creek, since the trail that continues up the south side of the valley leads to some vertical rock faces which will prevent you from reaching the lake.

Fourteen-acre Alpine Lake fills the bottom of a deep, narrow cirque gouged out of granite and metasedimentary rock. Rows of grotesquely eroded pinnacles thrust into the sky at the top of the cliffs. Brooding weeping spruce and firs are reflected in the dark water, while ghostly limbs of fallen snags reach from the depths near the outlet, and particularly on a cloudy day the entire aspect can be a bit somber. Only three fair campsites are in the rocks, brush and trees at the lower end of the lake. If all those sites are full, your hope for a sense of solitude will be greatly diminished, as the only icons missing from the usual campground experience will be the winnebagos and boom boxes. A slightly better site is above the south side of the valley below the lake. If you are the only one camped at the lake, enjoy the magnificent blessing. If not, carefully respect the desire of others for privacy.

Cross-Country Route to Smith and Morris Lakes

The first part of the route to Smith Lakes is by far the worst, involving steep bushwhacking as you climb out of the Alpine Lake basin. Once you have surmounted this obstacle, however, the travel becomes much easier. From Alpine Lake find the path that leads east along the northern edge of the meadow just below the lake. At the east end and slightly above the meadow in a clearing there is a dead snag, from which paths lead up into the brush on the hillside above. The goal is to find the least offensive route through this brush to open slopes above. There doesn't appear to be a "right" way to accomplish this goal, as many paths appear and disappear all along this slope. But, if you head for just above or slightly below the lower set of rounded dark granitic cliffs, you should be able to surmount this nasty section with the least amount of problems.

Once above the brushy section, the way does indeed open up and the climbing is much more pleasant as you ascend a gully north over mildly sloping granite slabs interspersed with low shrubs and dotted with occasional hemlocks and pines. While continuing to climb to the left (west) of the creek, head for a notch at the low point in the ridge above. Increasingly spectacular views greet you with each step.

Approximately 1 mile from Alpine Lake you reach the top of the ridge and are met with views of Mt. Shasta and Sawtooth Mountain. In most years you will encounter a patch of snow just beyond the saddle on the north-facing slope. Descend this slope to the west to a group of rocks. From this point you get a glimpse of a lake, not Smith Lake, but the smaller and slightly higher Morris Lake; Smith Lake, much larger, lies just out of view behind granite cliffs and ridges. Make an angling descent following a line of sight that corresponds to a ridge coming down from the summit of Sawtooth Mountain, over granite slabs, boulders and interlocking meadows to the point where the outlet creek exits Smith Lake.

Try to reach the lake near the outlet, as the slopes higher up around Smith Lake are quite steep and very difficult to descend. The outlet creek itself is wedged between granitic walls 20 to 30 feet high which makes the last part of the trip down to the lake a bit tricky. The easiest way seems to be right where the outlet creek leaves the lake, where you are able to scramble down some dirt ramps to a point where you can hop across the creek. The travel is much easier from here.

Smith Lake is a gorgeous subalpine lake surrounded by scattered hemlocks and rugged slopes that lead northwest up to the dramatic peak of Sawtooth Mountain. At the far end of the lake, a stream from above falls 50 feet over a sheer granite cliff before joining the exceedingly clear water of Smith Lake. Good-sized rainbow and brook trout inhabit the 24-acre lake, and fishing pressure should be minimal. Due to the length of time required and the difficulty of the route to get here, you should enjoy a reasonable level of solitude while appreciating the majestic environment at Smith.

Camping is limited to benches and shelves adjacent to and above the eastern shore of the lake just north of the crossing of the outlet stream. For those with enough energy left to reach them, there are even nicer campsites on the bench above the waterfall at the far end of Smith Lake. To get there you must climb up and over a rock knob, avoiding the steep cliffs below, descend slightly and traverse over to the bench. Wonderful places to camp are nestled under tall hemlocks and adjacent to streams that dance their way over granite slabs into delightful little ponds.

The route to Morris Lake heads west up from the bench across the streams and up slabs to the far left of the waterfall coming down from Morris Lake. As you work your way up the slabs you will draw closer to the water and actually follow the creek the last 200 feet up the channel into the basin. Cross over the creek and follow the beaten path along the right (north) side of the creek to the lake.

Morris Lake is a much smaller lake than Smith, but it possesses its own unique charm. While Smith is much more dramatic, Morris offers a more pastoral feeling. The topography around the lake is not as steep, consisting of rolling granite slabs interspersed with meadows, wildflowers and heather. You also get a much more intimate view of Sawtooth Mountain and the challenges it poses for the mountaineer. Camping is on the western shore in a grove of hemlocks not far from the inlet creek.

The route to Smith and Morris lakes is strenuous, but not particularly difficult by cross-country standards. With the exception of the brushy section just above Alpine Lake, the travel is enjoyable and straightforward. Plan on a good half-day to make the 2-mile off-trail climb with a pack.

Trip 4

Deer Creek and Four Lakes Loop to Long Canyon

Trip Type: Through trip of 5 to 8 days requiring a car shuttle or pick-up

Distance: 25 miles from Stuart Fork trailhead to Long Canyon trailhead

Elevation Change: 11,545 feet without side trips, average 462 feet per mile

Season: Early July to end of September

Topo Maps: *Rush Creek Lakes, Siligo Peak* and *Covington Mill* (all provisional 1982) 7.5' quadrangles

The Four Lakes Loop trail circles all the way around 8162-foot Siligo Peak, switchbacking over three spur ridges in the process. Along the way are views in all directions of the highest peaks and deepest canyons of the Trinity Alps. Each of the four lakes is different, in character as well as size, and each is delightful.

The approach up Deer Creek canyon from Morris Meadow is through a lush mix of forests, meadows and alder and willow flats. Sheer rock faces at the head of Deer Creek and several peaks over 8000 feet illustrate the mixed-up geology of this part of the Trinity Alps and offer rock-climbing opportunities. Wide expanses of fragrant wildflowers bloom in the high basins in July and August. Deer Creek and the Four Lakes Loop are less crowded than the Stuart Fork, but don't expect to be entirely alone. Deer Creek Camp and the meadows above it get constant use by horse packers coming in from the Long Canyon trailhead, and the trail over the ridge from Granite Lake is popular with backpackers. Stock use on the Four Lakes Loop is discouraged—the trail is steep and narrow, and there are no tie areas or suitable forage.

Echo Lake and Lake Anna can be reached by side trips from Deer Creek Pass and Bee Tree Gap. An alternate 44-mile loop trip back to the Stuart Fork trailhead continues south on the Stoney Ridge trail through Siligo Meadows

Trip 4
Deer Creek and Four Lakes Loop to Long Canyon

and Van Matre Meadows; then over Stonewall Pass and down Trinity Alps
Creek to the road near Trinity Alps Resort.

Starting Point

Directions to the Stuart Fork trailhead and description of 8.4 miles of the
Stuart Fork trail to the Deer Creek trail junction are in Trip 2.

Long Canyon trailhead is reached by a road up the north side of the East
Fork of Stuart Fork. From the Trinity Alps Resort junction (see Trip 2) drive
9.6 miles northeast on Highway 3 to a bridge over the East Fork of Stuart Fork.
Just before you cross the bridge, a sign points right to Guy Covington Drive.
Just beyond the bridge the paved, but narrow, East Fork road turns left. At 2.6
miles from Highway 3 a well-used dirt road turns right up the side of the
canyon from the East Fork road. A not very obvious sign at the junction points
to Long Canyon trailhead. If you come to a bridge across the East Fork, you've
gone .3 mile past the Long Canyon junction. The trailhead, with plenty of
parking space, is well marked and is on the left .3 mile up the dirt road.
Although the dirt road is a little rough and steep, a modern sedan should be
able to negotiate it without any trouble.

Description

Walking south out of Morris Meadows you turn southeast on the north spur of
the Deer Creek trail **Y** branching from the Stuart Fork trail at the south end of
the main meadow. Coming up the Stuart Fork you should look for the junction
of the south spur of the **Y** in open forest at the top of the last steep pitch .3 mile
below Morris Meadow. If you reach the junction late in the day, you may want
to camp at Morris Meadow—the first good campsite on the Deer Creek trail is
3.3 miles over the ridge at Willow Creek.

The two spurs of the trail join near the base of the big ridge between the
Stuart Fork and Deer Creek. The trail from here to the top of the divide has
been rebuilt in 10 long switchbacks. From the ridgetop, with an outstanding
view back at Sawtooth Mountain, you descend moderately for .3 mile, then level
off to contour northeast on the northwest side of Deer Creek canyon through
open forest that includes some very large ponderosa pines, sugar pines, Douglas
firs and some incense cedars. After dipping into a lateral gulch containing a
little creek, you climb out onto a bench above the steep-walled gorge that Deer
Creek has cut into alluvial material at the bottom of the canyon. Several more
small streams cross the trail as we climb away from Deer Creek through small
meadows and patches of oak brush interspersed with white fir and incense
cedar to a crossing of Willow Creek.

The Willow Creek trail junction and a good, large campsite are 200 yards
beyond where the creek tumbles over boulders in a jungle of alders. A sign for
the Willow Creek trail is on a three-trunked cedar up the hill north of the camp.
This trail crosses the Trinity Divide near Tri-Forest Peak and continues down
to Big Flat trailhead, 7.5 miles from the junction.

Continuing east on the Deer Creek trail you climb gently to moderately through wide meadows and alder and willow flats. A beautiful little stream, in the middle of one of the dense growths of willows, waters a splendid garden of head-high delphiniums. As the canyon turns gradually south, the trail climbs moderately on the east side over glacial till supporting sparse forest and ferny meadows dotted with white-flowering yampa and other wildflowers. At 1.5 miles from Willow Creek you turn to cross Deer Creek twice within one-quarter mile. The first campsites of half-mile-long Deer Creek Camp appear between the trail and the creek as you climb a rocky hillside above the second crossing. The Black Basin trail snakes up the steep east wall of the canyon from a junction halfway through this cluster of heavily used, but still good, campsites. The herds of cattle that used to graze here are long gone. However, the cattle have been partially replaced by horses and pack mules that now crowd the meadows at times. Fishing for both eastern brook and rainbow trout is fair to good in the creek below the camp.

From the Black Basin junction the Deer Creek trail descends slightly, then turns west to cross the little creek at the foot of a lush, wet meadow. You turn south again on the west side of the canyon well above a series of meadows and climb moderately for a mile to a grove of firs beside a cascade in the creek. As you turn up the side of the hill in the trees, a well-used, unsigned trail forks steeply to the right up the hill in loose, sandy soil. This is the old trail to Luella and Diamond lakes shown on the 1950 *Trinity Dam* quadrangle. You *can* go this way if you like, and pick up the newer Four Lakes Loop trail on the hill above Round Lake, but it is much easier to continue up the Deer Creek trail past the Granite Lake junction to the signed junction of the Four Lakes Loop turning west beside a tiny tributary of Deer Creek. If you are planning to go out to the Swift Creek trailhead by way of Granite Lake, it is 7.5 miles over the steep ridge from the Deer Creek trail junction (see Trip 6).

Round Lake is 200 yards west of the Deer Creek trail, surrounded by willows in a marshy flat. Although Round Lake is really more a pond than a lake, it is swimmable and a few 12-inch eastern brook trout have been taken from it. J. W. Cow Camp, dating from mining days, offers several excellent sites one-quarter mile farther along at the base of the hill below Luella Lake.

The rebuilt trail now climbs only moderately in six long switchbacks to a shelf below the cirque containing Luella Lake. The one fair campsite in the area is in the rocks above, and south of, the trail just before you dip into the little valley below the lake. You will have to tunnel through willows to the outlet stream in the valley or walk 250 yards to the lake to get water, and you will probably feel safer if you purify it. Firewood is virtually nonexistent, although a few foxtail and whitebark pines do manage to grow among the rocks.

Despite the snowbank that usually lingers for most of the summer above the south shore, the greenish waters of 2.5-acre Luella Lake are warm enough for hardy swimmers by mid-August. A few open spaces in the thick willows lining the shoreline, near where the trail approaches, may give you enough room to cast for pan-sized brook trout. Red metamorphic rock, extending most of the way around the lake, changes to granite on the south side leading up to the ragged crags of Siligo Peak. Siligo is a difficult climb from this side, but is a walk-up from the trail near Summit Lake on the south side.

The daily big attraction at Luella Lake is staged across the upper basin of Deer Creek as the shadow of the west ridge moves slowly up the sheer east wall across from your vantage point on the rock balcony below the lake. You may be so entranced that you forget to cook dinner as you watch the last flaming rays fade from the tops of the cliffs and the basin turn purple below—but the show is worth the wait.

From the shelf below Luella Lake you can see most of the trail to the top of the cirque ahead of you, switchbacking across talus slides on its way up the very steep west slope. You should carry water—there is no sure source of water between Luella and Diamond lakes. Begin the climb with a traverse north to a rim, then turn back southwest and start a series of long switchbacks, arcing around the west side of the cirque. A steep climb of .7 mile on sometimes rough tread is rewarded at the top with breathtaking views west across the Stuart Fork and east to Gibson and Seven Up peaks.

The top of the ridge is beautifully grassy under widely spaced, large foxtail pines, western white pines and red firs. You descend from the crest in moderate switchbacks across an open hillside, carpeted with grass and decorated with a myriad of wildflowers: mountain asters, mints, Indian paintbrushes and angelicas. Diamond Lake, hanging above yawning Stuart Fork canyon, comes into view from halfway down the slope.

The shallow, 2.5-acre diamond-shaped lake hangs on the lip of a shelf at the bottom of a U-shaped valley that funnels steeply down from a lateral ridge west of Siligo Peak. The one poor campsite at Diamond Lake is under a foxtail pine near the trail, the only large tree near the lake. Stone walls, built around the site by previous campers, give a clue to the overnight weather conditions you might expect on this unprotected perch. Good water is available from tiny streams above the lake, but firewood is nonexistent. On the plus side, the view of Sawtooth Mountain and the other peaks and ridges around the head of the Stuart Fork is overwhelming, and an amazing number and variety of wildflowers bloom around the grassy shoreline of the lake. Fishing is fair for eastern brook trout.

A new trail from Diamond Lake to Summit Lake runs around the east side of Diamond Lake and up to a shelf, then climbs east on 10 moderately steep switchbacks through a flower garden just north of a long, red-rock talus slide. Wild flax and stonecrop bloom in profusion among the many other wildflowers on the hillside. You traverse across the top of the talus, then climb another series of steeper switchbacks southwest through more flowers and rocks to a narrow crest.

Summit Lake, now in full view to the southeast, is so near the top of Peak 8059 that it appears to be in a volcanic crater. Peak 8059 is not volcanic—the basin was scooped out of sedimentary and metamorphosed rocks by the same glaciers that carved the rest of the local landscape.

The trail climbs gradually east along the crest, then contours level around the southwest flank of Siligo Peak to a junction 1.4 miles from Diamond Lake. The right fork descends a rocky slope .3 mile to the north shore of Summit Lake. The other fork continues east to Deer Creek Pass and Deer Lake. Four or five good campsites are distributed among scattered foxtail and whitebark pines above the north and west shores. Firewood is scarce and the lake is the only source of water. Summit Lake has no inlet or outlet streams except during peak run-off periods. The water should be purified before drinking.

Summit is the largest (13 acres) and the highest (7400 feet) of the four lakes around Siligo Peak. It is a lovely subalpine lake, its dark-blue water contrasting sharply with the stark red rocks of its surroundings. A base camp here will allow you to explore a lot of surrounding country on day-hikes and climbs. Fishing is fair to good for both rainbow and brook trout to 10 inches. Only the hardiest swimmers will stay in the chilly water very long at any time of year.

The trail to Deer Creek Pass and Deer Lake turns north from the junction above Summit Lake and climbs moderately steeply 200 yards to a notch in the solid rock ridge between Siligo Peak and Peak 8059. The terrain east of the crest is laid out below you like a map. Deer Lake lies a little north of east at the bottom of a giant, almost bare cirque. North of Deer Lake a steep drop-off hides the head of Deer Creek canyon. The trail we are on makes five switchbacks down a shoulder of Siligo Peak, then contours around to meet the trail snaking

Summit Lake sits in a crater-like basin near the top of Peak 8059

Trip 4
Deer Creek and Four Lakes Loop to Long Canyon

up from Deer Lake one-quarter mile below Deer Creek Pass on the south lip of the cirque.

An interesting botanical inversion can be seen on this crest. Whitebark pines, normally seen on the highest, most exposed ridges and peaks, stop short here and are replaced by wind-blasted, contorted Jeffrey pines clinging to the uppermost rocks. A few upright Jeffreys also grow down the west side of the ridge for a short distance.

You can begin a relatively easy "walk-up" climb to the top of Siligo Peak from almost any point on the trail between the Summit Lake junction and the top of the ridge above Deer Lake. A web of use trails leads up a steep incline of red rock, granite sand, patches of brush and blocks of granite to the summit, less than a half mile from the trail. The summit offers a superb panoramic view of all the peaks and canyons of the central Trinity Alps and three of the four lakes around the peak. Luella Lake is hidden under a ragged spur ridge to the north. Mount Shasta, northeast, and Lassen Peak, farther south, punctuate the eastern horizon.

The old trail from Summit Lake to Deer Lake ran almost straight down the southwest side of the Deer Lake cirque from the notch where the present trail crosses the ridge. The old trail was considerably shorter than the present one, but brutally steep. On the other hand, the switchbacks at the top of the new trail are so long and gradual that they present a great temptation to cross-cutters. Please try to resist.

After negotiating the switchbacks, you will have plenty of time to admire Deer Lake from several angles as you make the long traverse around the south side of the cirque to the junction below Deer Creek Pass. Deer Lake is about the same size and shape as Diamond Lake. The water appears jade-green from above, in vivid contrast to the red-weathered serpentine rock around it. Also, as

The crest of Siligo Peak overlooks Deer Creek canyon

at Diamond Lake, the only usable campsite is close to the trail on the east side of the lake, sheltered by the one large tree in the vicinity. Fly-fishing on quiet evenings at Deer Lake should get you a mess of pan-sized eastern brook trout for breakfast. If the wind comes up, forget it.

A steep quarter-mile climb from the Four Lakes trail junction takes you to the top of Deer Creek Pass, overlooking verdant Siligo Meadows to the south, Deer Lake and the upper valley of Deer Creek to the north. A fairly level .6-mile traverse east from the pass leads to Bee Tree Gap at the head of Long Canyon.

Side Trip to Echo Lake

As long as you're up this high, a relatively easy 4-mile round trip will take you down through Siligo Meadows, up over Little Stonewall Pass to gorgeous, isolated Echo Lake and back to Bee Tree Gap. Heavy cattle grazing in this area should prompt you to purify all drinking water.

The Stoney Ridge trail forks south from the Deer Creek trail just south of Deer Creek Pass and drops down a moderately steep, dry hillside through scattered foxtail and whitebark pines west of a deep ravine. Well-worn cattle trails from many years of grazing may confuse your way here, but if you keep just west of the ravine, then go directly south across the lush meadow at the bottom of the hill, you will see a large, erratic boulder beyond the gurgling creeklet that is the beginning of Deep Creek. You can pick up the not very obvious trail again, with the help of a few blazes and cut logs, south of the boulder in a belt of thicker forest. You will soon come to a more clearly defined track in the trees that leads into more open country and begins to climb moderately on the side of a ridge, still directly south, toward Little Stonewall Pass. The lower part of Siligo Meadows, including a number of small ponds with raised grass rims, stretches away below to the northwest where Deep Creek falls over the edge of Stuart Fork canyon. It is a very bucolic scene, including cows. Newer switchbacks have been added to ease the climb a little as you get closer to Little Stonewall Pass. Some different types of rock show up here in slides from the cliffs to the east: slates and serpentines as well as unmetamorphosed sandstones of various colors.

A quarter mile south of Little Stonewall Pass the trail levels off in a meadow. Look for a small pond among the erratic boulders at the east end of the meadow. If you walk around the pond and on east through a gap, you will see Echo Lake directly below you at the bottom of a large cirque. No official trail leads to the lake, but a number of use trails do.

Echo is a gorgeous teardrop-shaped, subalpine lake of 2.5 acres, outside the boundary of the old primitive area, but now included in the Trinity Alps Wilderness. Rock slides that reach almost to the tops of some of the cirque's cliffs have leveled out and filled in around the shoreline of the lake to form exquisite little meadows and flower gardens. Water seeps and gurgles through the slides on the east and north sides of the cirque, and enough soil has formed to support an amazing growth of flowers and ferns. A few stunted red firs, hemlocks and whitebark pines grow around the lake.

One poor campsite is on the southeast shore, too close to the lake. Much better places to camp are near the little pond above, or around Van Matre Meadow below. Fishing is fair for small brook trout.

You have two alternatives to backtracking over Little Stonewall Pass and through Siligo Meadows to Bee Tree Gap or Deer Creek Pass. One is to continue on through Van Matre Meadows, over Stonewall Pass and out to Trinity Alps Resort. The other alternative leads eventually to Long Canyon, not through Bee Tree Gap, but up the incline on the northeast side of the Echo Lake cirque, over the top and down past Billy-Be-Damned Lake to Lake Anna. From Lake Anna it is relatively easy to get down to the Long Canyon trail (see Side Trip to Lake Anna). The route is very strenuous, but offers solitude and fantastic scenery.

If you decide to return to Bee Tree Gap, you need not go all the way back to the junction by Deer Creek Pass. Instead, when you return to upper Siligo Meadow, cross the beginnings of Deep Creek and head for the hill to the east of the ravine that you stayed west of on the way south. Climb northeast on crisscrossing cattle trails, then continue on a faint track around the southeast side of a small meadow above. The well-defined trail from Deer Creek Pass to Bee Tree Gap crosses the upper edge of this meadow. You turn east on this trail and climb moderately steeply to the gap in the ridge.

Far beyond a distant arm of Clair Engle Lake and a series of purple ridges, Lassen Peak thrusts above the eastern skyline, 85 air-miles from your vantage point at Bee Tree Gap. Mount Shasta hides behind the crenelated bulk of Gibson Peak, towering above the north side of the green-floored basin directly below you at the head of Long Canyon. Closer up, gnarled red firs and mountain hemlocks, stunted lupines, pussy paws and stonecrops testify to the alpine character of the crest.

The Long Canyon trail first descends north in two short switchbacks, then turns back south to more switchbacks before rounding a spur ridge and contouring down to a delightful little meadow notched into the south wall of the canyon .9 mile from the summit. An icy little stream wanders from under a semipermanent snowbank to water the lush, green grass and refresh passers-by. Two good campsites are among the boulders around the meadow. Please don't camp in the meadow or forage stock here; the little patch of green could be ruined by just one such transgression.

The wide, rocky slope reaching up to the base of the cliffs on the crest, west and south of our little shelf, supports the thickest and most extensive growth of wildflowers to be found in the Trinity Alps. Acres and acres of Indian paintbrush, angelica and western pasqueflower reach almost as far as the eye can see. Under these taller flowers are amazing numbers of smaller varieties: bluebells, evening primroses and gilias for starters, crowding one another for space in the sun.

Side Trip to Lake Anna

Lake Anna gets more visitors now than in years past, but it's still a pretty safe bet that you won't be crowded if you decide to spend a night there. The deep, 4-acre lake is in the bottom of a steep-sided bowl of naked, red-weathered rock, hanging near the top of the ridge between Long Canyon and Bowerman Canyon.

The most direct, and probably the easiest, way to get up there is to climb the west side of the gully leading up south from the little meadow with the snowbank .9 mile below Bee Tree Gap in Long Canyon. Traces of a use trail lead up through the boulders, rock debris and occasional marshy spots. Miniature rock gardens of shade- and moisture-loving flowers grow along the banks of the gully. The first quarter mile is very steep and rough, easing to merely steep for the next quarter mile to a saddle where widely spaced, magnificent Shasta red firs shelter two good campsites. These would be excellent campsites except that firewood is scarce and the only source of water is the lake, 250 yards south and almost straight down.

It is a gorgeous lake, however, with remarkable views east over Bowerman Canyon and reflections of rugged cliffs to the west. Fishing is good for eastern brook trout to 10 inches, and the campsites above are grandstand seats for the finest sunrises you are apt to see anywhere.

You can also reach Lake Anna by a cross-country route along the base of the cliffs southeast of Bee Tree Gap. You avoid the steep climb that way, but the off-trail distance is farther and the route is rough and hard to follow. Confirmed masochists may want to try the climb up the outlet creek from the head of Bowerman Canyon, but it's not recommended for normal people. The Bowerman route is not even a good way to get *down* from Lake Anna.

From the little meadow hanging on the south side of upper Long Canyon the trail zigzags down on steep, rocky tread to cross the small creek in the bottom of the canyon, then turns east along the north slope. A series of meadows and willow flats, decorated with flowers in season, slopes moderately down for a mile to a narrower, wooded section of the canyon, where the trail drops steeply again on rough, worn tread. The tread gets a little better as the descent eases and the trail turns away from the creek, but disintegrates again on some newer switchbacks dropping steeply to the Bowerman Canyon trail junction, 3 miles from Bee Tree Gap. Heavy horse traffic has torn up this section of trail and makes it extremely dusty by late summer.

The junction is signed "BOWERMAN MEADOW TRAIL 8W22" on the fork to the southwest, and "FS ROAD 35N21Y" on our trail running on down the East Fork of Stuart Fork. A small, poor campsite, tucked under the trees near the junction, is the first since leaving the little meadow 2 miles back. Madrones and big-leaf maples begin to show up in the forest as you descend the next .7 mile of better, and only moderately steep, trail to the crossing of a good-sized tributary well up from the East Fork. A good campsite is on the east bank of the stream. You continue on an old road for the remaining .4 mile of gradual descent to the trailhead.

Trip 5

Deer Flat, Thumb Rock
Landers Creek Loop

Trip Type: Loop trip of 3 to 5 days

Distance: 19.7 miles

Elevation Change: 11,850 feet, average 602 feet per mile

Season: Mid-July to late September

Topo Maps: *Covington Mill* (provisional 1982), *Ycatapom Peak* and *Caribou Lake* (both provisional 1986) 7.5′ quadrangles

This is a strenuous trip involving almost 12,000 feet of elevation change, and the crossing of four major ridge systems. Some sections of trail are very steep and rough, and other sections are hard to find and follow. On the plus side, you will be rewarded with solitude and incomparable scenery once you get away from the thoroughfare along Swift Creek. No lakes are included in the basic loop, but you will be within easy side-trip distance of Twin, Shimmy, Lilypad and Landers lakes. Foster, Lion and Union lakes can be reached with more effort.

This trip is one of contrasts—you probably won't be able to walk a mile along Swift Creek without seeing other people, but on the traverse around Thumb Rock you may be the only people who have passed that way for weeks. Wind-blasted firs and Jeffrey pines are flattened against the rocks on the 7200-foot crest above Cub Wallow, while down in Swift Creek canyon straight boles of Douglas firs and ponderosa pines soar to 150–200 feet. The lush wet meadows at the head of Landers Creek supports acres of tropical-looking California pitcher plants—in contrast to near-desert and sagebrush around Shimmy Lake. Herds of deer graze Deer Flat in the evening and coyotes sing from the ridgetops, but in Mumford Meadow you're more apt to hear the electronic sounds of radios.

All in all, you will see more variety of flora, fauna and terrain on this trip than almost any other in the Trinity Alps.

Starting Point

Highway 3 crosses Swift Creek 29.5 miles north of Weaverville, just beyond the turnoff east to Trinity Center. The road to Swift Creek trailhead turns west .25 mile north of the Swift Creek bridge and .25 mile south of Wyntoon resort. The trailhead is 7 miles up this road, just as the sign at the junction indicates.

Narrow pavement on the Swift Creek road ends a mile from Highway 3. A well-graded dirt road wanders southwest, then west from the end of pavement, climbing steadily well above the south bank of Swift Creek. You pass a number of road forks, including two signed turnoffs to the Lake Eleanor trailhead, but the road up Swift Creek is clearly the main road at each fork. A small flat, 7 miles from the highway, offers auxiliary parking and a possible place to camp.

The trailhead, which includes a large parking lot, horse unloading and tie area, pit toilet, bulletin board and picnic table, is 200 yards up the road to the right. You would do well to ignore the camping symbol near the horse tie area. The "camp" consists of a slanted picnic table and fire pit on a rocky slope. A "STOCKWATER" sign shows the way to a beautiful, large spring below the parking lot. The source of the spring is protected by a split rail fence.

Description

The Swift Creek trail begins at the north end of the parking lot near a sign reading "FOSTERS CABIN 5, HORSESHOE LAKE 8, WARD LAKE 9." The trail was rebuilt in 1989 from the trailhead to Parker Creek, and is in good condition. The wilderness boundary is 200 yards from the trailhead.

You begin by descending through a dry gully and then coming out on a bench above Swift Creek .5 mile from the trailhead. The creek lives up to its name as it tumbles through boulders below some excellent campsites on the bench. Clumps of rare California pitcher plant grow in a marshy area farther on. Something you will undoubtedly notice very soon into the hike is the presence of old California license plates periodically nailed to tree trunks about 15 feet up from the ground. These markers have been placed along the trail to aid personnel in locating snow-survey equipment during the winter.

At 1.5 miles from the trailhead you begin to climb more steeply around the north side of a deep, narrow gorge that Swift Creek has cut through the solid metamorphic rock. You will hear the two waterfalls at the upper end of the gorge, but won't be able to see them until you walk over to the overhanging outcrops along the brink. The Granite Creek trail branches southwest above the gorge, 1.9 miles from the trailhead. Here our trail turns northwest to climb moderately steeply up the side of the canyon.

A small stream crosses the trail on a flat .8 mile from the Granite Creek junction. This little creeklet flows from Twin Lakes up on benches .4 mile north and a little east. Twin Lakes are two small ponds almost entirely covered with lilypads and surrounded by azaleas and California pitcher plants. The route up to the lakes on the west side of the stream involves bushwhacking and a scramble up a steep, muddy hillside. The lakes themselves have little to offer, but the azaleas are fragrant and beautiful.

The Swift Creek trail gets rougher and is steep in places as you climb again, moderately, to the crossing of Steer Creek. From the creek, you climb to a flat above the northwest bank, then soon drop down again to cross another small, unnamed creek. Two short switchbacks take you up to another flat, where you turn north to cross the little willow-lined creek twice, then follow it up .3 mile to the source in a small meadow. The trail turns northwest from the meadow over a low crest, and crosses another heavily forested flat to where a bridge once crossed Parker Creek. The bridge was wiped out, and the gorge was filled in, by a landslide in 1986. The trail now crosses the creek just above the former site of the bridge, then runs southwest for 200 yards along the brink of the gorge to a large camp area with a spring. A three-way trail junction is next to the camp 3.5 miles from the trailhead.

The two trails branching from the junction beside Parker Creek are: the Bear Basin/Swift Creek trail and the Parker Creek trail, which starts from the end of the campground and climbs northeast up Parker Canyon. You turn up Parker Creek on a steep, rocky trail, crossing the slide area to climb .5 mile to a junction with the Deer Flat trail at the foot of Sandy Canyon. Head down the lower trail, where 50 feet from the junction a trail sign attached to an incense cedar reads "DEER FLAT TRAIL 8W13, LILYPAD LAKE, SHIMMY LAKE."

Swift Creek Gorge

Sunrise at Shimmy Lake

You drop down 100 yards on the Deer Flat trail to cross Parker Creek and the creek from Sandy Canyon just above their confluence, then scramble up Sandy Canyon 50 yards before turning south across the side of the hill. The trail contours across several small, wet meadows covered with wildflowers early in the season, then rises steeply northeast up a gully to begin a series of switchbacks headed generally east. You top out approximately one-half mile from the Parker Creek/Deer Creek junction to head east on a gradually sloping bench overlooking Swift Creek canyon far below. This piece of trail is an absolute delight—little-used duff tread runs through open woods of ponderosa pines, Jeffrey pines, white firs and incense cedars.

Cairns and ducks mark the way as you come out of the trees and into a large meadow, then pick up the blazed trail climbing moderately in a belt of trees again before crossing another long strip of meadow where the trail disappears. Ducks guide you down to the next belt of trees and a little creek beside a large, developed campsite. Horizontal poles, wired between trees, identify this as a deer hunting camp. If you stay here for any length of time you probably will see some deer in the meadow.

The trail is not very clearly marked in the 10–15 acre wet meadow adjacent to the camp, but you can find it again by contouring around the edge of the meadow to the northeast side where a creeklet flows into the meadow. A very large cairn next to the creeklet signifies the resumption of the trail as it makes a steep, zigzagging, and sometimes boggy climb of 300 yards beside the stream up to a forested flat below yet another meadow. You climb moderately steeply a little east of north across this one and continue climbing up the forested hill above. At the edge of the next strip of meadow you turn east and soon come to the Deer Flat junction with the Lilypad Lake trail, 5.8 miles and 2700 feet higher than the Swift Creek trailhead.

Side Trip to Shimmy Lake

Shimmy Lake is .5 mile southeast down the Eleanor Lake trail from the Deer Flat trail junction. Vegetation thins as you descend moderately steeply on a few switchbacks not shown on the topo map. Sparse grass and clumps of manzanita grow in thin, rocky soil under widely spaced Jeffrey pines and white firs around the lake. Some sagebrush grows on the ridge to the south, adding to the desert-like aspect of the basin.

Comma-shaped 1.5-acre Shimmy Lake is lined with grass except for a pile of broken rock that has fallen into the west end from a blood-red outcrop above. From uncrowded grandstand seats in this rockpile you can watch the sun rise, almost out of the notch that marks the outlet, to reflect in the still water of the lake. If you're lucky, a doe and her fawn may be silhouetted against the pink sky of the rim.

Although the basin looks level at first glance, campsites are scarce. One fair site is next to a small meadow on the south side. The site under a large Jeffrey pine on the north shore is much too close to the lake. Shimmy Lake has no inlet streams, and the outlet stream usually dries up by midsummer. By late summer the lake water is brown and weedy, and should be purified for drinking. The somewhat unsavory water doesn't seem to have discouraged the few large, wary eastern brook trout that live in the deepest part of the lake off the rockpile. They make startling splashes after sundown, but are very choosy about what they eat.

Back at the Deer Flat junction, you climb north on the Lilypad Lake trail, first through thick manzanita brush on the crest of a ridge, then more steeply in open fir forest on the east side of the crest, going .5 mile to a bare, grassy saddle. The trail is hard to follow as it drops down to contour around the head of a small valley beyond the saddle—look for a rock cairn on the ridge northwest of a meadow at the head of the valley. A wider valley, falling away north toward Poison Canyon, lies below this second ridge. Ycatapom Peak (supposedly "the mountain that leans" in the local Indian language) thrusts up its ragged spires to the northeast. To the west the granite bulk of Thumb Rock looms above lush meadows and a series of small, terraced ponds.

At the crest two signs, both pointing northwest but on opposite sides of the trail, read "LILYPAD LAKE TRAIL 8W21, THUMB ROCK TRAIL, POISON CANYON TRAIL," and "THUMB ROCK TRAIL 8W16, POISON CANYON TRAIL, UNION CREEK TRAIL." If that isn't enough to confuse you, the prompt disappearance of the trail on the hillside leading down into the valley should do it. The solution to your dilemma is to continue across the head of the valley toward the southern side of Thumb Rock. The Lilypad Lake trail soon appears below, headed northeast across a

Ycatapom Peak rises above a pond at the head of Poison Canyon

pond-dotted terrace. Aptly named Lilypad Lake is a mile north in upper Poison Canyon; see Trip 8.

Your Thumb Rock trail is not quite as easy to find. Watch for rock cairns and tree blazes that will assist your negotiation across this trailless section, which lasts about 150 yards. The trail does reappear as it traverses the valley and then turns sharply uphill toward a gap in the ridgetop just southeast of Thumb Rock. Lightning-blasted Shasta red firs and foxtail pines in the gap and in cracks in the bare granite of Thumb Rock warn that this is not a good place to be in a thunderstorm. Splendid views of Mount Shasta on the horizon, and closer Ycatapom Peak and Poison Canyon reward your climb.

The trail is more evident as it winds through the gap and down southwest across open, grassy slopes and through scattered trees to a large meadow at the head of Sandy Canyon. It would appear that the trail would proceed though the meadow, but just as you reach it the trail bends slightly to the right and you climb uphill. A tiny stream in the meadow offers the last drinking water until you reach Union Creek, 3.4 miles away.

A clearer trail, marked with ducks and blazes, switchbacks moderately steeply to the crest of a red-orange rock spur ridge west of the meadow, then contours on the back side of the ridge to a junction with the Poison Canyon trail 8.5 miles from the trailhead. This well signed junction is just below the crest of a ridge running northwest from Thumb Rock, and dividing Parker Creek on the southwest side from Cub Wallow and Boulder Creek to the northwest.

The Poison Canyon trail to Union Creek soon climbs to the narrow crest of the ridge and then follows an undulating course northwest along that crest through manzanita, huckleberry oak and ceanothus bush. Through openings in the brush you can look out across the wide expanse of meadow in upper Parker Creek valley, and catch glimpses, almost straight down on the other side of the ridge, into secluded, trackless Cub Wallow, hanging above the abyss of Boulder Creek canyon. A half mile from the Deer Flat junction you turn more west, and descend slightly from the crest into open fir woods. Beyond the belt of trees you continue down around a grassy shoulder, covered with flowers in season, below a rounded, granite knob on the crest.

This part of the Poison Canyon trail is in excellent condition. Although the trail shows more deer tracks than boot or horse prints, it is still more heavily used than the Deer Flat trail around Thumb Rock. Below another band of firs, the trail runs through heavy brush in places as it descends gradually toward the saddle at the head of the Parker Creek valley. The open saddle marks the divide between Parker Creek to the south and Union Creek to the north. Your trail meets the Parker Creek/Union Creek trail right on the crest beneath two sets of signs on a twin-trunked red fir and a twin-trunked western white pine. Turn down Union Creek toward the junction with the Landers Lake trail.

The trail makes several moderately steep zigzags down the north side of the divide, then descends gradually through the east side of a large meadow. You come out on a rocky dike and, as you approach the little creek flowing from the ponds on the meadow, you will see a sign on an old, dead pine beside the trail which reads "LANDERS LAKE TRAIL 9W09, SWIFT CREEK TRAIL," .8 mile from the junction on the divide. Fill your water bottles here before you start up over the ridge toward Landers Creek.

Union Lake is 1.8 miles down Union Creek and back up a side canyon (see Trip 10). A number of excellent campsites are along Union Creek within the first mile below the Landers Lake trail junction. Landers Lake, 1.7 steep miles away, is the first good place to camp on the Landers Lake/Landers Creek trail.

A well-defined trail, marked by cairns, runs west from the Landers Lake junction at the head of Union Creek. You start climbing moderately southwest across a rocky slope, then northwest up the side of a main ridge west of the Union Creek valley. A short respite on a small flat brings you to the serious climb to the crest of the ridge on a zigzagging tread of loose rock and fine dust. The crest is in a gap .7 mile from the Union Creek trail junction. If you are a good off-trail route finder, you can avoid the steep, dry climb to the gap by making a traverse from the Parker Creek/Union Creek saddle around the head of the Union Creek valley to an intersection with the Landers Lake trail in the gap. If you choose this cross-country route, however, you will have to forego the refreshing waters of Union Creek. The jagged, red cone on the skyline west of the gap is Red Rock Mountain, rising behind the Landers Lake basin.

You continue moderately up the trail for 200 yards across the west side of the ridge to a small, dry meadow, then descend the rocky bottom of a dry gully southwest 300 yards to a junction with the Landers Creek trail coming up from Mumford Meadow and Swift Creek. The junction is at the lower end of a 10–12 acre wet meadow containing several small ponds lined with California pitcher plants. Landers Creek begins in the meadow.

Side Trip to Landers Lake

Landers Lake Spur trail 9W09A is mucky in places as it contours north around the east side of the wet meadow at the head of Landers Creek. You ascend moderately on a rocky slope north of the meadow, then turn west into a valley with a wall of red rock across its upper end. A short, steep climb brings you to a gap at the north end of this dike, from which you continue ascending moderately up a wider valley west to a final, steeper pitch over the rim of the bowl containing Landers Lake .6 mile from the Landers Lake/Union Creek junction.

Landers Lake has an eerie feel about it in late summer. The 3–4 acre lake has no outlet or inlet streams, and it shrinks back in its rocky bowl during the summer to expose acres of red and black boulders, striated with white watermarks and strewn with ghostly tree limbs. The dark boulders, the jagged red cliffs walling the wide basin, and the red cone of Red Rock Mountain all look volcanic, but are really metamorphosed sandstone.

A large, excellent campsite is beside the trail where it first climbs over the rim on the way to the lake. The trail continues one-quarter mile to another large site, often used by horsemen, northwest of the lake on the edge of the extensive meadows that carpet the upper part of the basin. A small, secluded site is in the trees near the northeast shoreline. In spite of having shrunk down so far by late summer, the water in the lake is clear and cold but it should be purified for drinking.

Deer congregate in the beautiful meadows in the evening, and a constant chorus of frogs rises from two small ponds on the northwest side of the basin. Small eastern brook trout are plentiful in the lake, but were hard to catch when we were there. If you make the effort to climb to the north rim of the basin, you can look directly down at Union Lake and Bullards Basin 1000 feet below!

Starting down Landers Creek toward Mumford Meadow, you snake down the east side of the wide, glaciated, upper valley through sparse forest to a dry meadow, then down through more trees to a group of fair campsites near the upper end of a large, wet meadow .6 mile below the Union Creek trail junction. The ponds in this meadow are lined and partly filled with California pitcher plants, as are the ponds in the wet meadow at the top of the valley.

Your trail skirts the east side of the meadow, then descends moderately through beautiful, open forest of Douglas fir, western white pine, Jeffrey pine and incense cedar above a grass floor. At 1 mile from the junction you turn west down two switchbacks to cross Landers Creek and climb moderately up the west bank to a junction with a trail branching west up Sunrise Creek canyon to Sunrise Basin and the crest above. Your trail gets rougher below this junction, descending south as the creek falls away southeast, and the last steep one-quarter mile down to wide Mumford Meadow is washed out and very rocky.

You cross the expansive meadow south to the signed trail junction with the Swift Creek trail, 1.6 miles from the Union Creek junction. As you turn east your feet will appreciate the level, well-graded trail after the steep, rocky

Red Rock Mountain is a rugged backdrop for Landers Lake

descent just completed. You will also discover where most of the people go from the Swift Creek trailhead—the many excellent campsites near the confluence of Landers and Swift creeks at the lower end of Mumford Meadow are usually filled to overflowing.

A half mile of delightfully easy descent, compared to the Landers Creek trail, brings you to Foster's Cabin and its clear, cold spring. A board-sided barn with a replacement corrugated-iron roof is the oldest building at Foster's. The original cabin has been replaced by a relatively new log structure that is off limits to the public. A curious, long, log-roof assembly without any shakes sits beside the trail, but there is no sign that there was ever a cabin under it. Several excellent campsites are east of the cabin between the trail and Swift Creek.

Below Foster's Cabin you walk beside Swift Creek past more good campsites along the south edge of big Parker Meadow. Several seeps and one delightful little creek drain out of the east end of the meadow and run across the trail before you turn away from Swift Creek and enter open forest. Good trail continues on a gradual descent past the Bear Basin trail junction to the three-way trail junction just west of Parker Creek, 1.4 miles from Foster's Cabin. The Swift Creek trailhead is 3.5 easy miles back down the Swift Creek trail.

Trip 6

Granite Lake,
Bear Basin Loop

Trip Type: Loop trip of 3 to 5 days

Distance: 17.2 miles

Elevation Change: 7955 feet, average 463 feet per mile

Season: Mid-July to mid-September

Topo Maps: *Covington Mill* and *Siligo Peak* (both provisional 1982), *Caribou Lake* and *Ycatapom Peak* (both provisional 1986) 7.5′ quadrangles

The upper part of this very pleasant and scenic loop goes all the way around 8132-foot Seven Up Peak, and from the traverse along the ridge west of Deer Creek canyon you have truly magnificent views across to Siligo Peak, Luella Lake and most of the central Trinity Alps. If you want to add two or three days and almost 10 miles to the trip, you can descend the long series of switchbacks from the Granite Creek summit down to Deer Creek and do the Four Lakes Loop.

Several small lakes, including Seven Up and Gibson hidden in the upper folds of the massive ridges, offer off-trail goals for those who may find Granite Lake overpopulated. A lot of backpackers go to Granite Lake, and some of them climb over the ridge to Deer Creek. Not nearly as many backpackers get to Bear Basin and Black Basin, but a good many equestrians go there because plenty of grass is available for stock. In spite of the heavy traffic, Granite Lake is still unique and beautiful, and it's still possible to catch a limit of fair-sized eastern brook trout from the evening rise. Swimming is delightful by mid-August.

Starting Point
You start from Swift Creek trailhead; see Trip 5 for directions.

Trip 6
Granite Lake, Bear Basin Loop

Description

The first 1.9 miles from the trailhead past the Swift Creek Gorge to the Granite Creek trail junction are described in Trip 5. The trail contours almost level from the junction 200 yards to a hump-backed, steel-truss bridge over Swift Creek. You climb up the south bank, then cross a 200-yard-wide bench before starting to climb south up the west side of the Granite Creek canyon. The trail from here to Granite Lake was rebuilt in 1990. The tread is steep and rocky until you cross two tributary creeks. Relatively new switchbacks have been added above the creeks to ease the climb. On a bench 1.3 miles from Swift Creek the trail turns close to Granite Creek for a short distance before climbing away again through mature forest of Douglas firs, white firs, incense cedars and sugar pines. You level out on a flat and cross another small tributary in a willow thicket, then dip into a dry draw before starting a moderately steep climb over a moraine liberally sprinkled with erratic granite boulders.

You come close to Granite Creek again where it cascades over a metamorphic rock sill 2 miles from Swift Creek. Above the cascade the trail is almost level, following the bank of the creek in a wider part of the canyon. A half mile farther on the canyon narrows again, and you climb over the toe of a red-rock talus slide past another cascade. Head-high azaleas and ferns line the trail in the lush dell above the cascade. As you come out into the open at the foot of a narrow meadow, you get a first good look at the looming bulk of 8400-foot Gibson Peak straight ahead up the canyon.

After climbing moderately beside the meadow and through a belt of trees the trail jogs northwest to climb over the end of a metasedimentary rock dike running all the way across the canyon. You turn southwest again through patches of meadow and brush on the floor of sparse forest to find an icy spring in the middle of a wide band of alders, willows and vine maples 3 miles from Swift Creek. At the edge of talus falling from a glacier-carved, red-rock hump on the northwest side of the canyon you turn south to snake up the side of another dike only to find yet another one, and another cascade, above it.

A short climb northwest up a ferny side canyon gets you to the top of the third dike, where you turn back south, then west to enter the lower end of Gibson Meadow close to a screen of willows hiding the creek. An excellent, large campsite, heavily used by horse packers, is in a grove of firs north of the trail here. The trail skirts the north and northwest sides of the large, wet meadow, passes two lily ponds, and then turns north away from alder-choked Granite Creek up a side canyon before climbing the final moderately steep pitch into Granite Lake's basin.

Most of the good campsites at Granite Lake are on a ledge which the trail crosses on its way around the northwest side of the deep, 18-acre lake. A thick belt of alders below the ledge, growing around almost half the shoreline, makes access to the lake difficult. Paths of a sort have been broken though the brush, across the outlet to a hump of granite sloping into the water on the east side of the lake, and to the west end of a swimming beach beyond the alders near the inlet creek. Overuse and poor sanitation practices have made the lake water and the outlet creek questionable for drinking. Better water is available from the inlet stream on the west side and a somewhat obscure spring in heavy brush on the east side. Please practice your very best wilderness ethics here to prevent further pollution.

Cliffs and huge blocks of granite around the south half of the lake lead up to the magnificent bulk of Gibson Peak. Sunset colors on the peak, reflected in the lake, are unforgettable. Some unbelievably large incense cedars grow around and above the campsites on the northwest side of the lake. They are worth the effort to search out and observe—they may well be the biggest cedars you will ever see. Fishing is still good in Granite Lake for eastern brook trout to 10–11 inches, probably because it is so difficult to get to and around the shoreline.

The climb from Granite Lake to the crest of the ridge above Deer Creek is best done in early morning or late afternoon, since it is steep and in full sun most of the day. The first quarter-mile of trail rises moderately to steeply through forest above the campsites, then crosses two little streams as it continues to climb west through rocks and brush north of the inlet creek. You come close to the creek .5 mile from the lake, and the trail might appear to cross to the other side, but it doesn't. Stay on the north side of the creek, and climb beside it as it tumbles through alders in the bottom of a gulch. This is the last drinking water on the trail until you get around to the upper end of Bear Basin, a lot of ups and downs away.

A meadow full of lupine, mountain asters, angelica, fireweed, corn lilies, and other flowers greets you above the gulch. The trail wanders through it, climbing moderately west toward a gap in the ridge between the red rock of Seven Up Peak to the north and the gray granite of Gibson Peak to the south.

Beautiful Granite Lake can still be cool in August

Trip 6
Granite Lake, Bear Basin Loop

Two steep to very steep pitches, with a slight respite between, lead to a flower-decked amphitheater just below the crest. A last, short, steep scramble up the west wall brings you to the crest, a trail junction and a set of sensational views. Castle Crags and Lassen Peak can be seen on clear days on the eastern horizon, far above the upper end of Clair Engle Lake. Seven Up Peak's ragged red cone rears up a little east of north behind skeletons of lightning-shattered foxtail and whitebark pines on the crest.

The view west from the crest is one of the most comprehensive views of the central Trinity Alps you will find. Luella Lake hangs in a pocket on the north flank of Siligo Peak directly across the wide, glacier-formed chasm of upper Deer Creek canyon. Sawtooth Mountain forms the skyline behind the west wall of the canyon, and leads up to the jumble of peaks culminating in Thompson Peak, highest point on the horizon. The convoluted trace of the Four Lakes Loop trail is clearly visible across the canyon, climbing from tiny Round Lake past Luella Lake to crest the west ridge on its way to Diamond Lake.

The Granite Lake trail, 8W14, continues west from the crest, switchbacking down 1.2 miles to junctions with the Deer Creek trail and the Four Lakes Loop trail on the floor of the canyon (see Trip 4). Our trail north to Black Basin and Bear Basin is designated on a sign at the junction as "SEVEN UP PEAK TR. 9W67."

This trail contours northwest around the flanks of Seven Up Peak, then turns northeast around a shoulder to drop down to the divide between Black Basin and Bear Basin 1.3 miles from the Granite Creek trail junction. Contorted Jeffrey pines and Shasta red firs add foreground interest to the views along the way. An open, vertical mine shaft is beside one of the switchbacks on the way down to Black Basin. Please don't try to climb down it, throw anything into it or even get close to the mouth—it is both dangerous and historic, so we don't need to add any bleached bones or contemporary artifacts to whatever is

The lower meadow in Bear Basin

already at the bottom. The miner's collapsed cabin is beside the Black Basin/ Deer Creek trail a short distance north of a junction at the foot of the hill.

Black Basin is a glacier-carved trough sloping northwest from the Bear Basin divide, then turning west to end as a hanging valley above Deer Creek canyon. Black Basin has only one small pond and no streams to speak of, but it is a pretty valley and is well worth a day of exploration if you have the time.

The Bear Basin trail, 9W10, rises moderately north from the flat at the head of Black Basin toward a red-rock knob, then turns east and down toward a small, permanent snowbank in a cirque under the north slope of Seven Up Peak. You descend on a steep, loose, dirt tread through a flower garden for 200 yards, then jog north around a knob of rock. As you snake down the rocky slope below the knob, you realize why you had to make the jog—a 30–40-foot escarpment of gray, metamorphic rock extends from the knob across the valley.

The trail turns northeast near the bottom of the hill and doesn't get closer than 300 yards to the inviting snowbank in the cirque. Of course you can walk up to it if you crave snow, but an icy little stream trickles through alders 200 yards down the trail to slake your thirst. From higher on the hill you can see an alder- or willow-lined pond across on the east side of upper Bear Basin. That pond disappears from sight on the way down, and we couldn't find it in an hour of searching.

Below an outstanding grove of large red firs and western white pines you follow excellent, almost level trail northeast above the northwest side of a wide meadow. This trail is not nearly as heavily traveled as the Granite Creek trail and, in an airy fir grove .8 mile from the Black Basin junction, you will fine several excellent campsites with plenty of firewood. The only drawback is that you have to go 200 yards down into the meadow to Bear Creek for water.

Below the fir grove you drop down a little more steeply toward the middle of the valley, then cross Bear Creek just above a grove of cottonwoods rising out of a tangle of alders. After climbing over a wide, low, grassy hump on the valley floor, you descend moderately through a band of forest to another big, beautiful meadow 2.6 miles below Black Basin divide. Excellent campsites abound here, some near the creek on the southeast side of the meadow, and others by springs flowing from the hill on the northwest side. Although Seven Up Peak is out of sight now, several rugged spires on the southeast rim catch the morning and evening sun above the verdant valley.

Below the lower meadow the valley narrows to a canyon, and the trail gets rougher in the steeper places as it wanders down through open, mixed forest. Several springs and creeklets flow across the trail. As Bear Creek drops away more precipitously, you turn north on the side of the canyon, back east down to a bench, then north again to a new steel-girder bridge over Swift Creek, replacing a bridge washed out in 1983. The Bear Creek trail joins the Swift Creek trail 250 yards east of the bridge, near the three-way junction above Parker Creek and 1.3 miles from the lower meadow in Bear Basin. Swift Creek trailhead is 4.4 miles down the canyon. See Trip 5 for description (in reverse) of the Swift Creek trail.

Trip 7

Boulder, Lion, Foster and Sugar Pine Lakes

Trip Type: Through trip of 3 to 5 days

Distance: 21 miles plus 1.5 miles side trip to Little Boulder Lake

Elevation Change: 11,200 feet, average 498 feet per mile

Season: Late July to mid-September

Topo Map: *Ycatapom Peak* (provisional 1986) 7.5′ quadrangle

Fishermen will love this trip—when they're fishing. When they're toiling up the last, brutally steep, crumbling half mile of trail to the crest above Battle Creek, they may not love it quite so much. Although it starts high and ends low, as all good through-trips should, this is a difficult trip. There is hardly a flat spot in the 21 miles. However, it does string together four outstandingly beautiful lakes, each with its own distinct character. Add tiny Conway Lake and a short side trip to Little Boulder, and you have an even half-dozen—all of them with good to excellent fishing.

In addition to fishing, you get a good look at most of the high country between Coffee Creek and Swift Creek. The pass above Lion Lake offers about the best view of Mount Shasta you'll find in the Trinity Alps. You will see other people on this trip, but no big crowds after you leave the Boulder Lakes. The basin at the upper end of Battle Creek is seldom visited, except by cows and cowboys.

You will need two vehicles for the trip. You are not apt to be able to hitchhike the 18 miles from the Sugar Pine trailhead to the Boulder Lakes trailhead. Of course, you could make a round trip from either trailhead, in which case you probably would eliminate the climb to upper Battle Creek. That would be a shame, because it's a scenic wonder.

If you want to shorten the through-trip by 7 miles and two sets of ridges, Lion and Sugar Pine lakes are only 1.5 miles apart on the map, and it's possible to make an off-trail shortcut over the ridge between them. Again, you would miss upper Battle Creek.

Starting Point

The road to Boulder Lakes trailhead turns off Highway 3 less than a half mile south of the Coffee Creek Road junction 40 miles north of Weaverville. Increased logging activity in the area requires that you drive these roads with extreme caution. Signs would normally guide your way easily to the trailhead, but in 1993 vandals had stolen every sign along this route. Report any suspicious activity to the rangers at Coffee Creek.

Proceed on Forest Service Road 37N52 for 3.3 miles to a junction along a curve. Turn right onto F.S. Road 37N53 and travel 1.1 miles to a Y where you bear left. From this point the main road is obvious and leads to the trailhead at a former log landing on top of the ridge between Little Boulder Creek and Boulder Creek, 10.0 miles from Highway 3. There is plenty of parking. The road is rough in spots, but should be passable to almost any vehicle.

The Sugar Pine Creek trailhead at the other end of the trip is 7 miles up the Coffee Creek road from Highway 3. At 1.2 miles past the end of pavement on the Coffee Creek road look for a sign pointing left. A couple of hundred yards of rough, narrow road leads to a footbridge over Coffee Creek. Park where you can beside Coffee Creek or along the road. The trailhead is 100 yards beyond Coffee Creek on the north side of Sugar Pine Creek. The south bank of Sugar Pine Creek is private property at this point.

Description

A new trail runs southwest from the present Boulder Lakes trailhead east of the top of the ridge for 1.3 miles to connect with the old trail to Boulder Lakes that climbed up from Little Boulder Creek. You ascend moderately, with a few steeper spots, on excellent duff tread through dense forest, predominately white fir. Although the first 300 yards to the Wilderness boundary are through a logged area, it is not all that noticeable. It was a good job of selective logging.

The first part of the old trail is now a switchback as you climb steeply back northwest. You level off on the brow of the ridge and contour southwest to a junction with the Little Boulder Lake trail turning east, a quarter mile from where you came onto the old trail.

Below the junction, badly worn old trail makes one switchback down a brushy, rock-strewn hillside, then turns west across the large basin containing Boulder Lake. A three-way trail junction is beside a large campsite with an old Forest Service stove near the lower end of the lake 2 miles from the trailhead. The trail turning south runs around the east shore of the lake, then climbs over a ridge to Poison Canyon. The trail turning north crosses the outlet creek, and eventually connects with the Boulder Creek trail to Lion Lake.

Trip 7
Boulder, Lion, Foster and Sugar Pine Lakes

Boulder is a medium-sized green lake—8 acres of algae-tinted water with a ring of lily pads extending out 100 feet from most of the grass-bordered shoreline. A wet meadow borders the upper (south) end of the lake, and thick trees back up the grass and willows around most of the rest of the shoreline. A craggy granite peak dominates the glaciated ridge to the south. Three or four fair campsites, including a large one by the trail junction, are around the lower end of the lake. A number of excellent sites are on a bench 300–400 yards above the east shore of the lake. Two more good sites are near where the Poison Canyon trail crosses the inlet stream. Firewood is scarce, and all water should be purified.

In spite of a few drawbacks, including swarms of mosquitos in early summer and too many people in midsummer, Boulder Lake is a pleasant place to relax for a day or two. You can make a day-hike to Little Boulder (see Trip 8). The scenery is beautiful up there. Fishing is difficult around much of the tree-lined Boulder Lake shoreline, but the evening rise off the log jam at the outlet will usually produce a fair catch of 8–9-inch eastern brooks. Wading the muddy bottom near the inlet streams can also be productive if you don't hang up in the lily pads. Swimming is good off the rocks on the west side by August.

Side Trip to Little Boulder Lake

Little Boulder Lake is 300 feet higher than Boulder Lake, hung in a steep-sided pocket on the north side of Peak 6994. Although they are only .6 mile apart on the map, a colder mini-climate in the small basin supports quite different vegetation from that at Boulder Lake in the large basin to the west. Lodgepole pines and red firs grow above pinemat manzanita and Labrador tea here, compared with white firs, sugar pines, big-leaf manzanita and ceanothus brush around the larger lake.

Morning at Boulder Lake

From the signed Little Boulder Lake junction you climb at a moderately steep rate southeast for a quarter mile, then straight up the nose of the ridge for 200 yards before crossing over to descend to the lake .4 mile from the junction and .8 mile by trail from Boulder Lake. Little Boulder Creek originates in the 4.5-acre lake and runs out the open north side of the basin and down into a very steep canyon below. The outlet of the lake is usually dry by midsummer, however, A low dam at the outlet once raised the lake's level, probably to supply more water for downstream mining activities. Lush forest surrounds all but the south shore, where solid granite rises out of the water at a fairly steep angle, leading up to Peak 6994 on the horizon.

Eastern brook trout to 10 inches swim lazily along the shoreline looking for something to eat. Camping is limited to three or four poor-to-fair sites that are really too close to the northeast shore. The water stays much too cold for comfortable swimming.

Lion Lake is five trail miles from Boulder Lake and 900 feet higher. You descend 800 feet into Boulder Creek canyon on the way, so the total elevation change is 2500 feet. Some of that 5 miles is pretty steep, but most of the scenery is fantastic.

From the three-way intersection by Boulder Lake, you follow the trail north. The trail crosses to the west bank of the outlet stream in a gully a little way below the lake. Your way down the steep gully is on worn and washed-out tread, leveling off only momentarily across a swampy, alder-choked flat. Below the alders, exposed roots, boulders and loose gravel make the descent even more difficult until you find a trail junction in a forested flat .7 mile from Boulder Lake. The trail turning east across the creek here leads to a jeep road coming up from Goldfield campground at the confluence of Boulder Creek and Coffee Creek, but no sign tells you so. The trail and the road are fortunately little used. A new sign points to Boulder Lakes and Lion Lake trail 8N20. An old sign on another tree reads "SALMON-TRINITY ALPS WILDERNESS AREA BOUNDARY," anticipating the facts by many years.

The trail toward Lion Lake makes a long S-curve out of the flat, then climbs steeply, with some zigzags, northwest around the shoulder of a ridge between this canyon and Boulder Creek canyon. This trail section is in much better condition than the trail down from Boulder Lake. After a very steep pitch .5 mile from the junction, you round the point of the ridge and begin a contour southwest along the wall of Boulder Creek canyon. You soon descend again and, just beyond a short switchback, an opening in the thick fir forest gives you your first look at the white granite wall behind Conway and Lion lakes far above.

The bottom of Boulder Creek canyon is 2.3 miles from Boulder Lake. You traverse a small alder thicket, cross a strip of meadow where 6-foot-high delphiniums and monkshoods bloom, and boulder-hop Boulder Creek in a channel lined with willows and alders. The creek probably has trout in it, but it is almost impossible to fish here. A use trail branching left on the west bank leads to only two good campsites above the creek.

Just .2 mile from the crossing, your trail turns north to a junction with the Lion Lake trail. Here you turn southwest again and begin zigzagging very steeply on rough, washed-out tread up the side of the canyon. A creeklet flows across the trail .5 mile from the junction, and beyond it the climb becomes merely moderate along a shelf far above Boulder Creek. Directly across the canyon, a lot of bare granite leads up to the basin containing Found Lake and to the peak on the horizon south of the Boulder Lake basin. Farther south, Boulder Creek falls out of a basin named Cub Wallow, tucked under the crest of the divide between this drainage and Parker Creek. The trail traverses a series of benches with steep pitches between them as it climbs higher. Patches of thick forest of red firs, Jeffrey pines and incense cedars alternate with flowery open meadows and alder thickets hiding tinkling little creeks. Pipsissewas, twinflowers and mahonia grow under the trees, while meadow flowers include mints, phlox, wild hollyhock, angelica, Indian paintbrush, owl's clover and sulfur flowers in the drier places.

The gardens end 1.5 miles from the Boulder Creek junction, and you turn north to climb very steep zigzags, crossing a little creek twice in a quarter mile before turning southwest again across the canyonside. The ascent eases to only moderately steep through meadows and patches of brush. At 4.7 miles from Boulder Lake you enter a dense red-fir forest and come to a junction signed Conway Lake to the left and Foster Lake to the right up the hill.

Shortly after you turn onto the Conway Lake trail, you come out of the trees into the upper edge of a large and beautiful wet meadow sloping down to little, lily-pad-covered Conway Lake on a rocky shelf above wide Boulder Creek canyon. West of the meadow and lake, a little creek falls through a slot in a sloping wall of glacier-sculpted granite. Lion Lake is up there, as indicated by a sign at the edge of the trees and end of the trail, reading "LION LAKE 1/4 MILE FOOT TRAFFIC ONLY." The location of this sign might indicate that you should climb the rock north of the slot. Not so—it's much easier on the other side.

A few poor campsites are in the edge of the trees at the top of the meadow. Better ones are in the rocks east of Conway Lake. Firewood is very scarce. Conway Lake harbors small eastern brook trout under its lily pads, and there are some in the little creek running through the meadow below the lake, but fishing is obviously difficult. Fishing is much better for good-sized eastern brooks and rainbows up in Lion Lake, but there is only one poor campsite.

The easiest route up to Lion Lake is across the creek at the bottom of the slot in the granite wall, around the first hump on the south side, and west up the gully there to the top of the dike east of the lake.

Lion is an almost perfect subalpine lake, filling a cup gouged from solid granite by a glacier. The 3-acre lake is vaguely heart-shaped, deep-blue and quite deep. Sheer walls of rock rise almost directly from the water on three sides. Even on the lower, east side, the shoreline is steep except for the slot that the outlet creek has cut through the dike there. A large slide has filled in the north side of the lake with broken rock almost to water level. The rest of the lake drops off very steeply from the shoreline. Only a few red firs, mountain hemlocks and patches of low brush cling to the walls. One small, poor campsite is on top of the dike where you climb up. Firewood is nonexistent.

Although people have been climbing through the pass between Lion and Foster lakes for possibly hundreds of years, no trail connected the two lakes until fairly recently. Now 1.5 miles of trail take you over what people used to do, straight up and straight down, in little more than a half mile. Oddly enough, the trail is still steep. You start with a series of switchbacks climbing steeply north through large red firs for a quarter mile before turning southwest across the side of the mountain above Lion Lake.

If you want to make the cross-country traverse to Sugar Pine Lake, continue to climb off-trail above the first set of switchbacks toward a gap in the ridgeline. Keep to the east side of Sugar Pine Lake's cirque after crossing the ridge, and work your way down to the east shore of the lake. It's a steep climb up and a steeper climb down, but it's only 1.4 miles compared to 8.5 miles by way of Union Creek and Battle Creek. You really should go on over to see Foster Lake first, though.

Lion Lake is directly below you at .6 mile from the Conway Lake junction, and you get a good view of the mass of broken rock filling the depths almost to the surface on the north side. A generally moderate ascent southwest with some ups and downs bring you to a final short switchback to the crest 1 mile from the junction above Conway Lake. Before you start down to Foster Lake, take time to climb one of the large blocks of granite on the crest and enjoy the view back down Boulder Creek and up and away to Mount Shasta on the horizon.

Foster Lake fills a north-south trench directly west of the crest. Beyond a series of short, steep switchbacks, rough trail turns slightly west of north to contour across granite ledges and around big talus blocks, descending moderately. From a point where you can see down to Union Creek, you turn back and drop down to a trail junction on a shelf south of the lake. It is only 200 yards from this junction across the outlet of the lake to an excellent campsite with an old Forest Service stove in a thick stand of mountain hemlock. A few more fair campsites are up in the rocks to the west. You will have trouble finding any firewood within carrying distance.

Old-time Trinity Alps hikers will tell you the name of the 5.5-acre lake is Bear Lake, not Foster Lake. However, since there are already a Big Bear and a Little Bear Lake in the Alps, it's probably just as well to stick with "Foster" for this one. Besides, the Fosters were one of the pioneer families here. Foster is one of the higher lakes in the Alps at 7150 feet elevation, and is truly subalpine. Snow lingers on the south wall of the basin until August in most years.

Sunset floods the cliffs above the east shore with vivid colors on most evenings. Grandstand seats for the daily light show are on ledges beyond two exquisite little lily ponds just south of the largest campsite. You get a double feature on still evenings—one on the basin wall and one reflected from the surface of the lake, accented by trout rises. If you would rather fish than look, try the log jam at the outlet or the drop-offs along the rocky east shore. A limit of 8–9-inch eastern brook trout is almost a sure thing if the wind doesn't blow. Sometimes the wind does blow like fury, the only flaw in this otherwise delightful spot.

The 1.5 miles of trail from Foster Lake down to Union Creek were rebuilt not very many years ago, but fairly heavy horse traffic has worn the tread badly in the steeper sections. After pausing at the lip of the granite ledge north of Foster Lake to admire the view across the wide, lush upper basin of Union Creek, you descend a moderately steep set of switchbacks northwest through boulders and brush. Below a steep pitch straight west down the side of the canyon, you traverse northwest into a belt of firs, then down again along the south edge of a beautiful, large meadow. Steep zigzags continue northwest through head-high ceanothus and other brush to an alder-lined dell 1.3 miles from the lake where a copious, ice-cold spring cascades across the trail. You will not find a finer source of pure, clear water anywhere.

Beyond the spring you soon come out onto the open floor of Union Creek valley, and a triple-trunked cottonwood tree by a dry stream course marks the Sugar Pine Lake trail (8W07) junction 1.5 miles from Foster Lake. A new sign on one of the trunks of the tree, facing toward Union Creek, points to Sugar Pine Lake and Coffee Creek road. A faint trail branches from the Foster Lake trail somewhere between the cottonwood with the sign and a line of cottonwoods beside Union Creek. A row of ducks indicates the trail's course north across the meadow into open forest.

The Foster Lake trail continues west to cross first Union Creek and then the Union Creek trail, and runs on around the shoulder of a ridge to join a trail running up a side canyon to Union Lake 1 mile from the Union Creek junction. Descriptions of Union Lake and the Union Creek trail are in Trip 10. A trail junction for Landers Creek and Landers Lake is 1.4 miles up the valley; see Trip 6. Many excellent campsites with an adequate supply of firewood are along Union Creek above and below the trail crossing. Unfortunately, Union Creek is a little too small to fish at this point.

Beyond the Union Creek meadow you begin to climb immediately on the Sugar Pine Lake trail. Short, steep switchbacks ascend east through open forest of firs and incense cedars and patches of meadow. The tread is well-defined and good here, not nearly as torn up as the Foster Lake trail. A half mile from the junction you turn northeast across a brushy hillside, then east up into the lower end of a steeply sloping meadow reaching all the way to the top of the mountain. The trail, marked by ducks, runs south across the bottom of the meadow, crosses a little stream, then ascends steeply northeast along the southeast edge of the meadow beside the stream. Farther up, you weave in and out of majestic fir forest and meadow, sometimes beside the tiny creek, where both white and purple monkshoods bloom along with several varieties of orchids. The rough track crosses the little stream almost at its source, then zigzags very steeply up the open face of the mountain before re-entering open forest 1 mile from the Foster Lake junction.

You soon turn north on narrow tread directly across the upper end of the long meadow. Midway on this traverse you look straight down a gully and rock slide all the way to Union Creek. A switchback on an open slope north of the top of the meadow takes you to the crest in a saddle 1.5 miles from the junction beside Union Creek.

At the saddle a wide panorama to the south and west rewards your climb. Caribou Mountain looms on the skyline almost directly west, then come the high Alps around the head of Stuart Fork, including Thompson Peak. Ragged ridges farther south lead up to Siligo, Seven Up and Gibson peaks. In the middle distance, beyond the wide upper basin of Union Creek, Red Rock Mountain stands out above the basin containing Landers Lake. On the other side of the crest you look north into the verdant basin at the head of Battle Creek. A row of rugged knobs and pinnacles runs along the east side of this basin, separating it from Sugar Pine Creek.

Foxtail pines on the crest between Battle Creek and Sugar Pine Creek

From the saddle, the trail drops very steeply down the headwall of the basin, then turns to contour along the east slope below the knobs and pinnacles. A spring waters a garden of angelica, delphinium, monkshood, corn lilies, sneezeweed, lupine, yarrow, yampa, Indian paintbrush and other flowers .3 mile from the summit. A whole hillside of wild onions grows below the trail. Beyond another, larger spring bursting from the hill just above the trail, you traverse a steep slope aromatic with angelica, mint and lupine. Then look for ducks pointing the way east uphill. You snake very steeply up to what appears to be the crest, only to find it is a spur of the main ridge, and you must traverse north, climbing moderately, before a final steep rise to the top of the ridge in a saddle 1 mile from the Union Creek crest.

Gnarled foxtail pines cling to the rugged rocks of the summit, adding foreground interest. Long views are fantastic. On the west side you look down the Battle Creek canyon to Coffee Creek, and up to the Scott Mountain crest. On the Sugar Pine Creek side, Mount Shasta crowns the distant skyline beyond a series of ridges, and jagged Sugar Pine Buttes face you across the canyon.

The trail to the bottom of Sugar Pine Creek canyon has been relocated. After a short, steep drop south from the crest, you begin a long traverse a little east of north along the side of the canyon. This piece of trail is not for those who fear heights—the slope is so steep you look almost straight down to the floor of the canyon and the Sugar Pine Lake trail running across a small, very green meadow. Beyond a switchback .6 mile from the summit, the descent steepens through patches of manzanita, and in a grove of firs you turn back southeast and descend to a bench. Headed northeast again, you cross a delightful little creek on this bench 1 mile from the Battle Creek summit.

You continue a moderate descent northeast for another mile through meadows and groves of trees, then begin a set of moderately steep switchbacks east to the floor of the canyon. Your trail becomes enmeshed in a network of cattle tracks as you cross the wide meadow named Cabin Flat to a junction with the more clearly defined Sugar Pine Lake trail. Signs for Cabin Flat, Union Creek trail 8W07 and Sugar Pine Lake trail 8W59 are on the stub of a large snag north of the indistinct junction. Hikers coming up Sugar Pine Creek must have a lot of difficulty finding the Union Creek trail on the side of the canyon.

The Sugar Pine Lake trail is hard to follow as you enter forest south of Cabin Flat. The relocated trail is well away from the creek, near the west side of the canyon. If you get on the old trail, confused by a maze of cattle tracks and piles of rocks, you're going to have a tough time getting over deadfalls and washouts. On the other side of the strip of trees, you cross another wide meadow, enter forest again and come close to alder-choked Sugar Pine Creek 1 mile from the last trail junction. All water in this canyon should be purified for drinking because of heavy cattle grazing and horse traffic.

A gradual-to-moderate climb through more forest brings you to the little meadow you looked straight down to earlier from the top of the west ridge. A quarter mile of pleasant trail winds perfectly level through large red firs south of the little meadow, and then you begin the final moderate climb to Sugar Pine

Lake through jumbled granite boulders and over a moraine ridge. The trail ends near the outlet of the 8-acre lake 1.8 miles from the junction in Cabin Flat.

Jagged pinnacles cap the high walls on three sides of Sugar Pine Lake's cirque. Except for a talus slide running into the water on the southwest side, trees line the shoreline, but only a few of them are sugar pines, belying the lake's name. Several good campsites are in a relatively flat area east of the outlet. You can even find some firewood with a little effort—Sugar Pine doesn't get all that much traffic, and it is surrounded by a lot of trees. Fishing is good for small eastern brook trout. An intriguing curiosity near the campsite is a stranded 8-foot aluminum boat that someone hauled in. The boat appears to have been stepped on by a giant, just as you might squash an aluminum beverage can. We can only assume that the weight of winter snows accomplished the feat, but it still seems unlikely.

Headed northeast down the Sugar Pine Lake trail from the junction in Cabin Flat, you descend gradually to the lower edge of the meadow, then more steeply on zigzagging trail down a rocky hillside in open fir forest. At .6 mile you skirt the edge of a steep-sided ravine with Sugar Pine Creek at the bottom and, .2 mile farther on, drop down a steep, gullied pitch to a small tributary flowing from the west side of the canyon. This is the first water you would want to drink, even after purifying, since leaving Sugar Pine Lake.

The trail next crosses a bench, descending only moderately, then more steeply on better tread through dense, lush forest. Some tall sugar pines are beside the trail 1.4 miles from Cabin Flat before you begin another steep descent on washed-out trail to another tributary in an alder tangle. Then you traverse on better trail again, far up on the side of a **V**-cut canyon, and cross three more side streams before coming to a steep descent down the side of the canyon through a thicket of willows, dogwoods, alders, vine maples and big-leaf maples. Beyond one more tributary you come to a gate in a drift fence. Be sure to close the gate behind you. The fence is there to keep cattle from moving up and down the canyon. New trail contours back into a ravine below the fence, where you cross a larger tributary.

The last 2.2 miles of trail from the drift fence to the trailhead have been relocated and rebuilt. The trail now stays well up on the side of the canyon, descending at a mostly moderate rate, with one long switchback. Black oaks and ponderosa pines appear in the forest below the switchback, with madrones and blue-flowering ceanothus added in the last mile. You finally get down to Sugar Pine Creek just before reaching the trailhead 4.2 miles from Cabin Flat.

Trip 8

Boulder Lake to Poison Canyon and Lilypad Lake

Trip Type: Round trip of 2 to 4 days

Distance: 4.6 miles to Lilypad Lake, 9.2 miles round trip, plus 1.5 mile side trip to Found and Tapie lakes

Elevation Change: 2780 feet, 604 feet per mile

Season: Mid-July to mid-October

Topo Map: *Ycatapom Peak* (provisional 1986) 7.5′ quadrangle

Although it is only a three-hour hike from the popular Boulder Lakes trailhead, Poison Canyon is a wild and lonely place. You will probably hear coyotes at night, and deer and black bear are plentiful. Raptors, including golden eagles and several species of hawks, soar above a wide, lush basin floored with forest and meadows around Lilypad Lake. Ycatapom Peak (supposedly "leaning mountain" in Wintu) is a marvelously textured backdrop, and can be climbed if you are so inclined. A series of terraces with flowery meadows and several pristine ponds lead up south to Thumb Rock, a huge granite hump on the ridge above Parker Creek

Possibly the name "Poison Canyon" discourages visitors. The steep ridge south of Boulder Lake definitely does, and swarms of mosquitos in early summer may be an added deterrent. Whatever the reason, you are not apt to see many other people around Lilypad Lake and, if you climb up to the terraces below Thumb Rock, you might not see anyone else for a month.

An off-trail side trip to Found and Tapie lakes is very scenic and a relatively safe route-finding experience over steep rock. The best place to start this side trip is from near the top of the ridge south of Boulder Lake, and since it ends back on the trail near the bottom of the ridge, you will probably want to do this route on the way out from Poison Canyon.

A number of alternative through-trips continue from Poison Canyon to trailheads at North Fork Swift Creek, Lake Eleanor, Swift Creek, Union Creek and Sugar Pine Creek. Careful map research will show the way. An interesting loop trip of 21 miles can be planned around Thumb Rock to the Poison Canyon trail above Cub Wallow, then down to upper Union Creek and back to Boulder Lake by way of Foster and Lion lakes. Most of this route is described in Trips 6 and 7.

Lilypad Lake, and some of the ponds above, have eastern brook trout in them, but fishing is virtually impossible because of the lilies. Swimming is difficult for the same reason. Fishing in Boulder and Tapie lakes is fair to good.

Starting Point

See Trip 7 for directions to the Boulder Creek trailhead.

Description

Description of the first 1.25 miles from the Boulder Lakes trailhead to the junction at the lower end of Boulder Lake is in Trip 7.

A good, level trail runs south around the east side of Boulder Lake just above the shoreline. You make a short climb east from the side of the wet meadow above the lake, up to a bench and an excellent, large campsite beside the trail. In the next one-quarter mile you cross two inlet creeks and some morainal humps between them. A fair trail, steep in places, wanders up west of the second creek through open forest and small wet meadows where a variety of wildflowers bloom, including leopard lilies, corn lilies, shooting stars, Indian paintbrush, mountain asters, daisies, sunflowers and yampa.

The ascent steepens on rough tread up a heavily wooded slot between humps of granite before turning east to recross the creek .7 mile from the Boulder Lake junction. The banks of the pretty little creek are decorated with parrot's beak, angelica, pink spiraea and columbine. Two genuine switchbacks ease the pain a bit before you turn southwest away from the creek and scramble straight up a very steep broken granite slope in open forest of mountain hemlock, red fir and western white pine. Gaps in the trees offer good views back to Boulder Lake and Tapie Lake, the latter hanging in a trough gouged from the rock southwest of the larger lake. A final, very steep zigzag brings you to the narrow crest of the ridge from which you look straight into the north face of Ycatapom Peak across Poison Canyon. Off to the northwest a granite peak rises above a wide expanse of glacier-sculpted rock, falling away to Tapie and Boulder lakes. Found Lake is around behind this peak.

Instead of diving straight down the side of the canyon the trail now turns back southwest over the crest, and contours before dropping down to a junction with the Poison Canyon trail on a bench 1.6 miles from the junction at Boulder Lake. Going down the Poison Canyon trail, you descend three switchbacks between benches and continue to descend on a very long diagonal through open forest and thick brush. The junction with the Lilypad Lake trail is in a flat near the bottom of the canyon 1 mile from the Poison Canyon/Boulder Lakes junction. Two trail signs and a large cairn designate the junction, which is fortunate since the trail at this particular spot is overgrown with tall grass.

Up the canyon, pleasant, almost level trail with duff tread runs southwest from the junction, paralleling small North Fork Swift Creek through dense fir forest. You cross the creek as the forest begins to thin, and then the plant life becomes brush as you recross the creek .6 mile from the junction. The creek is not very appetizing here, heavily mineralized and drying up in late summer. A moderate ascent on rock ledges south of the creek takes you up to the wide, flat basin containing Lilypad Lake. Good campsites are in the edge of the trees before you go out into the meadows around the lake .9 mile from the junction down the canyon. You will have to go up to springs in the rocks above the lake to retrieve good water, but plenty of firewood is not very far away.

Lilypad Lake is aptly named—by midsummer you can hardly see the water for the lilies. Two-thirds of the shoreline of the shallow 2-acre lake is lined with willow thickets. Everything considered, it is not the greatest recreational lake, however, the meadows around the lake along with the towering peaks and ridges on all sides are uniquely beautiful. The near assurance of solitude definitely has its own attraction.

A faint trail continues through the meadow south of the lake and up the steep ledges beyond to the terraces below Thumb Rock. The sky is caught here in a series of pristine little ponds set in the greenest of plush meadows. A junction above the terraces gives you a choice of going over the ridge to Deer Flat or around behind Thumb Rock and back up the Poison Canyon trail above Cub Wallow. The latter loop goes through some of the most remote country reached by trail in the Trinity Alps (see Trip 6).

Off-Trail to Found and Tapie Lakes

About 200 yards north of the crest between Poison Canyon and Boulder Lake, just below the steep switchbacks, is the best place to start the off-trail traverse to Found Lake and the other small ponds in a high, isolated basin behind the granite peak to the west.

You dip down into a delightful, flowery vale west of the trail at the head of one of the Boulder Lake inlet streams. Cross over the stream where brush permits and head northwest over glacier-sculpted rock to the edge of talus slopes below the vertical faces on the east side of the tor. Keep as high as feasible below the cliffs to avoid the thick brush tangles and crevices between blocks of broken rock on the slopes below. As you traverse northwest farther around the peak, Tapie Lake comes into plain view in the cleft above Boulder Lake. A deep gully, floored with broken rock, runs down from the north side of the peak to a pocket south of Tapie Lake. Cross this gully as near its top as you can; the going will still be a bit rough over large talus blocks.

Northwest of the top of the gulch, you enter open forest of lodgepole pine and mountain hemlocks on the rocky floor of a wide, open basin. Found Lake is less than one-quarter mile straight ahead, but you won't be able to see it until you almost step in it, because of the rock ledges in-between. Chances are, the first lake you come to won't be Found Lake, but its shallower, unnamed twin. Found Lake sits at the head of the basin and the rocky western shoreline rises steeply away from the lake toward the crest of the ridge above. The twin pond, .1 mile southwest of Found Lake, is shallower, and has gentler terrain around the shoreline. One-quarter mile northwest of Found Lake the rocks drop away steeply, and you gaze across the wide abyss of upper Boulder Creek canyon to the niche containing Conway and Lions lakes.

If you like solitude, you will enjoy a stay at Found Lake. The surrounding scenery is magnificent; you can climb the peak if you desire some exercise and a wider view; and there are ledges for sunning and lakes for dipping. You will have to climb down to Tapie Lake if you want to fish, as a multitude of frogs live in the lakes in the upper basin, but no fish. Many excellent campsites are scattered among the rocks, and there is a good supply of firewood. There are no streams that flow in or out of the lakes except during snowmelt, and drinking water should be purified.

The best route to Tapie Lake from the basin above is down the nose of the spur ridge just northwest of the big gully. Don't wander too far to the right (south). The scramble down is not too difficult, generally northeast back and forth over bare ledges, ending at the south shore of Tapie Lake.

Eons ago a glacier plowed a trough through weaker rock on the steep face southwest of Boulder Lake. Tapie Lake now fills part of that trough. The lake drains out the north end of the trough, but the south end is also open and only a few feet higher. A small lily pond in the meadow at the south end is barely separated from the lake. Thick fir forest lines the west shore, and brush covers the outlet, creating difficulties in getting around the lake, but a few open spots offer good fishing for medium-sized eastern brook trout and access for swimming. One small, poor campsite is above the south shore.

A very steep, rough descent is possible from the outlet of Tapie Lake to the western shore of Boulder Lake. A better alternative leads out of the south end of the trough, east down a gully, then around a shoulder of bare granite and south across a shelf. Stay above the tops of two brush-filled ravines and you will find the Boulder Lake/Poison Canyon trail in a strip of trees .4 mile from Tapie Lake.

Trip 9

North Fork to East Fork Coffee Creek Loop

Trip Type: Loop trip of 4 to 7 days

Distance: 27.5 miles, not including a side trip to South Forks Lakes

Elevation Change: 12,035 feet, average 438 feet per mile

Season: Early July to mid-October

Topo Maps: *Ycatapom Peak, Billys Peak* and *Deadman Peak* (all provisional 1986) 7.5′ quadrangle

From busy, dusty Coffee Creek road to a seldom-used, 2.6-mile sample of the Pacific Crest Trail on the Scott River divide, this trip offers you a series of contrasts. Several miles of steep, badly worn trail are balanced by pleasant, level strolls through idyllic meadows. Brushy hillsides and mixed low-level forest near Coffee Creek give way to subalpine vistas alternating with forests of giant red firs along the ridge between Granite and Doe lakes. And the lakes—oh, what lakes! They range from big, heavily used Stoddard, at 5900 feet elevation the destination of trail rides from Coffee Creek Ranch, to tiny, remote Section Line in its 7000-foot-plus cirque, where you might not see another party for a week or two.

The trip transects a good cross section of the country north of Coffee Creek up to the Scott River divide. Fishing is good-to-excellent along most of the way, including some golden trout in Salmon Creek and the upper reaches of the North Fork. Some of the trail is heavily used, but there is still plenty of opportunity for solitude in the higher part of the loop. Mining relics are common in much of the area and a few claims are still being worked. Until the mid-1930s a small town endured along the North Fork between Lick Creek and Granite Creek. The Forest Service has acquired a private inholding at Hodges Cabin, and all of the area is now a part of Trinity Alps Wilderness.

This isn't the highest and most rugged part of the Trinity Alps, but it does provide a very pleasant and interesting sojourn.

Starting Point

The Coffee Creek road junction with Highway 3 is 40 miles north of Weaverville and just beyond the Coffee Creek bridge. The Coffee Creek Ranger Station is 300 yards off the Coffee Creek road on the first road to the right after you turn off Highway 3. The East Fork Coffee Creek trailhead is 7.3 miles from Highway 3, just beyond the East Fork bridge. The North Fork trailhead is 1 mile farther up the road, before you get to the North Fork Bridge. Parking at both trailheads is beside the road.

Narrow pavement on the Coffee Creek road ends 1 mile below the Sugar Pine trailhead 6 miles from Highway 3. Goldfield Campground, .3 mile beyond Coffee Creek Ranch, is a pleasant, no-fee, no-services campground. The developed campgrounds around Clair Engle Lake and on up the Trinity River have piped water and are better places for car camping.

Description

We walked this loop beginning at the East Fork and ending at the North Fork, and from that experience strongly suggest that you do it in the opposite direction. Unless you have a vehicle at each trailhead, you will have to walk or hitchhike the last uphill mile on dusty Coffee Creek road going this way, but the first 2 miles up the East Fork are brutally steep and rough if you start in the other direction.

Both Coffee Creek and the North Fork look as if they should have lots of trout in them near the trailhead, but appearances deceive; you will work hard for only a few small rainbows. Fishing is much better a few miles up the North Fork.

You climb moderately to moderately steeply northwest on good trail for the first mile, well up the side of the steep, narrow North Fork canyon. The next .5

Two crossings of North Fork Coffee Creek are on steel-truss bridges

mile of trail contours almost level past an old cabin site and some excellent campsites perched on ledges and benches, then dips down to cross the North Fork on a steel-truss bridge. A large, idyllic campsite is on a flat beside the creek above the bridge, just beyond a tributary cascading down the west side of the canyon.

A marvelous, wider valley, wooded with Douglas fir, ponderosa pine and incense cedar, extends 1.7 miles from the first bridge over North Fork Coffee Creek to Hodges Cabin. This stretch of stream is what fly-fishermen dream about—a positively beautiful stream, flowing swiftly over a wide, open bed of gravel and rocks, with long riffles, deep pools and plenty of room to cast. More important, it has trout in it—nice fat rainbows plus a few goldens and hybrids. The excellent trail ascends gradually not very far up on the west slope, except for one place where it switchbacks higher to climb over a rock shoulder.

Hodges Cabin is a large, two-story rustic building across the creek from the trail, 3.2 miles from the trailhead. The Forest Service acquired this private inholding, including the cabin, horse barn and corral, outbuildings and surrounding land, in 1987. The cabin dates from the 1920s, and once boasted its own hydroelectric plant and extensive water system. Famous Jockey Billy Pierson owned the complex at one time. A volunteer couple lived here as caretakers in the summer of 1989, working hard to clear out the cabin, inventory historic items and conduct tours for passing hikers. One proposal for future use of Hodges Cabin is to operate a wilderness hostel in it.

The trail continues rising gradually on the west side of a wide, flat valley that shows abundant evidence of past mining efforts. No claims are currently being mined here.

A little over a mile from Hodges Cabin, and 4.5 miles from the trailhead, the trail turns to cross to the northeast side of the North Fork on another steel-truss bridge a short distance above the confluence of Granite Creek. The Granite Creek trail forks right from the North Fork trail in a wide flat 150 yards from the bridge. You could cut 5–6 miles and some steep ups and downs from the trip by turning up Granite Creek, and thence to Granite Lake, but you would be missing some marvelous scenery up on the crest. A number of excellent campsites are between the trail and the North Fork beyond the junction.

You continue up the northeast side of the North Fork on an excellent trail, climbing gradually, then a little more steeply as the valley narrows, .6 mile to the confluence of Saloon Creek.

You boulder-hop or wade across Saloon Creek at the edge of a small meadow, then follow up a rocky spit between the two creeks. As you start to climb on a spur ridge, you look down on a sometimes occupied, and quite unique, miner's cabin on a flat by Saloon Creek. It is unique in that it is tall and narrow and has stucco walls.

The junction of the North Fork and Saloon Creek trails is on a small bench .3 mile above the crossing of Saloon Creek. North Fork Coffee Creek 9W02 is the trail turning west to Schlomberg Cabin and eventually climbing to the Salmon River crest above Long Gulch.

Your trail, Saloon Creek 9W01, continues up Saloon Creek, rising moderately through open fir forest. You pass an unsigned north leg of the Schlomberg Cabin trail, then climb moderately for .5 mile on a series of benches crisscrossed by cattle trails before descending gradually to cross to the east bank. An excellent campsite is on the flat just before you go down the west bank of the creek and through a 3-foot-wide slot sawed out of a 5–6-foot-diameter deadfall that fell directly across the ford.

The trail junction for South Fork Lakes is on the east bank at the confluence of an east fork not named on the map. An old sign at the junction show 2 miles to the left to South Fork Lakes and 1.5 miles up the east fork to the Scott River trail. An idyllic campsite is on a small flat between the forks of the creek, but you may wish you had purified the water when you find out how many cattle are upstream. Small trout below the forks will sometimes rise to flies.

Side Trip to South Fork Lakes

Lower and Upper South Fork Lakes are just over the crest beyond the head of Saloon Creek. The lakes are the source of the South Fork Scott River, flowing north, east of the ridge dividing the Salmon and Scott River drainages. Little South Fork Lake, not to be confused, is the source of the Little South Fork Salmon River, and is west of Caribou Basin, 17 air-miles southwest. The distance from the forks of Saloon Creek to the South Fork Lakes is 2.3 miles, but the hike involves a climb of 1250 feet.

The first half mile is an easy rise on good, lightly used trail shaded by thick forest. Beyond the forest you climb more steeply on rough, stony tread up a dry creek bed and over wooded benches where a few fair campsites are between the trail and the creek. At 1 mile you come to a sloping quarter-mile-long meadow, overgrazed and trodden to dust by cattle by late summer. Look for ducks (mostly single rocks perched on large boulders) leading north uphill away from

Lower South Fork Lake provides good swimming in late summer

Saloon Creek. A duck and a blaze on a large cedar mark the way into woods again.

Patches of shorn meadow with ducks alternate with belts of trees with blazes leading higher to another, larger meadow where the trail runs to the right of, then in, a small, dry stream bed headed generally northwest. At the foot of the steepest part of the ridge, ducks lead you into solid forest, where an obvious, blazed trail climbs north. After .3 mile of very steep climb with only occasional zigzags, you level off for a short distance and find a sign pointing back to Saloon Creek and ahead to South Fork Lakes. This is not the top of the climb—you continue to climb west on the north side of the ridge and around a hump, then descend steeply 200 yards only to climb again over another hump of slate and metamorphosed sandstone. The next short downhill takes you out onto the floor of the valley containing the lakes. Lower South Fork Lake is 150 yards north of where the trail branches in many directions in dense timber. Upper South Fork Lake is one-quarter mile south through dense fir and hemlock.

The 4.5-acre lower lake is shallow and set in a ring of lush grass backed by tall firs and hemlocks at the lower end of a hanging valley. The outlet stream falls over an escarpment a few yards from the lake. Cattle had not gotten to this valley the summer we were there, and the lush growth and flowers were a delightful contrast to the denuded meadows on the south side of the crest. Lower South Fork is a marvelous swimming lake. Excellent campsites with adequate firewood are in the trees beyond the south shore.

Upper South Fork Lake is larger (6.5 acres), set in a cirque with cliffs around the south and west sides. It also has excellent campsites above the northeast shore. Small eastern brook trout rise in the evening to almost anything that touches the surface of the water. All in all, this basin is an ideal place for a one- or two-day layover. South Fork Lakes can also be reached by a trail forking from the Pacific Crest Trail 1 mile south of Carter Meadows Summit on Forest Highway 93.

The trail ascending 1.5 miles from the forks of Saloon Creek to a junction with the Pacific Crest Trail at the top of the Scott River crest is in worse condition than the one to South Fork Lakes. You soon leave the forest in the bottom of the canyon and climb at a steep-to-very-steep rate through manzanita and huckleberry oak on rough, washed-out tread. After a mile of this you top out momentarily on the nose of the ridge between the forks of Saloon Creek, then continue up steeply north through red-fir forest and out onto more open slopes that would be grassy if cattle hadn't eaten everything down to red dirt. The cattle have also pretty well obliterated the trail. The best you can do is to keep 200–300 yards west of the little creek on whatever trail you can find, and climb toward a point just west of the lowest notch in the skyline. Near the crest you will find some old road traces that lead to the gap and a junction with the Pacific Crest Trail (PCT). As late as the 1930s a road led from Callahan through this pass and down to the settlement around Hodges Cabin on the North Fork.

You will have no trouble recognizing the PCT when you get to it. In addition to the signs at the junction, the PCT east along the crest is all relatively new, and looks like a freeway compared to the trail you've just come up. In the other direction, north toward Callahan, the PCT follows a fairly good dirt road now closed to vehicle traffic.

The PCT turns southeast from the Saloon Creek junction through open red-fir forest and around a shoulder of peak 7649. A mile of almost level, smooth, 3-foot-wide trail brings you to the southeast side of the peak and a welcome break where an icy spring flows across the tread from the cut bank on the uphill side. The trail ascends moderately past more seeps and springs, then turns to contour east well below the Scott River crest. A mile from the spring you climb slightly around a rocky, manzanita-covered shoulder offering wide views across Granite Creek, North Fork and Coffee Creek canyons and, at 2.3 miles from the Saloon Creek junction, turn east again on top of the crest. At about the first place where you can see over the north side of the narrow crest, a use trail, marked by a rock cairn when we were there, leads down the north slope.

Off-Trail to Section Line Lake

From the cairn beside the PCT, the rough use trail drops steeply northwest down the north slope and disappears within 200 yards. Section Line Lake is .3 mile southwest from the point where the trail disappears. The way is a bit rough and rocky through open forest and across some humps and gullies. Be sure to stay above (south of) an area of large talus blocks.

Section Line is a gorgeous little lake of 2–3 acres in a cirque right under the Scott River crest. A white granite talus slope falls directly into the south side of the lake, and red firs, mountain hemlocks and a few western white pines surround the rest of the shoreline. By late summer the water level falls below the outlet, and the water temperature rises almost to comfortable swimming level. However, access to the water is somewhat difficult because of broken rock and deadfalls around the shoreline. The only established campsite is much too close to the northwest shore, but there is plenty of room farther back from the lake. Please try to leave as little evidence of your camp as possible. Firewood is abundant, and will continue to be if we all use it conservatively.

Surprisingly, rainbow trout outnumber eastern brook in Section Line Lake. The rainbows vary greatly in size, indicating that they are reproducing, although they normally spawn only in running water. They probably spawn during the snowmelt runoff, and both fry and adults return to the lake before the streams dry up. You're not apt to catch any trophies here, but the fishing is fun, and with a little luck you will have enough to eat.

The .3 mile northeast along the crest from above Section Line Lake to the junction with the Wolford Cabin/Mavis Lake trail is typical of newly built sections of the Pacific Crest Trail—boulders have been moved at least 3 feet to either side of a minimum 2-foot-wide tread that contours constantly to stay as level as possible, and 8-foot-wide swaths have been cleared through patches of manzanita.

From the trail junction you can see Mavis Lake in a basin north of the crest and, much farther north, the wide expanse of Scott Valley. Fox Creek Lake is out of sight behind a spur ridge to the northwest. These lakes and the trails to them from the north are described in Trip 29. In case of emergency or other reason to shorten your trip, you can reach a trailhead 4 miles down the Mavis Lake trail.

Our trail down to Wolford Cabin drops steeply southeast out of the sparse firs and hemlocks on the crest, then zigzags down a steep, sandy, open slope partly covered with sagebrush, grass, yellow bush daisies and pinemat manzanita. At the upper fringe of a red-fir forest you turn southwest and, as you enter the trees, come close to a tiny creek, first drinking water on the trail since the spring back at peak 7649. As you continue down southeast, a few new switchbacks have been added to moderate the rate of descent. Near the bottom of Wolford gulch you turn a little more south, cross a small tributary, and enjoy a gradual .3-mile downhill beside a cascading creek to Wolford Cabin, 1.2 miles from the PCT junction.

Wolford Cabin is a substantial log cabin in relatively good condition, reroofed with aluminum, and still used by cattlemen and trail and snow-survey crews. It sits unlocked in the center of a verdant forest glade. You are welcome to use it if you need shelter, but please leave it at least as clean as you found it and don't take any souvenirs. An excellent campsite is between the cabin and the creek.

Exterior and interior of Wolford Cabin

An obvious, but unsigned, trail junction is in the glade beside the cabin. The trail leading east across Wolford Gulch Creek climbs 1.7 miles to Eagle Creek divide and a junction with the Eagle Creek trail and the Bloody Run trail (see Trip 31). The trail to Granite Creek and Granite Lake descends moderately to moderately steeply southwest from the clearing at Wolford Cabin, well up on the northwest side of Wolford Gulch, .5 mile to a junction with the Granite Creek trail. Turning east on the Granite Creek trail, you drop steeply into Wolford Gulch, cross the creek, and climb up to continue a gradual ascent east above Granite Creek. The trail turns south to cross Granite Creek .4 mile from the junction by Wolford Gulch.

The first quarter mile southeast from the Granite Creek crossing is almost level through park-like forest and meadows. The rest of the mile up to Granite Lake is on rough, moderately steep trail snaking up brushy hillsides and across wooded benches. The trail does not approach the lake directly, but circles above the east and south shores.

This Granite Lake, sometimes called "Little Granite Lake," isn't as big or as glamorous as the Granite Lake in the Swift Creek drainage, but it doesn't have as many visitors either. At 6400 feet elevation, the 6-acre, shallow lake has lily pads floating in it and grass growing on the ends of water-soaked logs sticking out of the water. Swimming isn't the greatest because of lily pads and debris on the bottom, but the lake does support a good population of average-sized eastern brook trout. Several campsites around the north and south sides of the lake rate only fair, and firewood is scarce.

After circling the south side of Granite Lake, you start up the Doe Lake trail. This 3.6-mile piece of new trail connects Granite Lake with Doe Lake by a steep climb to the top of a 7000-foot-plus, east-west trending ridge and a traverse along its length before the descent to Doe Lake. Be sure to fill your water bottles; you may need a drink or two before you reach the top of the ridge. Soon after circling the south shore of Granite Lake, you start switchbacking up northwest. After topping out on a rocky spur ridge west of the lake, you zigzag down the other side, then contour around the head of a small valley before beginning the very steep, switchbacking climb south to a saddle on the main ridge.

After the first steep-to-very-steep mile from Granite Lake to the saddle on rough, dusty trail, you can begin enjoying the long traverse of the ridge. The first 300 yards rises gradually on top of the narrow crest; then you begin to contour southeast around a granite peak. Once around the flanks of this peak you continue to climb moderately east below the crest of the ridge through open red-fir forest and across slopes of granite and sand, decorated with bush daisies, sulfur flowers and mints. A little over a mile of easy travel on good trail brings you to a delightful dell with a sweet, clear spring, the only water on this side of the hill.

From the spring you climb more steeply out onto a granite ledge with stupendous views across Coffee Creek canyon to the highest peaks of the Trinity Alps, including Sawtooth Mountain, Thompson Peak and Caribou

Mountain. The next .5 mile of trail ascends moderately at first, but ends with 200 yards of scrambling up zigzags in broken granite to a saddle between two granite knobs overlooking the Doe Lake basin. You can now see Mount Shasta on the horizon to the northeast and Castle Crags directly east.

A few more steep zigzags take you down into a hanging valley. At the east and lower end of this little valley you drop very steeply over a granite ledge, then traverse east across a steep slope to the north shore of Doe Lake .4 mile from the top of the ridge.

Doe Lake is a beautiful, 4–5-acre subalpine lake in a very-steep-walled granite cirque beneath a rugged, twin-peaked mountain to the southwest. A few good campsites are among the boulders above the northeast shore. Although Doe Lake doesn't get a lot of traffic, very little firewood is available, so be sure to bring your stove. Fishing is good for eastern brook trout, but they don't seem to get bigger than 8–9 inches. The water is warm enough for swimming in the shallower areas by mid-August.

From Doe Lake you descend east down a wide valley littered with erratic granite boulders, first on the north side of the outlet creek, then crossing to the south side. At the lower end of the valley the trail wanders through a maze of alder thickets and meandering stream channels, and is hard to follow until it emerges into several acres of corn lilies at the upper end of half-mile-long Doe Flat.

In the middle of gently sloping Doe Flat you pass the junction of a trail turning north across a burnt-over ridge to Bloody Run and connecting with the Eagle Creek trail and the Pacific Crest Trail near Eagle Peak. A mile of rough trail, steep in places, twists down a little south of east from Doe Flat to a

The ridge trail between Granite Lake and Doe Lake

Doe Lake offers good fishing

well-signed junction with the East Fork Coffee Creek trail in the East Fork's upper valley. As you leave the flat and start down the hill, you walk through spotty burned areas left by the fires of 1987. The openings made by the fires offer wide vistas of the valley below and Billys Peak, high point of the massive ridge rising behind Stoddard Lake to the southeast. A tiny creek on the hillside offers better drinking water than does the cow-tainted East Fork below. The remains of Stoddard Cabin, several excellent campsites and the junction of one of the trails to Stoddard Lake are a quarter mile east up the East Fork trail from the Doe Lake junction. The East Fork Coffee Creek trailhead is 6.5 miles southwest down the trail.

Side Trip to Stoddard Lake

Stoddard Lake is a large (25 acres), deep, blue lake, sharing a wide, forested basin with smaller McDonald Lake. Stoddard Lake has a good population of small-to-medium-sized eastern brook trout. A little mountaineering will get you up to exquisite Little Stoddard Lake on a shelf gouged out of the side of Billys Peak. Plenty of good-to-excellent campsites are in the Stoddard Lake basin.

It all sounds idyllic, but there are a few drawbacks—cows, horses, people and mosquitos in about that order of importance. A large herd of cattle grazes the area every summer, and Coffee Creek Ranch runs a trail ride to the lake two or three times a week during the tourist season. Logging roads have encouraged visitation by bringing the Ripple Creek/Stoddard Lake trailhead within 3 miles from the southeast. Elevation of under 6000 feet and a marshy area between Stoddard and McDonald lakes combine to produce clouds of mosquitos through July. In spite of all this, it is still a very pleasant place.

Two trails lead to Stoddard Lake from the East Fork trail—one from Stoddard Cabin and the other from .7 mile west, at the upper end of the rugged East Fork canyon. Hikers will probably prefer the trail from Stoddard Cabin, since it has much less horse traffic. From the junction beside the tumbled logs of the old cabin, the trail heads south to cross, within 200 yards, two little streams that are the beginning of the East Fork. You continue south across a lush flat, then as you start to climb moderately through open, grass-floored woods, you will see tufts of beargrass. Tall candles of white flowers identify beargrass in early summer; later only dried seed stalks remain.

This trail is not often maintained, so you will probably have to climb over a few deadfalls, but it is well-defined until you run into a maze of cattle paths near Stoddard Lake. You skirt some brush patches higher up the hill and turn a little more east to top out on a rim overlooking Stoddard Lake 1 mile from Stoddard Cabin. This point on the rim is a trail junction, although the only sign in sight says "KEEP THE LAKE CLEAN," and the ground is so trampled you can't see any trails. To the east a trail goes over the ridge to the Ripple Creek trailhead. In the opposite direction a trail follows the rim to a junction of the other East Fork trail. Use trails lead from the south shore .3 mile to McDonald Lake. Little Stoddard Lake is another .5 mile south of McDonald and up a steep rock face.

Trip 9
North Fork to East Fork Coffee Creek Loop

To take the other trail back down to East Fork Coffee Creek, find the junction with the trail around the lake 250 yards east of the outlet. The badly worn, dusty trail starts off north almost level, then turns northwest to parallel the outlet creek down 1 mile to the East Fork. Some lodgepole pines appear in the open forest on the moderate to steep descent. The well-signed junction with the East Fork trail is north of the creek, 100 yards from the crossing.

A small tributary chuckles across the East Fork trail 300 yards below the Stoddard Lake junction, providing better drinking water than the East Fork or Stoddard Lake. Below another small tributary, .5 mile of gradual descent farther down, the creek drops away in a steeper canyon, and the trail descends more steeply on the northwest slope through a towering forest of Douglas firs, ponderosa pines and Jeffrey pines plus an occasional sugar pine and white fir. A giant snag that has fallen parallel to the trail a little farther down will give you a better idea of just how big these trees are. You come close to the creek again 1.4 miles from the Stoddard Lake junction. A tremendous flood and slide came down a tributary from the north here in 1983, completely covering a flat along the East Fork with rocks, mud and forest debris. This was the site of the Holland Mine. Now the mining relics are gone or covered, and the only thing remaining to mark the site is a sign on a tree by the relocated trail.

You climb out of this devastated area to pick up the track of an old road, then descend moderately, crossing two tributaries of the creek before coming to a road fork. Your route is on the upper, right-hand fork—the other fork leads down to the ruins of some more recent mine buildings that have collapsed into the bottom of the canyon.

The road soon disappears again, and you turn more south on foot trail to continue down, steeply at times, above a steep rock-walled gulch cut into the bottom of the canyon by the creek. The trail gets rougher and dustier as you round a shoulder of rock. After a steep drop with a few switchbacks across the remains of an old wooden flume, you will see an incongruous sheet-metal outhouse perched on the hillside below. It wasn't put there for the convenience of trail users; it served a miner's cabin around the corner of the canyon. The creek has cut its way far below you here in a rugged canyon of gray metamorphic rock.

Two more long switchbacks take you down to intersect the miner's road 2.3 miles from Holland Mine. Most of the trail below Holland Mine is fairly new, and the road shown all the way up the canyon on some maps doesn't exist. After .7 mile of moderately steep, dusty downhill on the road you are directly above the East Fork trailhead, and a stub trail switchbacks down to it. However, if you are walking back up the Coffee Creek road to the North Fork trailhead, you might as well stay on the miner's road until it joins the Coffee Creek road after turning around the corner of the two canyons. Please don't try to drive up the miner's road—there is no place to park or turn around until you get to the claim, and that is private property.

Trip 10

Union Creek and
Dorleska Mine to Big Flat

Trip Type: Through trip of 2 to 5 days

Distance: 10.3 miles plus 2.6-mile side trip to Union Lake

Elevation Change: 5125 feet, average 397 feet per mile

Season: Late June to mid-October

Topo Map: *Caribou Lake* (provisional 1986) 7.5′ quadrangle

Union Creek canyon isn't as spectacular as some other Trinity Alps canyons, but for being just plain nice it can't be beat. The trail is easy, and so many excellent campsites are available that you can actually pick and choose where you want to camp and have enough wood for a small campfire without worrying about shorting the next visitor. Fishing is excellent in Union Creek for feisty, pan-sized rainbow trout up to the confluence with the creek from Bullards Basin. Fishing isn't quite as good up at Union Lake, but the side trip will give you an opportunity to swim and do some rock scrambling up to Landers Lake if you want more exercise.

Although a road once ran all the way up into Bullards Basin, most of the magnificent forest in Union Creek canyon is still intact. Bullards Basin is another story. Most of the trees around the Dorleska Mine were cut in the early 1900s to construct buildings, timber the mine shafts and rifts, and fire boilers to operate the mine and mill. Mining was concentrated in the ridge between the Union Creek drainage and South Fork Salmon River to the north. You pass the Yellow Rose Mine on the way down the north side of the ridge to Big Flat. The heavy machinery now rusting away at both historic mines inspires wonder as to how men and mules ever brought it in and set it up in a virtually roadless wilderness. Gold was a powerful incentive, as the huge piles of rock, dug and moved essentially by hand, still testify. A little bit of placer mining is still going

Trip 10
Union Creek and Dorleska Mine to Big Flat

on near the mouth of Union Creek on private land, but the rest of the canyon is virtually untouched.

Cattle still graze along Union Creek, but haven't had the devastating effect that they have in other parts of the Trinity Alps.

Since this is a through-trip, you will need a second vehicle or someone to pick you up at the Big Flat trailhead. However, it is fairly easy to hitchhike the 9 miles of the Coffee Creek road from Big Flat to Union Creek trailhead if you need to.

Starting Point

Union Creek trailhead is 11.5 miles up the Coffee Creek road and .5 mile east of Union Creek. If you cross the Union Creek bridge, you've gone a half mile too far. A trailhead sign on the side of the Coffee Creek road disappears periodically. The first part of the trail is an old logging road turning south up the side of Coffee Creek canyon through broken rock. Parking is below a locked gate 50 yards up the hill, or along the side of the Coffee Creek road. Please do not block access to the gate.

Big Flat trailhead is beside Big Flat campground, 20.5 miles up the Coffee Creek road from Highway 3. Coffee Creek road junction with Highway 3 is 40 miles north of Weaverville.

Description

For the first 300 yards above the gate on the old road, you climb east at a moderately steep rate, then turn back southwest along the side of Coffee Creek canyon, headed for the mouth of Union Creek canyon. A "NO MOTOR VEHICLES ALLOWED" sign at the trailhead seems to have been effective—no vehicles appear to have been on the road for many years. A deep gulch washed through the road by a little creek .5 mile from the trailhead may have something to do with that happy fact.

At .8 mile the road turns south into Union Creek canyon, and you continue a moderate ascent well above the creek. Beyond the first mile you are looking down at the tops of a fine stand of sugar pines in the canyon below, and some large specimens drop their foot-long cones in the road a little farther along. A few large ponderosa pines are also beside the road, emphasizing the difference between these two valuable species.

As the road levels off and begins to descend gradually 2 miles from the trailhead, another little creek flows across, partly through an iron pipe under the roadbed. A half mile farther on, you can see Union Creek in a bed of boulders below as you come to a series of slides across the road. Union Creek has washed out the road beyond the slides, and you climb along the top of a bank to a bridge across the creek's steep-sided gulch 2.3 miles from the trailhead. This bridge washed out 1983, and was replaced in the summer of 1986. Excellent campsites are on both sides of the creek near the bridge.

The trail above the bridge follows a road trace apparently much older than the one below the bridge. You turn away from the creek by a meadow, and climb moderately to a crossing of good-sized Pin Creek .5 mile from the bridge. This ford was paved with concrete years ago, and part of the tread remains, seeming quite out of place in this sylvan setting. The trail continues south, rising gradually through a beautiful forest of Douglas firs, incense cedars, sugar pines and a few ponderosa pines. A few open meadows are between the trail and Union Creek, and excellent campsites are everywhere. If Union Creek is not too high, eager 7–8-inch rainbow trout will rise in almost every hole in its rocky bed between the bridge and the confluence with the creek from Bullards Basin. Once in a while a 10-incher will surprise you.

You come close to the creek from Bullards Basin 1.3 miles above the Union Creek bridge. The steel tread from a large crawler tractor is a jarring note beside the old road trace as you follow the creek for 200 yards before crossing to the other side. The trail, which has been in excellent condition to this point, gets a little bit rougher as you continue south, out of sight of Union Creek, in heavy forest. In an area of seeps and springs you leave the road trace and cross a small tributary that runs down into a wet meadow full of wildflowers. You soon turn toward Union Creek again, and skirt the bottom of a large meadow leading up to the foot of a rugged ridge separating Union Creek and Union Lake basin from Bullards Basin. The Dorleska Mine trail junction is beside this meadow 4.9 miles from the trailhead.

Side Trip to Union Lake

The Union Creek trail continues up the canyon in thick woods, within hearing distance of Union Creek, to a crossing of the little creek flowing down from Union Lake .4 mile from the Dorleska Mine trail junction. You turn right at a signed junction 100 feet beyond the ford, and follow good duff tread south into a wide valley between two high spur ridges. At .4 mile from the last junction, a trail from farther up Union Creek (see Trip 7) that has run around the nose of the eastern spur ridge joins your trail. You cross the creek again .2 mile above this junction and begin a somewhat steeper rise up the open top of a low ridge dividing the upper part of the valley.

Long, narrow Union Lake is in a depression on the east side of the ridge 1.3 miles from the Dorleska Mine trail junction. A tiny creek meanders through a wet meadow carpeted with wildflowers west of the ridge. Many excellent campsites are among widely spaced firs along the top of the ridge. Despite heavy use, there is still an adequate supply of firewood. Drinking water should be purified.

Lush growth of grass and willows lines most of the irregularly shaped shoreline. Except for one deeper spot in the lower end, the 3.5-acre lake is quite shallow, with logs protruding from the surface. It does have good-sized eastern brook trout in it, however. Sometimes they rise, sometimes they don't. By midsummer the water is warm enough for swimming, but the banks are mucky. Plenty of forage in meadows to the west and north makes Union Lake very popular with equestrians. For the same reason, you are apt to have deer in your camp at night.

A marvelously textured rock wall with hanging gardens and meadows rises above the south end of the basin. If you're inclined to steep off-trail exploration, a tiny, unnamed lake nestles under the shoulder of Red Rock Mountain to the southwest, and the Landers Lake basin is less than a mile away in a straight line over the south crest.

The Dorleska Mine trail turns sharply right from its junction with the Union Creek trail, and climbs moderately west above the top of a big meadow at the base of a spur ridge. Down at the bottom edge of the meadow, you can see the Union Creek trail you followed earlier. A steep rise of 200 yards beyond the meadow takes you around to the northwest side of the ridge, where the forest changes from mostly Douglas fir to mostly white fir, and the climb eases a bit.

Beyond another short, steep rise you cross the bottom edge of another large meadow, then turn west across the floor of Bullards Basin. The trail crosses a tiny stream in open forest and then, 1.2 miles from the Union Creek junction, crosses the rocky channel of the main creek draining the basin.

The steep climb up the west ridge begins immediately beyond the creek crossing. The rough trail zigzags generally west, very steeply at times, up a rocky slope through an open forest of Jeffrey pine, white fir, incense cedar, western white pine and the stumps of old-time logging. Farther up you climb

Union Lake and the climbers'
route to Landers Lake

One of the steam engines
at Dorleska Mine

beside a little stream and a wet meadow before leveling out on a bench just below the tailings pond and one of the rock dumps of the Dorleska Mine. As soon as you climb around the old tailings pond and dump, you are looking up at the remains of Dorleska's large stamp mill 2 miles from Union Creek.

Eight heavy stamps in two stands pounded away here from the turn of the century to the mid-'30s, powered by steam from a wood-burning boiler. Two steam engines and the boiler are still in place among the debris of a building that once sheltered them. The mill stands are not in as good shape. The giant camshafts have fallen, and the stamps lean on one another like a line-up of drunks. We can only wonder today how men and mules managed to get all the heavy machinery up here without benefit of a road beyond the lower end of Bullards Basin.

As you climb up to the next bench above the mill, an old sign beside the trail tells about the mine and how it got its name. The sign reads: "Gold discovered in 1898 by R. D. Lawerence. Mine named after his wife Dorleska. All machinery and material hauled in by mules. Last operated about 1934."

A spring behind the sign drains into a willow swamp below. Boards from miners' shacks have been recycled to develop a rather elaborate campsite beside the willows and under the only tree in the immediate area. Please don't burn any of the boards or carry away any souvenirs—everything here has historic value. Two little ore cars still sit on rusting tracks near the caved-in mouth of a drift running into the side of the ridge at the west edge of the bench. No buildings are still standing at Dorleska.

Between this bench and a larger flat above to the southwest, you walk on old road trace again. That's all the road there was. It was used to haul ore from the upper diggings down to the stamp mill. Another boiler sits near a large rock dump on the upper flat. It may have been used to operate a draw works, although there is no evidence of a headworks or shaft now.

Rough, gravelly trail snakes southwest up the steep, bare slope beyond the upper diggings to the crest of the ridge .5 mile from the stamp mill. Forests on the benches and the side of the ridge have never really recovered from being cut to fire the boilers and build the mine works and shacks. Contorted western white pines, foxtail pines, Jeffrey pines and hemlocks on the crest were spared, however.

From the crest you look down into the South Fork valley south of Big Flat and across to Packers Peak, northwest, and Caribou Mountain, southwest. Josephine Lake hangs in a slot on the side of Caribou Mountain, and the Caribou Lakes trail switchbacks up its brushy north shoulder. Preachers Peak is the high point on the rocky crest directly north.

From the summit, you descend moderately at first, then more steeply, heading slightly west of south across the west side of the ridge. The trail cuts through two dumps from prospect holes on the way down and then, a half mile from the crest, turns straight down the side of the ridge to meet the Big Flat/Sunrise Basin trail. Turning north on this trail soon brings you to the Yellow Rose Mine diggings, where the trail ducks down to pass below a large rock dump, upright boiler and remains of a rotary rock crusher.

Trip 10
Union Creek and Dorleska Mine to Big Flat

A short walk along the top of the dump will bring you to the mouth of a caved-in drift running into the hill. A small stream of water runs from the drift, but it looks and smells too mineralized to drink. A funny little two-story shack leaning to the south up the hill from the drift may not continue to stand through many more winters.

From the Yellow Rose Mine the level trail runs north on a flat for 300 yards, then begins to descend moderately steeply northwest across the side of the ridge. The first mile below the mine is mostly in fir forest, with occasional open or brushy spots. You cross several little streams and seeps, but they are all mossy and heavily mineralized. The trees get thinner and the brush gets thicker as you continue your descent on fair trail, very rough in steep places. Finally, 1.8 miles below the mine, a crystal-clear little stream flows across the trail in the bottom of a steep gully.

Past a grove of Douglas firs you can see Big Flat below and Mountain Meadow Ranch across the valley. Traversing past more brush and sparse Oregon oaks, you come to the grove of big Douglas firs at Big Flat 2.3 miles from the Yellow Rose Mine. The sign at the trailhead says 3 miles, but that must have been measured by someone walking *up* the trail on a hot afternoon. The trailhead parking lot is across the main road before you get to the campground.

Caribou Mountain from the crest above
Dorleska Mine

Two-story shack at
Yellow Rose Mine

Trip 11

South Fork Coffee Creek Loop to Trail Gulch and Long Gulch Lakes

---

Trip Type: Loop trip of 3 to 5 days

Distance: 17 miles

Elevation Change: 9135 feet, average 537 feet per mile

Season: Mid-July to mid-September

Topo Map: *Deadman Peak* (provisional 1986) 7.5′ quadrangle

South Fork Coffee Creek has a misleading name—it flows in from the north, well north of North Fork Coffee Creek and almost at the northernmost point of Coffee Creek's crooked course through the northern Trinity Alps. The only things that can be considered "south" about this pretty little creek are that it flows south from the south side of the South Fork Salmon River divide.

A very pleasant trail leads up the South Fork—not too steep, well shaded except for the upper meadows, and quite scenic. Above the confluence of Steveale Creek the steep-sided lower canyon gives way to a wide glaciated valley, with flowery meadows backed by granite ridges and peaks. Once you've climbed the last steep half mile to the crest of the divide, you drop almost directly into the dramatic cirque containing Trail Gulch Lake.

Trail Gulch and Long Gulch are charming, subalpine lakes, each 12–15 acres in size and typical of the string of lakes along the north side of the Salmon/Scott River divide. Although the two lakes are only a mile apart on the map, the trail between them crosses and recrosses the divide in 3.4 tortuous miles. Of course, you could avoid some of the climbing by going all the way down Trail Gulch and back up Long Gulch, but you would miss a lot of gorgeous scenery, and it's almost 6 miles that way.

Both lakes are within easy day-hiking or riding distance of trailheads on the north side of the divide, but the remoteness of those trailheads helps keep visitation to only moderate. The lakes are warm enough for good swimming by mid-August, and fishing in them is fair to good for rainbow trout to 10 inches. South Fork Coffee Creek supports a good population of pan-sized rainbows below Steveale Creek, but you have to crawl down into the canyon to get at them.

The return side of the loop trip across the upper basin of North Fork Coffee Creek and down through Steveale Meadow is mostly downhill and offers distinctly different scenery. You will have to learn to get along with grazing cattle, however; they are an integral part of the scenery.

Starting Point

South Fork Coffee Creek trailhead is 15 miles up the Coffee Creek road from Highway 3, and 8.3 miles beyond the North Fork trailhead. Directions to the Coffee Creek road and Coffee Creek Ranger Station are in Trip 9. The signed turnoff to the trailhead is .4 mile above the road bridge over the South Fork and beside an area of previous heavy dredging along Coffee Creek. Four or five vehicles can park here if you are careful not to block access. Don't park above the gate across the turnoff road—if it's open when you go in, it may be locked when you come out. If the parking space is full, you may find room in one of two wide turnouts within the next .5 mile up the road near the Lady Gulch and Adams Lake trailheads.

Description

A Forest Service gate, 50 yards from the Coffee Creek road, is intended to block vehicular access to the jeep road that is the beginning of the South Fork trail. The road ascends gradually north for 150 yards, then you begin to climb steeply northeast, first in a washed-out gully, then on switchbacks up the side of a ridge.

At .6 mile you round a shoulder of the ridge in thick Douglas fir forest and level off headed north on the old road contouring the west slope of the South Fork Coffee Creek canyon. Large Douglas firs, ponderosa pines and sugar pines shade the way to a road fork, 1 mile from the trailhead. The left-hand fork is signed "SOUTH FORK TRAIL." The right-hand fork disappears in the trees toward the bottom of the canyon.

The road ends .2 mile farther on at a cabin site just beyond a small stream. A rusty bedspring and the remains of an enameled kitchen range sitting on a concrete slab indicate the relatively recent vintage of the cabin, but the structure itself has completely disappeared. This is a good campsite if you don't mind the pile of trash in the gully below. An old Forest Service sign on a tree show a distance of 1 mile back to Coffee Creek road and 6 miles to Trail Gulch Lake. Don't put too much trust in either figure.

You climb moderately now, on good foot and horse trail, out into ferny meadows before turning to ford the South Fork 2 miles from the trailhead. A few good campsites are beyond a screen of willows on the east bank. However, you should purify the water because of the many cattle in the meadows above.

A short, steep climb east from the crossing brings you to a bench where you level off at a junction with the Steveale Meadow/North Fork trail at .3 mile. The sign on the South Fork trail at the junction lists the Taylor Creek trail as the destination to the northwest, which may be confusing, since that is the way to Trail Gulch Lake. The Taylor Creek trail forks west from this trail on the crest above Trail Gulch Lake, so the Taylor Creek sign shows the right direction unless you want to do the loop in the other direction up Steveale Creek to Long Gulch Lake first.

On the South Fork trail you ascend moderately northwest across forested benches and heavily grazed meadows to cross a small tributary .3 mile from the trail junction, and come close to the South Fork again. This tributary is the last drinking water on the trail before you climb over the divide and down to Trail Gulch Lake, 3.5 miles away.

From the watering spot you continue to ascend moderately through fern-filled meadows, and as the trail turns more northward, a massive, glacier-carved, granite ridge comes into view across the valley. Steeper pitches of trail lead higher as Shasta red firs and foxtail pines begin to appear in patches of forest between meadows. Above a sandy flat the last .5 mile to a gap in the Salmon River divide is steep to very steep.

A multiple trail junction marks the top of the divide. The Taylor Creek trail branches west to cross the divide through another gap and run down Taylor Creek to the South Fork Salmon River. Northwest across the gap a dim track contours along the side of a spur ridge and eventually crosses over to descend to Fish Lake. Except for the view from the top of the spur ridge, the side trip to Fish Lake isn't worth the effort. Fish Lake is really a pond, and the

Ferny meadow at the head of South Fork Coffee Creek canyon

once-beautiful meadow around it has been almost destroyed by grazing cattle.

Your trail to Trail Gulch Lake leads northeast over the crest and you soon see the sparkling, deep, blue lake nestled in the cirque below. Five moderately steep switchbacks, built since the topo map was published, descend the north face of the divide to an unsigned trail junction .3 mile west of the lake. From here the Trail Gulch trail continues north 2.8 miles to a trailhead near Carter Meadow. The trail to the lake wanders east through broken granite, climbing slightly over a rim before running along the north shore below a number of excellent campsites in open red fir and hemlock forest 6 miles from the South Fork trailhead.

Deadman Peak towers to 7600 feet directly above the south shore of 14-acre, 6500-foot elevation Trail Gulch Lake. Granite cliffs and talus slides surrounding more than half of the shoreline reflect in the usually placid water. A mammoth rockfall has formed a small island near the south shore that you can swim to if you want more seclusion. In spite of heavy fishing pressure, it's still possible to raise a few 10–11-inch rainbow trout. All in all, it's a very nice place to spend a day or two. There is usually plenty of room in the many good-to-excellent campsites, but don't expect to find much firewood.

Bound for Long Gulch Lake you follow the trail to the outlet at the northeast corner of Trail Gulch Lake, then turn north in the edge of the trees past a large horse-camping area. About 75 yards from the lake you will see a small clump of blazed and initialed lodgepole pines beside a tiny meadow. The trail runs east across the meadow, crosses the outlet creek, and continues through a gap in the thick alders on the other side. Beyond the alders you turn back toward the lake, then go east again at a duck to climb past a campsite and look for more ducks leading east up the open, cow-tracked hill. As you approach a rock wall at the top of the moderately steep slope, the trail, still marked by ducks, turns northeast below a thicket of alders and climbs into dense forest. A well-defined trail snakes up through mature Shasta red firs and mountain hemlocks north of the alders to a 200-yard stretch of very steep, gravelly, open slope. Some of this material is loose, and you tend to slip back two steps for every three you climb. The tread improves a little after you pass this obstacle course, and you zigzag east through younger, open forest and broken rock, very steep at times, to the crest .8 mile from the outlet at Trail Gulch Lake. Superb views north to the Marble Mountains and west across Trail Gulch reward your climb.

An old Forest Service sign propped against a snag just south of the summit reads: "NORTH FORK COFFEE CREEK TRAIL 9W02, SCHLOMBERG CABIN, COFFEE CREEK ROAD." You can make an off-trail traverse from here along the south side of the crest for about .8 mile and pick up the trail again where it crosses the crest above Long Gulch Lake, but you will find the going very rough and probably not worth the effort. Your trail plunges over the south side of the divide in a few zigzags, then makes two long traverses, not shown on the topo map, before crossing a granite shelf and continuing down southeast, guided by ducks through broken rock, to a flat meadow of 10–15 acres. Most of this route is south of the trail shown on the *Coffee Creek* quadrangle.

In the meadow you go south through a gap in a row of alders, then look for ducks leading northeast away from the meandering streamcourse ahead of you. A cairn by a row of rocks marks the exit from the meadow, and you continue northeast across a little flat and past another duck into woods where blazes mark the trail. Follow the lightly used trail east and northeast through more woods and patches of meadow and, 2 miles from Trail Gulch Lake, drop down to a trail junction beside a tiny intermittent stream flowing southeast in a thicket of alders. The heavily used trail coming in from the south is the Steveale Meadow trail that you will use to complete the loop when you come back this way. A new sign on a fir tree points ahead northeast to Long Gulch Lake and back the way we've come to Trail Gulch Lake. The Steveale Meadow trail has no sign. From the junction the well-defined Long Gulch trail climbs moderately to steeply north-northeast .4 mile to a gap in the crest above Long Gulch Lake. A junction with the North Fork/Schlomberg Cabin trail is just below the top of the pass on the south side.

Long Gulch Lake, almost a twin of Trail Gulch Lake, comes into view to the northwest as you reach the top of the divide. Your trail dives steeply down the north side of the divide through a dense forest composed almost entirely of mountain hemlock to a granite ledge, then descends more moderately north across the west side of a ridge on the east side of Long Gulch. You turn west .3 mile from the crest, to zigzag steeply down an open slope to the lower end of a lush little meadow. You might be tempted by your view from above and by the topo map to believe that an easy approach to the lake lies up this meadow and over a spur ridge. Wrong!—you would end up struggling down a rough talus slope in heavy brush. The easy way is on down the Long Gulch trail one-quarter mile to a trail junction, then back up the east side of the outlet creek to the lake.

The cirque walls around 10-acre Long Gulch Lake are darker granite than those around Trail Gulch Lake, and also contain some metamorphic rock strata. Otherwise, the two lakes and their settings are quite similar. Rainbow trout fingerlings along the shoreline and in the outlet creek show that the trout are spawning well here. We had trouble catching any fish more than 6–7 inches long, however. The Long Gulch trailhead is less than 2 miles north of the lake, so visitation and fishing pressure are greater than at Trail Gulch. A large number of good campsites in a wide, wooded area above the north shore would be classified excellent except for heavy use and absence of firewood. Swimming is excellent by mid-August.

After enjoying Long Gulch Lake retrace your steps back over the Salmon River divide 1.3 miles to the Steveale Meadow trail junction—unless you've decided to turn down the North Fork to Schlomberg Cabin. It's 9.3 miles from Long Gulch Lake to the North Fork trailhead that way.

From the Trail Gulch/Long Gulch trail junction, the Steveale Meadow trail wanders a little west of south across the valley, skirting some large flats of alders. A junction with a little-used trail going northeast across the valley to connect with the North Fork trail is at the foot of a spur ridge on the south side. A sign at the junction reads: "STEVEALE CREEK TRAIL 9W61," and points to "LONG GULCH LAKE" and "SOUTH FORK COFFEE CREEK TRAIL." The trail to the North Fork has no sign.

From this junction you climb moderately southeast for 250 yards, then turn southwest around the shoulder of the ridge to begin tracing a long contour around a wide, upper basin draining east into North Fork Coffee Creek. This piece of trail has been built above the old trail that dipped down into the basin on the *Coffee Creek* quadrangle. The traverse offers panoramic views across the basin to the ridges east of the North Fork, including the top of Mount Shasta on the skyline. On the other side of the basin, the trail turns southeast on the crest of the divide between the Steveale Creek and North Fork drainages and descends to a saddle at the head of Steveale Meadow.

Steveale Meadow slopes steeply south from the saddle in a half-mile spread of grass and alder thickets before dropping into the steep-walled canyon below. As you start down, you can line up the tip of distant Caribou Mountain in the notch of the lower canyon. A half mile down the moderately steep trail on the east side of the meadow you enter a strip of fir forest and, as you emerge into meadow again, you are next to Steveale Creek, burbling under a thick cover of alders. This is the first fast-running water since we left Long Gulch Lake, but you may want to check the number of cattle grazing the meadow before you drink it. A hand-carved sign at a much-used campsite in the lower end of this piece of meadow dubs the site "CAMP SIBERIA." It was probably carved by a lonesome cowpoke who had to herd cattle up here.

An important, but unsigned, trail junction is few yards below the campsite. Although it looks like all the other cow paths, the track diving into the alders and crossing to the west bank of the creek is the Steveale Creek trail. The faint trail continuing down the east bank soon turns up a ravine and eventually climbs to Chipmunk Meadow. A good-sized mine once was operated in the lower end of the ravine, and it's not far away if you want to check it out.

Steveale Creek falls away in a steep-sided canyon as our trail continues almost level above the west bank. You turn a little southwest, then northwest around the point of a ridge between Steveale Creek and South Fork Coffee Creek. A moderate-to-steep descent of .3 mile through dense fir forest brings you to the junction with the South Fork trail 1.8 miles from the divide above Steveale Meadow. Halfway down this last hill a little run of clear, clean water crosses the trail.

It's 2.3 miles of easy going from the Steveale Creek trail junction back down to the South Fork Coffee Creek trailhead.

Trip 12

Adams Lake

Trip Type: Round trip day-hike or overnight

Distance: 2.3 miles one way

Elevation Change: 1160 feet, average 504 feet per mile

Season: Late June to early October

Topo Map: *Caribou Lake* (provisional 1986) 7.5′ quadrangle

Adams Lake is a very pleasant place to visit, ever since vehicle access was blocked several years ago. It is now a half-hour horseback ride or a vigorous hike of a little more than an hour from the Coffee Creek road, and the amount of use and corresponding amount of trash left behind have been reduced accordingly. The trail goes only to Adams Lake and cross-country travel beyond the lake is very difficult, so don't plan to connect with anything else.

At 6200 feet elevation, Adams Lake isn't alpine or even subalpine, but it is a pretty place. A lush, flower-dotted meadow leads up to the little, 1-acre lake and a 7500-foot granite mountain rises directly behind it. A unique feature is a patch of cattails near the outlet. It's hard to say how they got there—we didn't find any in any other lakes in the Trinity Alps. Fishing is fair for pan-sized eastern brook trout. The banks and bottom of the lake are too muddy for good swimming.

Starting Point

The Adams Lake trailhead is 15.8 miles up the Coffee Creek road and .8 mile beyond the South Fork Coffee Creek trailhead. The trailhead is not very obvious—it is an old jeep road that has been chopped off by a 3-to-4-foot cut on the north side of the Coffee Creek road. It is marked by a small sign a half mile beyond the Adams Creek bridge, just before you get to the present rework area of the Upper Nash Mine. Parking is in a turnout between Adams Creek and the trailhead. A sign at the Lady Gulch trailhead, between Adams Creek and the

Trip 12
Adams Lake

South Fork trailhead, lists Adams Creek as a destination, but the Lady Gulch trail does not go to Adams Lake and does not connect with the Adams Lake trail.

Directions for getting to the Coffee Creek road and South Fork Coffee Creek trailhead are in Trip 9 and Trip 11.

Description

Don't be discouraged by the "TRESPASSING ABSOLUTELY FORBIDDEN" sign nailed to a tree beside the jeep road that is the beginning of the Adams Lake trail. It's perfectly all right to walk up the road. A steel-bar Forest Service gate 100 yards up the road bears the usual "NO VEHICULAR TRAFFIC" sign, which may be a bit redundant considering the 3-to-4-foot vertical bank where the jeep road meets the Coffee Creek road.

The road snakes north .3 mile to the top of the ridge between Adams Creek and Coffee Creek, where an old miner's ditch also crosses the ridge on its way from the Adams Creek canyon to the workings down on Coffee Creek. Our road-trail turns a little south of west, directly up the crest of the ridge through a magnificent, mature forest of Douglas and white firs with occasional sugar pines, western white pines and incense cedars. Surprisingly, the old road is in very good condition, although it is steep to very steep with no checks or culverts to prevent washing. At .8 mile from the trailhead you turn northwest over the side of the ridge and follow a contour above the Adams Creek canyon.

After a "zig" south up a ravine and a "zag" northwest over a little spur ridge, the trail contours west to come close to Adams Creek, trickling through thick alders in a steep-sided gulch. You continue west just south of the gulch, and at 1.6 miles from the trailhead a gap in the alders allows easy access to the creek. After a quarter mile of moderate climbing between the creek and a small meadow, you cross to the north bank and continue up the glaciated valley as it turns south to a larger meadow and Adams Lake, which lies in a grassy cup at the meadow's upper, southwest side.

The water in Adams Lake is green and unappealing by late summer, but the setting is still lush. Willows border about half of the muddy shoreline from the cattails near the outlet around to talus falling into the south side from the mountain above. A sweet little spring offers drinking water near a built-up campsite in the trees northwest of the lake. Tables, grills and mounds of trash testify to previous four-wheel-drive access, but now with less use it's all beginning to merge with the forest floor. You may meet a trail-ride group from Mountain Meadow Ranch, but they seldom stay overnight.

Trip 13

Caribou Basin
and Sawtooth Ridge

Trip Type: Round trip of 2 to 5 days

Distance: 9.6 miles one way to Big Caribou Lake

Elevation Change: 3975 feet, average 414 feet per mile

Season: Mid-July to mid-September

Topo Map: *Caribou Lake* (provisional 1986) 7.5′ quadrangle

Talk to any "oldtimer" in the Trinity area for any length of time and one of the stories you're sure to hear is about a pack trip to Caribou Basin in the "good old days." The story will probably include prodigious number of trout as long as your arm, at least one marauding bear, a pack mule that fell off the mostly vertical trail over Caribou Mountain and an early fall snowstorm with 100-mile-an-hour winds. If your "oldtimer" happens to be an incurable romantic, you may also hear of moonlight on white granite, the delicious fragrance of angelica blooming in lush meadows and a thread of wood smoke drifting across Big Caribou Lake at dawn from the camp of the only other party in the basin.

Times have changed, of course, but you may still be able to recognize Caribou Basin as the same place the "oldtimer" talked about. The 100-year-old trail over the top of Caribou Mountain is still there, but few people, or horses or mules, use it any more—the new trail around the mountain is 2 miles longer, but has only one or two short pitches that are more than a moderate grade. You're welcome to use the old trail if you like—it's a lot less dusty, and it gives you the opportunity to detour off-trail to Little Caribou Lake, something few people can say they've done these days. The moon still shines on white granite, and angelica still blooms sweetly in the meadows. If you are especially unlucky, you might see a snowstorm and a marauding bear, too.

Trip 13
Caribou Basin and Sawtooth Ridge

Caribou Basin is certainly not the pristine wilderness that it was when the first dudes were packed into it 75 or so years ago, but the scenery is still stunning, and most of the attributes of wilderness are still there. The deep, blue lakes still reflect untouched cliffs and peaks. It's still possible to catch a limit of eastern brook and rainbow trout, but both the limit and the trout are smaller than they used to be. The views from Sawtooth Ridge are still superlative and, as you explore along the crest, you can imagine for a little while that there is no one else in the world.

Caribou Basin is heavily visited but, contrary to general impression, not as heavily visited as some other areas in the Trinity Alps. The tendency of visitors to congregate around Snowslide Lake and tiny Middle Caribou Lake gives the impression that the basin is more crowded than it really is. A little thought about where you camp and how you camp will help a lot in preserving the wilderness atmosphere. The purity of the water in the lakes has been in question for several years. Bad sanitation practices, too many pack animals and the inability of a solid rock basin to absorb wastes have all contributed to the problem. Please be considerate of those who follow you.

Starting Point

The trailhead is beside Big Flat campground, 20.5 miles up the Coffee Creek road from Highway 3, and .7 mile past the road that forks right to Mountain Meadow Ranch. If you come to a gate across the road and signs for Josephine Creek Lodge (formerly Carter's Resort), you've gone .3 mile past Big Flat. Think twice about camping at Big Flat—the campground is small, primitive and usually overcrowded. Car camping is much better back by Clair Engle Lake.

Directions to Coffee Creek junction and description of the Coffee Creek road are in Trips 9 and 11.

Description

A "CARIBOU TRAIL" sign by the backpackers' parking area above Big Flat campground marks the wide, heavily used trail descending 200 yards south to cross the South Fork Salmon River. The trail divides just before you get to the little river—left fork to a foot-log, right fork to a ford. Another left fork leads south to Kidd Creek. The South Fork may be big enough to be a little scary early in the season, but the crossing shouldn't be really dangerous.

The trail forks again at the bottom of the steep bank on the other side of the stream. Take the left fork up the bank; the right fork is the old trail going around the ridge ahead of you and up Caribou Gulch.

In the flat above the bank you turn west, pass yet another trail branching south toward Josephine Creek Lodge and the Kidd Creek trail, and, 100 yards farther on, come to a trail register at the foot of the ridge. A series of moderate switchbacks takes you halfway up the hill, where you begin a long, gradually ascending traverse south across the face of the ridge in heavy brush. Welcome, cool shade greets you in a strip of fir forest .7 mile across the slope. On the other side of the trees you get a first close-up look at the glistening granite slopes of Caribou Mountain before turning back in another strip of trees to begin the next long traverse north.

Panoramic views of Big Flat, Mountain Meadow Ranch and the trail slanting up the ridge across the valley to Yellow Rose Mine open up as you traverse .8 mile before turning back south again. You soon turn southwest on this final traverse, and enter signed Caribou Meadow in a saddle on top of the ridge 4 miles from the trailhead. The old Caribou trail crosses the new trail in the meadow; you have the option of turning south on it to climb over Caribou Mountain if you like. Consider, though, that the old trail is not maintained, and is a lot steeper and rougher than the excellent tread you've been on this far. If you decide to climb the old trail, and want to make the off-trail side trip to Little Caribou Lake, you should start looking for an off-trail route west across the bare granite a little more than a mile above Caribou Meadow. The lake is in a cirque less than a half mile from the old trail. Solitude is almost guaranteed at Little Caribou, and you'll even find enough wood for a campfire, but it's a thousand feet higher than Caribou Meadow.

On the new trail you follow a level contour around the west side of the ridge you just climbed, and soon come out of woods onto the solid granite northwest face of Caribou Mountain. Rough tread, blasted out of the rock, climbs moderately northwest for a half mile. Beyond a strip of sedimentary rock you cross two small streams, dry in late summer, at the head of Caribou Gulch, then follow a contour all the way around a north-facing shoulder of the mountain to Brown's Meadow. Your trail runs across the bottom of the large, steeply sloping meadow, and dives into a thicket of alders on the west side concealing a sluggish little stream. A few fair campsites are under trees above the trail close to the alders. Drinking water that probably should be purified is available from a spring flowing through a pipe beneath the trail 300 yards west up the hill.

Four long, dusty switchbacks take you up the mostly forested slope of the next spur ridge. You climb directly up the crest for 100 yards, then turn gradually southwest and south around the mountain, climbing moderately through dense forest on old talus slopes. Seven miles from the trailhead you head southeast across a very steep, open, granite slope overlooking the awesome chasm through which Caribou Creek drains northwest. A panorama of glacier-carved rock rises on the other side of the canyon, leading up to Thompson Peak on the southwest horizon. Big Caribou Lake and Lower Caribou Lake soon appear in the giant basin above the head of the canyon, but Snowslide and Middle Caribou lakes remain hidden behind folds of rock.

Pinemat manzanita carpets some of the granite, and sparse red firs, mountain hemlocks, Jeffrey pines, whitebark pines and mountain mahoganies cling to cracks and ledges. Halfway along the canyon wall the trail turns and descends into a chute gouged into the side of the mountain. From the middle of this chute you have an unobstructed view between your toes of the bottom of the canyon a half mile below—not for those who suffer from vertigo. Three short, steep switchbacks take you up to the next point of rock, and you continue mostly level to a belt of trees sloping a little less steeply toward the lower end of Caribou Basin. On the other side of the trees you look down a brushy slope directly into Snowslide Lake, nestled in a trough between a granite dike and cliffs on the west side of Caribou Mountain. The old Caribou trail rejoins the new trail somewhere in the trees, but the junction is hard to find.

Four long switchbacks in and out of the trees and a few zigzags at the bottom of the slope lead to a small meadow at the north end of the dike west of Snowslide Lake. A fine spring flows across the trail halfway down the hill, providing the best water in the basin. Even this water should be purified, however. Overused campsites cover the dike and fill the basin around Middle Caribou Lake below the south end of the dike. If you camp in this area, please be very careful to dispose of human waste and wash water well away from the lakes where it can't drain back in to the lakes. Also pack out all your garbage— you won't find enough firewood to burn it. Less crowded campsites are around Big Caribou Lake, but they are exposed to wind and weather. Although the Forest Service declared Caribou basin water drinkable as of 1981, you probably should purify all drinking water.

Ten-acre Snowslide Lake has no inlet or outlet streams, and its level fluctuates as much as 2 feet during the summer. Both rainbow and eastern brook trout live in its cold depths and, if you're lucky, you can still hook an occasional 12-incher during the evening rise.

Trails branch in all directions through the scrubby mountain hemlocks, firs and lodgepole pines on the dike above Snowslide Lake. Most of the trails lead to the pocket in the rocks containing half-acre Middle Caribou Lake, or on northwest to Lower Caribou Lake. Middle Caribou is a grassy pond below a waterfall in the stream flowing from Big Caribou to Lower Caribou Lake. Lower Caribou is a steep-sided, 22-acre lake, very difficult to get around and producing only small eastern brook trout for your trouble. There are no good campsites around Lower Caribou.

The trail from Snowslide Lake to Big Caribou Lake runs along the south shore of Snowslide below a rock rim, then climbs southwest on short, steep switchbacks up over granite ledges. The route is not very well defined in the jumbled, glacier-gouged granite above the initial climb. It wanders generally southwest, marked by occasion ducks, to the north shore of big Caribou Lake and an unsigned junction with the lightly used trail to Little South Fork Salmon River, northwest over two high ridges.

Big Caribou Lake is the commonly used, and appropriate, name for this 72-acre, deep, subalpine lake, although it's just plain "Caribou Lake" on the topo map. After all, it is the biggest lake in the Trinity Alps, and many people say it's the most beautiful. It sits in the bottom of a very large cirque beneath Caribou Mountain, Sawtooth Ridge and an unnamed spur ridge to the west. Two thirds of the convoluted shoreline, from the northwest around to almost south, is granite. Low cliffs overlook indigo depths. Moving shadows of surface wavelets cross ledges that slope into crystal clear water, then rise again as tiny islets offshore. Many "bathtub" lakes and ponds fill hollows and troughs in the glaciated granite around the lake. Erratic boulders perch everywhere, and dwarfed and wind-contorted trees cling to cracks and crannies.

Where granite gives way to metamorphic rock around the south shore, pocket meadows and other greenery replace bare rock to some extent, and a few tiny, gravelly beaches offer easier access to the lake. Farther around to the west, fingers of talus from the west ridge slide directly into the water between strips of upright firs and hemlocks. A startlingly white vein of quartz slashes diagonally across the red-stained cliffs toward the top of the west ridge.

Many good campsites are in the rocks above the north and east shores of Big Caribou, and a few more are on the edges of pocket meadows above the south shore. Please don't camp in the meadows—they are very fragile.

Sawtooth Ridge views: Caribou Basin, top; Stuart Fork canyon and lakes, below

Firewood is scarce to nonexistent. When the wind isn't blowing too hard, fishing for both rainbow and eastern brook trout is good in Big Caribou, but don't expect any trophy fish.

The jagged top of Sawtooth Ridge forms the horizon all the way across the sky south of Big Caribou Lake. A trail climbs to the crest from the south end of the lake, then drops 2200 feet of elevation in 1.8 miles of switchbacks to Portuguese Camp at the bottom of the Stuart Fork canyon. Horses are prohibited on this trail.

You won't find any signs pointing the way to the Sawtooth Ridge crest, but you can see the trail from below, near where it crosses the crest, so you can't get very lost. The trail around the east side of Big Caribou Lake is crisscrossed by deer trails and tracks leading to campsites, and is anything but obvious but, again, you can see where you want to go. A half mile of clambering over the rocks should bring you to the meadows above the south shore. Head southwest up the hill on whatever track you can find and, as you come near the top of the series of little meadows and intervening ledges, you should find a more definite trail climbing southwest, then southeast, across the steep, grassy slope. Above a sparse grove of mountain hemlocks you zigzag directly south up a very steep slope on crumbing rock to a gap in the crest 1.3 miles from the trail junction on the north shore of Big Caribou Lake.

The views from the gap where the trail crosses are breathtaking, but if you explore a little east and west of the crest, you will discover even better overlooks. The awesome bulk of Sawtooth Mountain looms up directly across Stuart Fork canyon. You can see down the canyon southeast to Morris Meadow and beyond. Emerald and Sapphire lakes glitter like their namesake jewels in the granite basin below snow-capped Thompson Peak at the head of the canyon. Caribou Basin is laid out like a map back the way you came, and you can trace the route back to Big Flat, contouring around a massive shoulder of Caribou Mountain.

The best thing that can be said about the trail going south over the crest to Portuguese Camp is that going down it is probably better than climbing up it from the canyon below.

Trip 14

Sunrise Basin, Horseshoe Lake, Ward Lake Loop

Trip Type: Loop trip of 3 to 5 days

Distance: 19.5

Elevation Change: 10,560 feet, average 543 feet per mile

Season: Mid-July to late September

Topo Map: *Caribou Lake, Ycatapom Peak* (both provisional 1986) and *Siligo Peak* (provisional 1982) 7.5′ quadrangles

Historic mines, high peaks, high mountain lakes and flowery meadows are the main attractions on this strenuous loop trip. You will see other people, but certainly not as many as you would on the Caribou Basin trail out of Big Flat or on the alternate route up Swift Creek to Horseshoe and Ward lakes. If you want to get away from people and climb some peaks, a whole row of them is along the crest you cross twice, from Red Rock Mountain on the north end down to Tri-Forest Peak on the south.

A side trip to Landers Lake is a relatively easy endeavor, either off-trail or on. An extended loop of 29 miles would add Landers Lake, upper Union Creek, Parker Creek and Parker Meadow to the itinerary (see Trip 6). Careful study of the maps will reveal a number of other extensions and alternatives.

Fishing in Horseshoe and Ward lakes is apt to be frustrating. Both lakes seem to have plenty of eastern brook trout in them, but the fish tend to sneer at all artificial lures. Swimming in the lakes is cool at best.

It's something of a toss-up as to which direction you should take to do this loop. If you get a late start, you will probably be better off to walk up the Carter's Lodge road from Big Flat, and camp somewhere up Kidd Creek. The disadvantage of that direction is that the steepest, roughest piece of trail on the trip is at the head of Kidd Creek, and you would be going up it instead of down.

Trip 14
Sunrise Basin, Horseshoe Lake, Ward Lake Loop

Similarly, in the direction the trip is written, the trail up the side of the ridge past the Yellow Rose and Leroy mines can be brutally hot in the afternoon, and there is very little water.

Starting Point

You start and end at Big Flat trailhead 20.5 miles up the Coffee Creek road. Trailhead parking is just off the main road before you get to the campground. Don't plan to camp at Big Flat campground; it is almost always full, and if you do manage to find a site, it is primitive and crowded. You will be much more comfortable car-camping at one of the excellent fee campgrounds around Clair Engle Lake. The Coffee Creek road junction with Highway 3 is 40 miles north of Weaverville. For a description of Coffee Creek road, see Trips 9 and 11.

Description

The trail to Sunrise Basin begins on the east side of the Coffee Creek road above the Big Flat trailhead parking area. A sign there says 3 miles to Yellow Rose Mine; it's really 2.3 miles. Description of the Yellow Rose Mine and the trail between the mine and Big Flat is in Trip 10. The first water up the steep, dusty trail is .5 mile from the trailhead. The next water is just beyond the Dorleska Mine trail junction, 2.5 miles from the trailhead. You would have to try hard to get off this trail before you get to the Yellow Rose Mine.

The Dorleska Mine trail junction is .2 mile up the hill from the Yellow Rose Mine on rough, steep tread, and from the junction you continue climbing south across a meadow. A tiny spring is below the trail halfway across the meadow, the reason for the riveted iron pipe beside the trail near the junction. The water is potable, in contrast to the streams and seeps at and below the mine.

Beyond the meadow, you climb over a shoulder of the ridge, then rise more gradually along a bench in open forest of white fir and western white pine. A short, steep, washed-out pitch at the south end of the bench takes you up to the Leroy Mine, 3 miles from the trailhead. A clear little stream flows beside the cabins here, and several campsites provide the first good place to camp since the trailhead.

A short climb from the Leroy Mine leads to a long contour, turning gradually southeast around the side of the mountain through open forest. The full face of Caribou Mountain soon comes into view across the South Fork canyon. Until you've seen it from here or from an airplane, it is had to realize what a tremendous mass of granite the Caribou Mountain monolith is.

An old prospect hole and a spring, badly trampled by cattle, are below a short, steep drop as you enter a basin at the head of Gulick Creek 1 mile from the Leroy Mine. The tip of Tri-Forest Peak peers over the south wall of the basin. The trail contours around the northeast side to a little meadow just below the headwall. Several springs run across the trail, but pollution by grazing cattle makes the water undrinkable.

The trail snakes east up the headwall without benefit of any real switch-backs. A quarter mile of steep-to-very-steep climbing over broken rock brings you to the crest above Sunrise Basin, 4.6 miles from the trailhead. Western white pines and foxtail pines stand among the rocks on the way up, but only foxtails survive at the summit. Back the way you came, you look all the way down the South Fork Salmon canyon and up to Packers Peak on the horizon.

Red Rock Mountain rears its fractured red bulk above the crest to the north. Landers Lake is in a basin less than a mile away behind the east shoulder of the mountain, but you need to be a pretty good mountaineer to get there from here. Beyond Sunrise Basin, spread out at your feet, you can see down to Parker Meadow on the floor of Swift Creek canyon far below.

An old sign on the crest says it is 3.5 miles to Landers Lake through Sunrise Basin, which is about right. Another old sign, nailed to a tree on the Sunrise side, gives distances of 1.5 miles to the Leroy Mine, 2 miles to the Yellow Rose Mine and 5 miles to Big Flat. The first two are about right, but it's really only 4.6 miles to Big Flat.

Going down into Sunrise Basin, the trail contours south below the crest for 200 yards, then turns down to a ravine north of a small ridge of shattered rock. Two switchbacks at the bottom of the ravine take you down to a dry bench, which you traverse northward. From the bench, the trail wanders down the north side of the basin, steeply at times, across more benches and wet and dry meadows.

You skirt the foot of a huge pile of broken red rock that has slid off the side of Red Rock Mountain, then descend more steeply across a strip of dry meadow and down a gravelly slope to the foot of a wet meadow where a mass of California pitcher plants grow. A substantial stream falls down a lush ravine 1 mile from the crest. You follow this creek down and cross it and two more cascading channels just above where they disappear into a huge mass of willows, then circle around the south side of the willows to a large, level meadow on the floor of the basin. Even in late summer many flowers still bloom here—goldenrods, sunflowers, yampa and several varieties of daisies.

The stream course across the meadow is dry below the willows by August, but the creek reappears from underground in a ravine in the forest east of the meadow to provide filtered water for the excellent campsites there. Not many people go through Sunrise Basin, and it is a fine spot to relax for a couple of days if you want to get away from crowds. If you want to be entirely alone, try climbing over the south wall of Sunrise Basin and around into French Cove. Neither place offers any fishing or swimming, unfortunately.

The trail on down to Landers Creek is south of Sunrise Creek. You cross two more small meadows, then descend at a moderately steep rate through open fir forest to a junction with the Landers Creek/Landers Lake trail 6.5 miles from the trailhead at Big Flat. If you want to make a side trip to Landers Lake, it is 1.8 miles north up the canyon. Descriptions of the trail and the lake are in Trip 6.

The .7 mile of trail down Landers Creek to Mumford Meadow is also described in Trip 6. Suffice it to say that it is steep and washed out.

Trip 14
Sunrise Basin, Horseshoe Lake, Ward Lake Loop

When you come to the edge of Mumford Meadow in the bottom of Swift Creek canyon, look for an unsigned branch of the Landers Creek trail that runs southwest across the meadow to connect with the Swift Creek trail in a row of trees by the creek. The Swift Creek trailhead is 6 miles southeast down the canyon. After the steep, rough descent down Landers Creek, the trail west up Swift Creek offers very pleasant walking, smooth tread rising gradually through alternating forest and meadow not far from the creek.

The trail and the canyon turn southwest about a half mile from the Landers Creek junction, and you cross some boggy spots where small streams flow across to Swift Creek. At the head of Swift Creek, 1.8 miles from Landers Creek, you turn west in a basin and climb moderately through a grove of white firs and across a small meadow toward a granite wall north of a red peak. Above an unlikely grove of large cottonwoods at the edge of the meadow, a little creek runs down a steep pitch of trail, making climbing difficult.

You soon get out of the creek, only to attack a steeper set of zigzags over broken rock and glaciated outcrops and though manzanita brush up to a small flat. A grove of large red firs beside a small meadow offers a good spot to rest, but you will have to go a quarter mile farther up the trail to find water. Shooting stars, lupines, yarrows and mountain asters bloom beside the little creek as you climb higher to the junction of the Horseshoe Lake/Ward Lake trail in another small grove of red firs, 1.9 miles from the Landers Creek trail junction.

Horseshoe Lake is in a granite cirque a half mile southwest of the junction. The rough trail snakes up over ledges, through a flat and over a rock dike to the outlet of the 4-acre lake. Its shape, bent around a hump of glacier-resistant

Mountain hemlock at Ward Lake

Meadow above Swift Creek canyon

granite on the floor of the cirque, gives Horseshoe Lake its name. The outside curve on the west side has a lot of brush along the shoreline. Sparse mountain hemlocks, western white pines and lodgepole pines grow among the rocks above the east shore and on the granite hump in the middle of the lake. The inside curve of the horseshoe has a more open shoreline, with rock ledges that drop off into deep water. Fishing is fair for small eastern brook trout.

Two good campsites are on ledges east of the lake. Firewood is scarce. Please don't camp on the hump in the middle of the lake—it is obvious that wastes will drain directly into the lake.

Back at the Swift Creek trail junction, the Ward Lake trail ducks down north to cross a little creek, then climbs into a grove of large red firs, all snow-bent at the base of the trunks. An old sheet-iron sheepherder's stove, not the standard cast-iron USFS model, sits in a fair campsite under the trees. Small streams and seeps muddy the trail across the top of a wet meadow above the grove. The water runs down into small, deep pothole ponds that reflect the sky in the flower-filled meadow.

A steep climb north on rough trail takes you across a brushy hillside and up to some very large scattered red firs. One or two of these trees must be more than 10 feet in diameter at the butt. Beyond strips of meadow and more brush, you climb very steeply around a granite shoulder, and turn west into a red, metamorphic rock basin. A narrow, grass-floored gully with a still stream in it leads to the outlet of Ward Lake .7 mile from the Horseshoe Lake/Swift Creek junction.

Gorgeous green meadows slope down to 5.5-acre Ward Lake from the steep south and west sides of its basin. The lake is bent around a hump of rock in the opposite direction from Horseshoe Lake, so the outside of the curve is to the east, with the outlet running out of the east part of the curve. The shoreline is rocky except where the meadows extend to the shore, and the water is very deep off the rocks on the inside of the curve. Two large, excellent campsites are above the south shore. Several other fair sites are near the outlet and above the north shore. Adequate firewood is available up the sides of the basin.

A few spots in the steeply sloping meadows might be level enough to tempt someone to camp in them. Please don't do it. Any heavy use of these subalpine grasslands will cause damage that will not repair itself for many, many years.

Ward Lake seldom gets warm enough for comfortable swimming, and its large eastern brook trout tend to ignore all temptations cast their way, but a sunset and sunrise or two, reflected in the still water, are worth more than the admission price. Several deer may wander through your campsite. Some of them have become pests because previous campers have fed them. You should also be careful not to inadvertently feed the resident black bears. They don't beg food—they just take it if it's where they can get at it.

Most of the rock around the shoreline of Ward Lake is granite, but as you climb away from the north shore on the way to Kidd Creek, you soon come to the kind of red metamorphic rock you see in the crest ahead. After skirting the north shore of the lake, the trail dips into the edge of the wet meadow sloping down to the west shore, then climbs into a grove of firs with a few more fair campsites.

Beyond another strip of meadow north of the trees, you discover that the trail is not heading for the low gap in the ridge to the northeast, as you hoped, but straight north toward what appears to be the highest point on the steep ridge. You will see from higher up that the valley beyond the ridge to the northeast leads back down to Swift Creek. Take a breather as you scramble up the very steep, rocky slope, and look back at the magnificent panorama to the southeast. A lush, green vale falls away directly below into Swift Creek canyon in the middle distance. On the far side of the canyon, hanging valleys decorate the walls leading up to the serried ranks of central Alps.

The crest above Kidd Creek is .6 mile from Ward Lake. In addition to the panorama back east and south, you can now see all the way down Kidd Creek and across the South Fork Salmon canyon to Mountain Meadow Ranch and Packers Peak. Snow-capped tops of the Marble Mountains form the horizon to the northwest, and Red Rock Mountain straddles the jagged ridge to the north.

A set of short, very steep switchbacks takes you down the north side of the crest and into a cleft filled with huge red and gray talus blocks. Lingering snowbanks here suggest that you should not attempt this route early in the season. The trail snakes down the cleft, in and out of talus on tread of broken rock and loose gravel, then turns out onto a steep hillside on the southwest side of the canyon. The trail is better .5 mile from the crest, as you pass a series of little ponds at the head of a meadow sloping north into the main canyon.

A good campsite is beside Kidd Creek in a grove of red firs and western white pines .3 mile farther down. Heavy cattle grazing in the meadows on the floor of the canyon should prompt you to purify all drinking water.

On the southwest side of a large meadow, you continue a moderate descent northwest, then drop off more steeply as you enter mixed forest 1.5 miles from the crest. A waterfall in Kidd Creek is beside the trail at 2 miles. The next quarter mile of more moderate descent brings you out on a point of rock where you look directly across at the face of Caribou Mountain. The trail turns south from the point of a ledge, then steeply west down the side of the hill to a set of switchbacks. Douglas firs predominate in the forest where you reach a junction with the South Fork Salmon trail, 3.8 miles from Ward Lake.

A confusing old sign at the junction says Kidd Creek and Ward Lake are up the South Fork trail. That trail actually climbs south to the head of the canyon and over a crest west of Tri-Forest Peak. You turn north at the junction, and soon cross the rocky bed of Kidd Creek. The creek is usually underground here by midsummer. North of Kidd Creek the trail has been relocated to climb around the Josephine Creek Lodge property.

You switchback down again to level trail leading north through beautiful, open forest, and come to a crossing of the Josephine Creek Lodge road. You now have a choice of continuing on relatively new trail across the road or turning right on the road. Either way leads to the Big Flat trailhead in 2.5 almost level miles. The trail is much more scenic and pleasant walking.

Trip 15

Canyon Creek Lakes
and "El" Lake

Trip Type: Round trip of 3 to 5 days

Distance: 9 miles one way to "El" Lake, 18 miles round trip

Elevation Change: 3545 feet, average 394 feet per mile

Season: Early July to mid-October

Topo Map: *Mount Hilton* (provisional 1982) 7.5′ quadrangle

If you can take only one trip into the Trinity Alps, Canyon Creek is your best choice. It provides at least a sample of most of the sights and activities that make the Trinity Alps such a unique and marvelous place. Thompson Peak, highest of the Alps, soars in snow-tipped splendor above the deep, blue waters of Canyon Creek Lakes in the upper basin. Higher up, in a side pocket of granite, contorted little "El" Lake reflects permanent snowbanks and minarets on the north side of Sawtooth Mountain. A relatively cold microclimate contributes an almost subalpine character to the basin and its lakes despite relatively low elevations (5606 feet at Lower Canyon Creek Lake to 6529 feet at "El" Lake). Weeping spruces and foxtail pines appear here at lower altitudes than in other parts of the Alps.

Big brown, rainbow and eastern brook trout reside in the two lower lakes and are occasionally caught by expert anglers. Smaller eastern brooks succumb to almost anyone at "El" Lake. Surrounding cliffs, peaks and steep granite slopes offer opportunities for all classes of rock climbing.

On the way up the easy Canyon Creek trail you pass three notable sets of waterfalls and dozens of lesser ones. Oaks, madrones, dogwoods and big-leaf maples in the lower forests give way to white firs, red firs, Jeffrey pines and sugar pines higher up. You are apt to see deer anywhere in the canyon, but they are most prevalent in the lush forests and meadows at about the midpoint. You just might see a black bear on the trail too, although they are not as plentiful here as in other parts of the Alps. A wide variety of birds and wildflowers greet you along the trail. The lower reaches of Canyon Creek support an excellent population of native rainbow trout.

If this all wounds too idyllic to be true, it is. Canyon Creek is to the Trinity Alps as Yosemite Valley is to Yosemite National Park, and has many of the same problems. People are loving it to death. Access probably should be limited, and camping around the lakes should be eliminated. When you make this trip, which you should, just as you should see Yosemite Valley at least once, please camp below the lakes and try to keep your impact as light as possible. Because of the heavy use, you should carry a stove and purify all water. The crowds thin out after Labor Day and the fishing is better, but then you won't see the midsummer wildflower displays.

Canyon Creek and its lakes are still breathtakingly beautiful. Don't miss them, but please don't wear out your welcome.

Starting Point

Canyon Creek road turns north off Highway 299 in Junction City, 8 miles west of Weaverville and .1 mile east of the Canyon Creek bridge. The road is paved, but unsigned. If you are traveling east on Highway 299 from Eureka/Arcata, a short-cut road forks left 3 miles west of Junction City before you get to the Junction City BLM campground. This unsigned, paved road snakes over a ridge to intercept Canyon Creek road on the east side of the canyon 2.5 miles above Junction City.

From this intersection, narrow and sometimes steep pavement continues up the east side of the rugged canyon overlooking a number of rustic miners' shacks clinging precariously to the rocks below. You cross to the west side of the creek at Fisher Gulch 7.9 miles from Junction City, and keep to the right at a fork 1.4 miles farther on. A one-lane bridge soon takes you back to the east bank and up to an open flat where the town of Dedrick once stood. People lived and mined here into the 1930s, supporting a saloon, a general store and a post office. Little remains today to show where Dedrick was, primarily because none of its mining claims were patented and, after being abandoned during World War II, the land reverted to the federal government.

Just beyond Dedrick townsite, you see where the 1987 fire burned on the hillside east of the road. Most of the burn area you drive through between Dedrick and the end of the road burned only on the ground and has recovered very rapidly. Within a few years it will be hard to tell where the fire burned.

Small, undeveloped and very pleasant Ripstein campground is between the road and Canyon Creek 12.3 miles from Junction City. The campground was untouched by the fire. Pavement ends less than a mile beyond the campground, and at 13.8 miles the road ends in a turn-around loop at the trailhead.

Ample parking is along the sides of the loop. A sign near a pit toilet off the northeast side of the loop points north to wide, well-used Canyon Creek trail and east to little-used Bear Creek trail. The Bear Creek trail goes over the east ridge and down the Boulder Creek that flows into Stuart Fork to a junction with the Alpine Lake trail and thence to the Stuart Fork trail.

Description

The first quarter mile of the Canyon Creek trail rises slightly. You then level off well up on the side of the canyon before turning east into the shaded side canyon of Bear Creek. A few spots of fire burned across this part of the trail. Lush stands of dogwood and big-leaf maple line the descent to the crossing of Bear Creek. Beyond a boulder-hop across the creek, you climb a short, steep pitch to a shoulder far above Canyon Creek, and continue north through open, dry, hillside forest of canyon oak, black oak, ponderosa pine, Douglas fir and a few incense cedars. At 1.5 miles a few fair campsites are on a bench in more lush forest, but it's a long way down to Canyon Creek for water.

At 2.5 miles from the trailhead you skirt the top of a cliff above boulder-strewn Canyon Creek. Across the canyon, tongues of fire ran down the east-facing canyon wall in 1987. Lightning strikes started the fire on the west-side crest, and it is easy to see that it burned its hottest there.

The *Helena* 1951 quadrangle shows McKay Camp beside the trail less than 2 miles from the trailhead. The trail has been rebuilt and relocated, and a junction turning left down to the present McKay Camp is 3 miles from the trailhead. Rough trail descends steeply 200 yards through heavy brush to a large flat—actually an island between two channels of Canyon Creek. Both channels are usually dry by midsummer. The creek disappears in "The Sinks"

Lower and Middle falls of Canyon Creek

upstream, buried by a huge rockslide, to emerge again at the downstream end of the island. A number of excellent campsites are on the island and on another flat west of the creek. Fishing for native rainbow trout to 10 inches is excellent below McKay Camp and in holes in the rockpile upstream. The old trail on the *Helena* quadrangle ran on up the bottom of the canyon from here, but you will have trouble finding a trace of it now.

Back on the wide, smooth tread of the present-day Canyon Creek trail, you climb moderately, far up on the east side of the canyon, with a view across to the wide scar left when a big piece of the west wall fell, creating "The Sinks." A half mile from the McKay Camp junction a fresh-looking little creek falls from above and flows across the trail. Don't get water from it at the first crossing because the trail switches back and crosses it two more times. You should purify the water, wherever you get it.

Not far above the switchback you will first hear, then glimpse, the high cascade that used to be known as *the* Canyon Creek Falls. The old trail on the floor of the canyon climbed up right beside it, but you will have to crawl back down the creek to find it now. The new trail comes close to the creek just below another, less spectacular fall now known as Lower Canyon Creek Falls. A beautiful swimming pool is at the base of this fall, offering a refreshing dip after the 3.8 miles of trail you've traversed so far. Several weeping spruce trees grow beside the trail here. Long fronds hanging straight down from the branches distinguish these trees from other conifers. Ignore the small, poor campsites beside the trail here—better ones are in a grove of mature firs .5 mile farther on just below Upper Canyon Creek Meadows. There is even a cave under a huge boulder, if you didn't bring your own shelter. You will see no further evidence of the 1987 fire beyond this point.

Almost level trail along the east side of Upper Canyon Creek Meadows runs through shoulder-high ferns on the forest floor. Masses of flowers bloom in the marshy meadows in mid-July. Above the meadows the trail deteriorates badly, as you climb moderately over exposed roots and rocks away from the creek. At 5 miles from the trailhead you climb over some granite ledges just above the creek, then turn up the side of the canyon again on rough tread through rocks and brush.

A large, heavily forested flat, littered with boulders and crossed by several midsummer-dry watercourses, begins 5.5 miles from the trailhead. Several fair-to-good campsites are among the boulders not too far from Canyon Creek. As you approach a cliff at the north end of the flat, a use trail branches west to the foot of Middle Falls, a spectacular cascade over granite ledges into a deep granite bowl. The creek spreads in a number of overgrown channels below. Somewhere on the west side of the flat, Boulder Creek merges with one of these channels, but you would have to search hard to find it.

A difficult, steep, cross-country route to Morris and Smith lakes runs up the south side of the gulch east of this flat and over the top of the ridge south of Sawtooth Mountain. The first and most difficult obstacle on this route is a band of heavy brush in rock falls at the base of the ridge. Once beyond that problem, the way is very steep and requires good orienteering and mountaineering ability, but is generally considered to be an easier approach to Morris and Smith lakes than the route up Bear Gulch from Morris Meadow on the other side of the ridge.

The main trail turns east at the base of a cliff at the flat's north end, and soon begins a series of moderately steep switchbacks north beside a little creek. At the top of the switchbacks you enter a forested, azalea-floored dell, where the well-signed Boulder Creek Lakes trail forks west 6 miles from the trailhead. If you follow the Boulder Creek Lakes trail .2 mile west across bare granite and down to Canyon Creek, you will find many excellent campsites in forested flats on both sides of the creek.

Continuing up the Canyon Creek Lakes trail, you come close to the creek again above the azalea dell, pass more good campsites, and then turn east to climb another set of switchbacks around the next set of falls. A small, fair campsite nestles under fir trees near the top of the falls as you approach the creek again. This is the last campsite before the climb up to the lakes. The rough trail climbs moderately steeply through rocks and brush up the east side of the canyon, then turns north to the outlet of Lower Canyon Creek Lake 1.4 miles from the Boulder Creek Lakes junction.

The very deep, blue, 15-acre lower lake sits in a bowl of solid granite, which is very steep on the east side leading up to massive Sawtooth Mountain, but lower and shelving on the other three sides. Only a few clumps of brush and scattered weeping spruces, Jeffrey pines and red firs break the expanse of smooth, glaciated granite sloping up from the west shore to a row of cliffs. Beyond more cliffs and rugged ridges, snow-capped Mount Hilton towers into

Lower Canyon Creek Lake

the western sky. To the north, the jagged top of Thompson Peak fits nearly into a notch at the head of the canyon.

Be very careful crossing the outlet of the lake if the water is at all high. A woman was swept away and drowned here in 1983. Beyond the crossing, look for orange-painted blazes on rocks showing the way northwest to the base of some cliffs. Your route turns north below these crags, and from this vantage point it is easy to see why you should not camp at this lake. The only possible places to camp are on the sloping shelf of rock below you, and it is obvious that any waste deposited there will inevitably wash into the lake. The painted blazes lead to a gully through which you climb northwest to your first awe-inspiring view of Upper Canyon Creek Lake. From your viewpoint at the west end of a granite dike between the lakes, you look north to vertically tiered strata resembling irregular slices of toasted bread rising directly from a deep bay. Jagged Wedding Cake and Thompson Peak top the granite skyline beyond. Canyon Creek flows in several meandering channels across lush green delta to enter the lake from the northeast. A frozen cascade of glacier-rounded granite falls to the east shore from the cirque containing "El" Lake. A strip of grass and gravelly beach, backed by willows and alders, runs from the outlet at the east end of the dike around to the bare granite south of the inlet meadow.

Upper Canyon Creek Lake and Thompson Peak

You will find more orange-painted blazes marking the way east along the top of the dike. The outlet of the upper lake runs through a steep-sided cut where a wood-timbered dam once raised the level of the lake 6–8 feet. Although no evidence of ditches or flumes remains, the additional impounded water was probably used for mining somewhere down the canyon. Crossing the outlet can be dangerous when the water is high.

A few poor campsites are in the pockets of brush and trees on the dike and on a little strip of beach. None of them should be used. Please camp in the canyon below the lakes—it's not that far to walk and you will be more comfortable while helping to preserve the fragile beauty of the lakes basin.

Brown trout up to five pounds and eastern brook and rainbow trout almost as big have been taken near the outlet and the inlet.

Off-Trail Side Trip to "El" Lake

No real trail leads up the steep granite slopes between Upper Canyon Creek Lake and little "El" Lake in its secluded cirque, but there is a route, marked by ducks and orange-painted blazes. To find the route, walk north along the strip of grass and beach on the east side of Upper Canyon Creek Lake to where vertical granite blocks your way. Climb up a gully behind a very poor campsite that should not be used, turn northeast across the top of the first granite knob and you should soon pick up ducks and orange blazes marking the route south of some cliffs.

You continue generally northeast, very steeply at times, up and up over ledges, through gullies and past two small ponds. Along the way you have spectacular views back across the Canyon Creek Lakes and up to Mount Hilton on the horizon. At .7 mile from the start of the climb, you top out on a ledge overlooking a very green valley, through which the outlet stream from "El" Lake wanders. The lake is beyond a shoulder of rock to the east, in a cirque surrounded by an amazing tableau of cliffs and peaks.

Permanent snowbanks on the towering north face of Sawtooth Mountain, the south wall of the cirque, reflect in the quiet, rock-dotted surface of "El" Lake. The 2-acre lake obviously gets its name from its shape, a contorted L that wraps around rocks and plush little meadows. Weeping spruce, mountain hemlock and red fir grow in pockets of soil along the steep west shore and up the walls to the base of the cliffs. Talus slopes at the base of the upper cliffs are so white they look like snow at first glance.

The timbered ridge across the valley north of the lake is the divide between this drainage and the head of the Stuart Fork. A strenuous cross-country route runs through a saddle in this ridge and down to Mirror and Sapphire lakes in the giant cirque beyond. The part of this route running around the head of the Stuart Fork cirque to Mirror Lake is potentially dangerous due to unstable rock, and should be attempted only by experienced cross-country hikers.

A small, poor campsite in the rocks where you first reach the shoreline of "El" Lake is too close to the lake and should not be used. Look for better sites along the edge of the meadows below the lake. Small eastern brook trout rise to almost anything that touches the surface of the lake on summer evenings.

Trip 16

Canyon Creek
to Boulder Creek Lakes

Trip Type: Round trip of 3 to 5 days

Distance: 8.6 miles one way to Upper Boulder Creek Lake; 17.2 miles round trip

Elevation Change: 3440 feet, average 400 feet per mile

Season: Early July to mid-October

Topo Map: *Mount Hilton* (provisional 1982) 7.5' quadrangle

The Lower Boulder Creek Lakes are only a little over 2 miles off the heavily traveled Canyon Creek trail, but they are lightly visited compared to Canyon Creek and its lakes. A half mile of the roughest, steepest trail in the Trinity Alps on the way up probably eliminates many potential visitors.

Upper Boulder Creek Lake is seldom visited at all, primarily because it's almost impossible to get through the brush that chokes the lower end of the steep-sided cleft it occupies. It's worth the effort, though—it's a uniquely beautiful little lake, with a permanent snowfield at its upper end.

Lower Boulder Creek Lakes consist of two connected bodies of water large enough to be called lakes and a half-dozen murky ponds full of tadpoles and frogs. All these lakes and ponds fill depressions scooped out by glaciers from the stage of a giant amphitheater halfway up the granite ridge west of the Middle Falls of Canyon Creek. None of the lower lakes and ponds has a permanent inlet or outlet. The upper lake is the source of Boulder Creek. Only a few trees dot the wide expanse of rock, and the only shelter is under overhanging ledges, but you can see forever. It is not a good place for walking around during thunderstorms.

Fishing is fair for small eastern brook and rainbow trout in the lower lakes. You can climb Mount Hilton from the northwest side of the basin without needing more than class II climbing skills. If you want more challenge, there is plenty of good, vertical granite on all sides. Unlike the Canyon Creek Lakes, the Boulder Creek Lakes are warm enough for swimming by August. Fair campsites are on ledges and in pockets in the rock around the lower lakes. There is no firewood. Water from Boulder Creek above the lakes is better than the water in the lakes, but probably should still be purified.

Starting Point

See Trip 15 for directions to the Canyon Creek trailhead and description of the Canyon Creek trail to the Boulder Creek Lakes junction above Middle Falls, 6 miles from the trailhead.

Description

The Boulder Creek Lakes trail branches west from the Canyon Creek trail, crosses a shelf of bare granite, and descends through low brush to a crossing of Canyon Creek. This crossing could be very dangerous in early season. A good foot-log is 100 feet upstream from the ford, and many excellent campsites are upstream on both sides of the creek.

A good trail turns south from the ford, and you climb moderately through open forest and some brush around a buttress of the west ridge and up into the lower valley of Boulder Creek. As the trail turns southwest at the lower edge of the wide, flat-floored valley .6 mile from the Canyon Creek junction, you can see Boulder Creek falling over an escarpment to the south. A half mile of pleasant, almost level walking takes you through lush meadows and groves of trees, including some small aspen, to a close-up view of a line of cliffs running across the canyon.

You turn west as you approach the escarpment and begin to climb moderately steeply through heavy brush on rough, rocky tread. You soon come

Boulder Creek lakes, left, Upper Boulder Creek Lake, right

to the atrocious .5 mile of trail mentioned in the introduction. Parts of it seem almost vertical, in heavy brush and over loose rock and big boulders. Two traverses across the face of the canyon wall relieve the strain a little bit. Beyond a final, very steep pitch, you turn south on a shelf above the north end of the cliffs. As you follow ducks higher on a hump of granite, the lower lakes come into view directly south, but you soon realize that they are beyond a wide crack in the floor of this wide amphitheater. Little Boulder Creek froths through the bottom of this vertical-walled slot after cascading down from Upper Boulder Creek Lake. Cairns and ducks show the way southwest across bare rock to a point where the chasm is only a few feet deep and relatively easy to cross.

From the creek crossing, you pick you way around a large hump of granite and down to the largest lake, 2.3 miles from the Canyon Creek trail. The 5-acre, shallow lake is in a depression scooped from solid granite by the last glacier to flow from the ridge into Canyon creek. A later glacier gouged out the valley below and left the escarpment below the lakes. A 1-acre lake to the east is joined to the larger lake when the water level is high. Patches of brush grow in pockets of soil around the lakes, but only a few single Jeffrey pines, red firs and weeping spruces interrupt the wide expanse of rock.

Slabs of granite, sloping into the water, offer excellent sunbathing opportunities and easy access to the water. However, a layer of silt on the bottom is easily stirred to muddy the water. Bashful skinny-dippers have a problem in this wide-open basin—there's no place to hide. Small rainbow and eastern brook trout rise morning and evening to well-places dry flies.

Many fair to good campsites are scattered among the rocks. Please don't camp in sites that are obviously too close to the lakes, and be very careful of your waste disposal.

Off-Trail to Upper Boulder Creek Lake

You can easily see where Upper Boulder Creek Lake is. It's in the notch up there on the west wall from which Boulder Creek pours. The problem is to get up there.

Actually, you can climb up on either side of the creek, but the north side is probably a little easier, and you will run into fewer blank walls of rock. The brush gets thicker as you climb and, when you get into the notch above the cascade, you still have 300 yards of solid brush and broken blocks of granite to negotiate to reach the east end of the gorgeous little lake. The lake sits in the upper end of a very steep-sided, deep cleft in the side of the ridge. A permanent snowbank, shaded by cliffs, is beyond a tiny, bright-green meadow at the upper end. Large red firs grow among fallen blocks of granite around the lower end. Steep talus slopes slide directly into the deep water along both sides.

Small trout feed on the surface all day in the deep shade, but it's very difficult to get around the shoreline to fish for them. There is no place to camp. All in all, Upper Boulder Creek Lake is a beautiful place to visit, but you wouldn't want to stay there.

Trip 17

North Fork Trinity River to Grizzly Lake

Trip Type: Round trip of 4 to 7 days

Distance: 17.5 miles one way, 35 miles round trip

Elevation Change: 4650 feet, 266 feet per mile

Season: Mid-July to early October

Topo Maps: *Thurston Peaks* (provisional 1982), *Cecil Lake* 1979 and *Thompson Peak* 1979 7.5′ quadrangles

This is the "relaxed" route to Grizzly Lake for those who have enough time to enjoy it. You start out easy, climbing only 1000 feet in the first 10 miles of excellent trail in the bottoms of the lush, deep canyons of the North Fork Trinity River and Grizzly Creek. You will see an amazing variety of trees, ferns and flowers along the way and, if you're lucky, a school or two of big steelhead or salmon finning lazily in one of the deep, green pools. Picturesque cabins sit on benches along the river, and a plethora of old time mining relics are along the trail. It is quite likely that you will see present-day miners in wet suits working Venturi dredges on a few active claims. If you're what the mountain folk refer to as a flatlander, by the time you reach the last steep mile of "trail" to Grizzly Lake you should be well acclimated for higher elevations. Don't expect to be alone at Grizzly Lake, or for that matter at Grizzly Meadows. Even though the routes to get there are either long or strenuous, the drama of Grizzly Falls, along with the beauty of Grizzly Lake and the majesty of Thompson Peak, lures many visitors. If, however, you chose the longer route, you will have the first 13.5 miles of trail substantially to yourself.

If you're in a hurry, as most hikers to Grizzly Lake seem to be, you can take the short and strenuous route, a 13-mile round trip from the China Creek trailhead on the north side of the Salmon River divide; a route involving 5340 feet of elevation gain and loss. Directions to the trailhead, a long way from most points of origin, along with the trail description to the junction with the Grizzly Lake trail, are in Trip 31.

Grizzly is the quintessential high mountain lake. The deep, blue waters reflect perpetual snowfields and remnant glaciers which drape the north side of 9002-foot Thompson Peak. Small pockets of red fir, whitebark pine and mountain hemlock shelter a few campsites and soften the harsh outlines of the granite bowl that cradles the lake. As magnificent as the peak and the lake are, the most spectacular feature of Grizzly Lake is the outlet stream. Within 10 yards of the north shoreline, Grizzly Creek leaps clear from the top of an overhanging granite cliff and plunges nearly 100 vertical feet, crashing upon the rocks below and cascading another 100 feet through a rocky cleft to the meadows farther below.

Hauling a backpack up the steep and rough last mile to the lake is a difficult endeavor, and along with the fact that the area surrounding the lake is a fragile ecosystem, you may want to consider camping at one of the excellent sites around Grizzly meadow and day-hiking to the lake and beyond. If you can't resist the temptation to camp at the lake, please limit your stay and keep your impact as light as possible; build no fires, camp only in previously used sites and dispose of wastes and wash water very carefully. With the increased popularity of Grizzly Lake these practices are essential for the preservation of its natural beauty.

Starting Point

The Hobo Gulch trailhead is 17 miles north of the turnoff to the ghost town of Old Helena from Highway 299. Driving west from Weaverville on Highway 299,

Old Helena

Relics from 19th-century mining

you top Oregon Mountain Summit at 4 miles and .4 mile further on come to a historical monument on the left featuring a hydraulic miners "Long Tom." It is worth a short pause to read about the La Grange Mine, look at the "Long Tom" and gaze south to the scars left from the early 1900s, when the entire side of the mountain was washed down Oregon Gulch.

8 miles west of Weaverville, Junction City, dating from the early mining days, is beside the Trinity River at the bottom of the Oregon Mountain hill. 7 more miles along the river, alive with gold miners again, brings you to a bridge across the North Fork Trinity River and, just beyond, the turnoff signed "OLD HELENA."

The main feature of this old town is a solid, square, two story red brick building, possibly 100 years old, which until a few years ago was the location of an active Post Office. A few old frame houses, vacant feed store and stable, and a row of giant black walnut trees shading the road are also noteworthy.

North of the townsite, the narrow paved road crosses the North Fork and then continues up the East Fork of the North Fork 2.7 miles to the junction of the Hobo Gulch road, turning left up the side of the canyon. The narrow, very crooked and sometimes steep gravel road climbs more than 8 miles to the top of the ridge between the North Fork and its East Fork. A steeper downgrade of 5 miles brings you to the trailhead .3 mile above the Hobo Gulch Campground. The primitive campground is under large ponderosa pines and Douglas firs on a quarter-mile-long flat beside the river. The only water, which is of doubtful quality, is from the river. Two pit toilets serve the usually crowded campground, and since the Forest Service no longer hauls out garbage and many campers seem too lazy to, it can be a pretty unsavory place by late summer. Probably the best option is to camp elsewhere and then park your vehicle at the trailhead, not in the campground.

Description

The trail starts out almost level from the trailhead in dense mixed forest, leads .2 mile to a junction with a spur trail coming up from the campground, and then climbs moderately steeply for a short distance before descending the east slope to cross Backbone Creek .6 mile from the trailhead. If you plan to fish for the salmon, steelhead or rainbows that populate the North Fork, you will need to check on the current regulations, as the California Department of Fish & Game had closed the river and its tributaries to fishing during the 1993 season. A somewhat confusing three-way trail junction confronts you on the north bank of Backbone Creek. Farthest to the right, trail 11W07, signed "RUSSELL CABIN," heads up Backbone Creek. The trail to the left, leading almost straight beside the river, signed "PAPOOSE LAKE-LOW WATER TRAIL, & BEAR WALLOW MEADOWS," travels upstream a short distance, fords the North Fork and then branches. The branch to Bear Wallow Meadows turns west up Whites Creek, but the faint low-water trail continues alongside the west bank of the North Fork through

Trip 17
North Fork Trinity River to Grizzly Lake

brush and soggy tread until fording back over the river farther upstream. The correct trail, signed solely Papoose Lake, is the middle one, which turns somewhat to the right and heads steeply uphill.

Your steep climb moderates eventually as you head up the spur ridge between Backbone Creek and the North Fork, then travels north along the east side of the canyon. Very pleasant open forest includes madrones, canyon oaks, and an occasional sugar pine, as well as the more common Douglas firs and ponderosa pines.

You soon drop down to meet the trace of the low trail again .6 mile from Backbone Creek, in a beautiful flat shaded by incense cedars and Douglas firs. An entire army could set up camp between here and China Creek and still have an adequate supply of firewood. Another flat with excellent campsites is higher above the river just north of China Creek, 2.3 miles from the trailhead.

The trail divides once more at the upper end of the flat above China Creek. The left trail heads down to the river, where more campsites can be found. The trail to the right is the main trail, which climbs up and then down again, and after a few more ups and downs, passes the remains of Strunce Cabin. About one-quarter mile from the remains you reach the junction with the Rattlesnake Creek trail in a broad flat with plenty of campsites, 4.5 miles from the trailhead.

Your trail to the left, signed "GRIZZLY LAKE," fords Rattlesnake Creek, which is a good-sized creek, and the ford can be difficult when the water is high. The trail passes an excellent campsite on the north bank of Rattlesnake Creek, then climbs the ridge north of the creek in five moderately steep switchbacks before turning around the nose of the ridge and continuing north well up on the east side of the North Fork canyon. Here you continue on a contour, then make a

Jorstad Cabin   Camp on upper Grizzly Creek

steeply descending traverse as the trail diagonals across an almost vertical rock face to another contour and then a descent to a flat below Morrison Gulch and Morrison Cabin. A sign posted on a tree at a trail junction states "RATTLESNAKE LAKE" with an arrow pointing to the left, and "GRIZZLY LAKE" with an arrow to the right.

New trail, not shown on the *Cecil Lake* quadrangle, climbs from the upper end of this flat and stays up on the steep east bank of the river as it makes a horseshoe turn around the spur ridge on which Morrison Cabin is perched. The old trail fords the river to a junction with the Rattlesnake Lake trail, then continues past the cabin and up the west side of the river to another crossing near Jorstad Cabin, farther upstream. Morrison Cabin, nestled under ponderosa pines and Douglas firs, was built in conjunction with an old mining claim and abandoned in 1989.

Your trail along the east side of the North Fork runs almost level through deep woods until it comes out into the open again at Pfeiffer Flat. The trail delivers you almost at the doorstep of Jorstad Cabin, 8.2 miles from the trailhead. George Jorstad built this cozy little cabin back in 1937 and was still living in it, hand-placer-mining his claim, in 1983, even though he was over 80 years old. The cabin, which is now under the care of the Forest Service, has escaped the calamities of fire and vandalism—at least so far. This idyllic site deserves your utmost consideration and respect.

The continuation of the trail passes through an old wooden gate approximately 100 feet to the right of the cabin. An easy half-mile amble under towering ponderosa pines, incense cedars and Douglas firs brings you to Pegleg Camp at the confluence of Grizzly Creek and the North Fork Trinity River. There is room for three or four tents and plenty of firewood.

Leaving the North Fork you turn east from Pegleg Camp up the narrower canyon of Grizzly Creek on good trail, built up on the south slope since the canyon bottom is steep and choked with alders. A ford without any foot-logs, .9 mile from Pegleg, takes you to the north side of the canyon, where you climb moderately steeply above more alders and willows, then level off in a jumble of rock piles that marks the old mining site of China Gardens. A fire burned through this area in 1987 punctuating the eerie sense of devastation begun by miners long ago. The rapid recovery of the understory is a good testament to the healing capacities of nature, but occasional downed logs and 8-to-15-foot scars on standing evergreens remind you of the destruction that fire can bring. Beyond the diggings you climb steeply for 200 yards to an old ditch, walk along it for a quarter-mile to a tributary creek and another steep pitch, then ascend more gradually to Mill Gulch, 3 miles from Pegleg.

Trail junctions are close together in Mill Gulch. At the creek a seldom, used and never maintained, trail designated "TRAIL 11W02, CECIL LAKE" climbs upstream. Just beyond the creek another trail heading across Grizzly Creek and up Specimen Creek is signed "PAPOOSE LAKE; SPECIMEN CREEK, NORTH FORK, HOBO CAMP." Your trail, which continues up Grizzly Creek, is clearly defined at all junctions with signs as well. On your return trip you should probably avoid the temptation to shorten the distance to Papoose Lake by climbing up the Specimen Creek trail to Bob's Farm and down the other side. Reportedly this trail is one of the steepest and roughest in the entire wilderness, and just about anyone who has tried it will tell you that it's better to go the full distance back down the North Fork and up Rattlesnake Creek. In addition, the top and the south side of the ridge, including the trail, were badly burned by the 1987 fire. An old-timer named Bob really did grow vegetables for the early miners on top of the ridge. His burros carried the vegetables down, and Bob just had a little bit of gold to carry back up the ridge.

Your Grizzly Creek trail gets steeper between the Specimen Creek junction and the China Creek junction, 1.7 miles farther up the canyon, just beyond a clear, cold, little creek cascading down a gully from the north. From this junction the China Creek trailhead is 2.5 miles north over the Salmon Divide, 1350 feet up to the crest and 1600 feet down the other side. Continuing up Grizzly Creek you begin to turn south in thick woods well away from the creek. At 1.3 miles from the last junction you climb out of the woods and over the top of a glaciated metamorphic rock outcrop offering the first long views since leaving the trailhead,14.4 miles back. The higher valley above shows the typical **U**-shape left by glaciers, in contrast to the unglaciated **V**-shaped canyon below.

Traverses along the east side of the more open upper valley alternate with switchbacks to gain altitude across patches of broken rock and brush. From openings 3 miles above the China Creek junction you get your first glimpses of Thompson Peak and the perpetual snowfields that cling to its northern side. Small meadows, willow flats and groves of red fir soon replace brush on the more level floor of the upper valley, and good campsites appear above and below a spring flowing across the trail. You then climb moderately steeply for one-half mile beyond the spring, over exposed rock and through belts of firs to the north edge of Upper Grizzly Meadow. Directly ahead of you, beyond lush grass and wildflowers, the outlet of Grizzly Lake leaps from a precipice to dissolve in cascades of white foam and mist in the tumbled blocks of granite below.

Good to excellent campsites are in groves of fir on the south and west sides of the meadow and between the trail and the creek below the meadow. Be sure to protect your food and equipment; the deer and rodents seem to be more of a problem than the bears, but your food should still be hung away from the reach of all of them.

Route to Grizzly Lake

Contrary to what is shown on the *Thompson Peak* quadrangle map, the trail does not end a half mile below Upper Grizzly Meadow but continues across the meadow, through the trees at the upper end and into the pile of talus on the east side of the meadows. The Forest Service has improved the trail from this point over the years, but it is still a long way from being what you would normally consider a "trail" to be. The route up to Grizzly Lake from the meadows has been designated as a "scramble" trail, the purpose of which is to define a single route up the very steep slope, but not to encourage people to carry backpacks up to camp at the lake. Above the lower talus a virtual granite staircase has been constructed and is marked by cairns. Approximately half way up the slope a spring flows down a rock channel. Pass over the spring and pick up the dirt trail, which can be slick and muddy in spots, until you reach a rock outcropping. Behind the outcropping is a steep path through a cleft marked by cairns that leads alongside the upper channel of the spring and crosses over to a field of wildflowers. Cross another branch of the spring, and easier trail, somewhat indistinct, passes over boulders, through lush vegetation, and over another watercourse, and makes an angling traverse across the slope. The trail becomes more distinct again in an area of scattered evergreens and brings you to the shoreline of spectacular Grizzly Lake.

The full expanse of deep, blue Grizzly Lake and its magnificent basin lies before you. Almost level slabs of granite ease into the water west of the outlet, offering opportunities for pondering, sunbathing and quick, cold dips into the icy waters. Mountain hemlocks, red firs, foxtail pines and whitebark pines grow in cracks and on ledges around the solid granite basin. Lush gardens of wildflowers bloom in tiny meadows long after their counterparts have faded in the valley below. Above the first cliffs to the southeast a large, higher cirque and shelf on the north face of jagged 9002-foot Thompson Peak hold perpetual snowfields and near-glaciers.

The handful of usable campsites are on the rock slabs along the north shore and among trees on a ridge and peninsula above the northwest shore. If you do decide to camp at the lake, you most likely will find no firewood, and if you do it should not be burned.

Old-time packers and hikers in the Trinity Alps tell tales of taking limits of rainbow trout, all over 12 inches, from Grizzly Lake. Heavier visitation and the corresponding increase in fishing pressure have taken a harsh toll, and today you'll be lucky to catch enough trout for breakfast.

Rock climbers and scramblers will find plenty of good vertical and overhanging rock both above and below the lake. For the more prosaic, who desire to reach the summit of the highest peak in the Trinity Alps, the route to the top of Thompson Peak is straightforward: From the north shore of Grizzly Lake, work above the granite cliffs to the southwest. Angle across the granite slabs above, which may be snow-covered in early season, to the low point on the ridge leading up to the summit. Follow the back side of the ridge to the top. The views are superb.

For cross-country enthusiasts, the route to diminutive Lois Lake can be traversed in a short time. To get there, climb clefts in the ridge southwest of the north shore of Grizzly Lake until you reach the top of the ridge. Turn left (west) along the ridge and climb to the saddle where another ridge meets it from the northwest. Carefully drop down southwest from the ridge, to where you can see Lois Lake below, sitting serenely in its basin. Descend approximately 350 feet to the lake. For those who desire a closer glimpse of Thompson Peak but have neither the desire nor the time to climb to the summit, excellent views can be had at the top of the ridge above Lois Lake, including a 270° panorama with Mount Shasta to the east.

One final note: The route to Grizzly Lake is steep and strenuous, and only experienced hikers should attempt it. Only those with cross-country experience, familiar with map and compass orienteering, should attempt any of the off-trail routes.

The waterfall from Grizzly Lake

Trip 18

North Fork Trinity River to Papoose Lake

Trip Type: Round trip of 3 to 6 days

Distance: 12.5 miles one way, 25 miles round trip

Elevation Change: 3695 feet, average 296 feet per mile

Season: Mid-July to early October

Topo Map: *Mount Hilton* (provisional 1982) 7.5′ quadrangle

The Rattlesnake Creek trail to Papoose Lake traverses one of the most intensely mined areas in the entire Trinity Alps. Enormous rock piles, pits, ditches and relics, dating from the early '49er days to the present, litter the first 4 miles of steep-walled Rattlesnake canyon from the confluence with the North Fork Trinity River up to Mill Creek. Fifty to one hundred Caucasians, along with a larger and unrecorded number of Chinese, lived and grubbed here in the mid to late-nineteenth century. Most of the gold that they extracted from Mother Nature now lies hidden away in man-made vaults, but the evidence of their labor will remain for centuries to come. Present-day activity is minimal, although claims are still posted throughout the canyon; large-scale mining efforts now require lengthy environmental impact statements and numerous permits.

The scars that the miners left behind should not deter you from taking this trip, however, as Papoose Lake is a beautiful gem tucked into a deep cirque rimmed with serrated cliffs. Opportunities abound for climbing or exploring the peaks and ridges above, and the fishing can be quite good. Unlike increasingly popular Grizzly Lake just 2.5 air miles to the north, Papoose Lake offers relative solitude even during the peak of the backpacking season, and is just as spectacular.

Trip 18
North Fork Trinity River to Papoose Lake

Starting Point

The trailhead for the Papoose Lake trail is the same as the one described in Trip 17 for Grizzly Lake. From Hobo Gulch trailhead follow the description for the North Fork Trinity River trail 4.5 miles to the junction of the Grizzly Lake and Papoose Lake trails.

Description

At the signed trail junction just before the trail to Grizzly Lake fords Rattlesnake Creek, trail 11W05 to Papoose Lake forks northeast on an old, level wagon road. The wide floor of Rattlesnake Creek's lower canyon is a maze of pits and rock piles, mementos of bygone mining days. Heavy growths of alders, willows and big-leaf maples have softened the raw contours over the years and blocked views of the creek.

Approximately one-third mile up the trail you encounter the first evidences of the fire that swept through the canyon in 1987. Burn scars reach up tree trunks as high as 25 feet in places, and downed trees are scattered randomly across the forest floor. The forest fire was not completely destructive and, in fact, destroyed only small amounts of timber in selected areas. The destruction has been further mitigated by the remarkable recovery of the underbrush, which now flourishes wherever soil, water and light conditions allow. If there were no other reasons to take this hike, just the mere observance of the recuperative powers of nature would be justification alone.

As the canyon narrows, the trail climbs moderately up the southeast slope away from the old road, and passes a sign declaring "RATTLESNAKE TRAIL, BROWNS MINE" and "PAPOOSE LAKE," all with arrows pointing straight up the trail. After a brief excursion into Martin's Gulch the trail rejoins the old road and follows it until your progress is impeded by three log rounds approximately 2 feet high and 3 feet in diameter. A sign marked "TRAIL" redirects your travel to the left, down through rock debris toward the ford of Rattlesnake Creek, 1.7 miles from the junction.

There are no foot-logs to assist you across the creek. You will have to get your feet, as well as your legs, wet as you ford the creek, and the crossing could be difficult in high water. A campsite is along the creek immediately beyond the ford. You soon climb up to the old road again on the northwest side of the canyon, and then ascend moderately with a few steeper pitches through mixed forest above Rattlesnake Creek as it falls in and out of deep pools in a steep-walled gorge. A long terrace on the other side of the canyon is covered with hand-piled boulders for more than a half mile. If you have the time and the energy to climb down into the gorge past an abandoned 1940s vintage winch and dump truck, some surprisingly large rainbow trout may rise to dry flies in these pools.

You won't have any trouble at all recognizing Brown's Mine 1.8 miles from the ford of Rattlesnake Creek. Piles of mining junk are spread in all directions around a sign nailed to an old Douglas fir. In addition to the usual items—

riveted pipe, gears, valves, boiler grates, corrugated iron, bed springs and wire rope—a strange welded steel object resembling a 6-foot guitar case puzzles everyone who passes by.

A short, steep climb brings you to a junction with the brutally steep trail that leads up to Bob's Farm and down again to Grizzly Creek. (See Trip 17 for comments regarding this trail.) Your Papoose Lake trail continues east above Rattlesnake Creek until you come to a clearing in a grove of manzanita where you can see more evidence of the '87 fire. Your trail climbs steeply, then descends just as steeply as it dips down to cross Mill Creek at the lower end of its long cascade from Lois Lake, located in a high basin to the northeast. A single campsite lies next to the creek.

Above Mill Creek you climb moderately on good foot trail through Douglas firs and black oaks and across brushy hillsides for .5 mile to a crossing of the Middle Fork Rattlesnake Creek, which combines a boulder hop and a log jam to complete. Another 2 miles of somewhat steeper ascent, now headed southeast, brings you to Enni Camp (Enos on the quadrangle map) in a glacial moraine area 6.3 miles from North Fork Trinity River. The area on either side of Enni Camp suffered the effects of the '87 fire, but fortunately the camp itself and the immediate surroundings escaped. Giant red firs shade the excellent site, which has room for 12–15 campers. A little-used trail leads northeast from the camp up the side of the canyon to Bear Valley Meadows.

The trail to Papoose Lake continues on a well-defined track, climbing steeply east of the creek. Effects of the fire become evident once more, and at about a half mile from Enni Camp you must pay close attention to the direction of the trail as downed logs, debris and new growth combine to slightly confuse the route. About .75 mile from the camp, you encounter large granite boulders and cross to the south bank as the creek turns east. Ducks show the way east across a sloping bench through ceanothus and manzanita brush and over more boulders. Just to the left of a red fir at the upper end of this bench you begin a steep climb along the top of a cliff above the creek. At the bottom of a vertical face of metamorphic rock you follow the trail south, then double back to zigzag up through a crack to a ledge above. You cross this ledge eastward, climbing over granite boulders, and look for ducks leading south to two less vertical faces with a ledge between. Above the third rock face you continue south along the west edge of a deep gorge through which the outlet creek falls from the lake. Beyond a hump of solid granite, showing some glacial striation and polish, you overlook gorgeous, teardrop-shaped Papoose Lake.

A sharp dividing line runs diagonally across the Papoose Lake cirque; the southeast side is granite, the northwest side is gray metamorphic rock. A large granite slab slopes into the water east of the outlet, offering an excellent viewpoint and fishing perch, as well as a great place to sunbathe and to inch into the icy waters for a dip. From ledges a little farther along the eastern shore you can gaze down into the deep water at 12–15 inch rainbow trout cruising out of reach beside vertical drop-offs. A few of them will come up for flies around sundown, if you can find the necessary room to cast. The problem then becomes discovering a way to extract them from the water. It's relatively easier to catch a panful of smaller trout near the outlet.

Seeps and pockets of soil among the rocks around Papoose Lake support a marvelous profusion of wildflowers—pink spiraea, Indian paintbrush, wild onions, bistort, multicolored monkey flowers, leopard lilies, angelica, mountain aster and Queen Anne's lace are just a few of the many species present. Sparse trees include mountain hemlock, whitebark pine and red fir.

A number of campsites near the outlet are badly overused. Excellent spots farther up in the rocks above the northwest shore provide excellent views of the lake and cliffs. One word of caution, however, is that if your tent requires staking, your choice of campsites will be limited, as most of them have only an inch or two of decomposed granite over solid rock. Firewood is extremely scarce.

Scramblers will find plenty of chances to explore the divide above Canyon Creek, and experienced mountaineers can test their skills on Mount Hilton, which is just out of sight beyond the divide. For the rest, Papoose Lake and environs offer marvelous photographic opportunities and a pleasant atmosphere for contemplating life. The fact that there are no shortcuts to get here, in combination with the mass pilgrimage of backpackers to the shores of more popular Grizzly Lake, makes for relative solitude at Papoose Lake. Two small notes of caution: Although chances are you won't see either, hang your food above bear height; and watch carefully for snakes, particularly in the lower parts of the canyon. Rattlesnake Creek did get its name for a reason.

Trip 19

New River Divide Loop

Trip Type: Loop trip of 3 to 4 days

Distance: 25.5 miles including side trip to Whites Creek Lake

Elevation Change: 9880 feet, average 387 feet per mile

Season: Early July to mid-October, depending on when you can ford North Fork Trinity River

Topo Maps: *Thurston Peaks* (provisional 1982) and *Cecil Lake* 1979 7.5′ quadrangles

Solitude and scenery are the primary attractions of this trip. The only time the southern part of the New River Divide trail sees much traffic is during deer season in late September and early October. It is virtually deserted during the rest of the year. The same is true of the trail up Whites Creek to Bear Wallow Meadows and Hunters Camp. The segment from Rattlesnake Camp down to Morrison Cabin is traveled more often since it is the main route between New River and North Fork Trinity River, but you still won't be crowded there. The 6 miles of the loop along the North Fork Trinity River trail is a different story—that trail is sometimes called a freeway by people who like to be alone.

Views from the New River Divide are truly awe-inspiring. You overlook the entire New River drainage and a series of ridges farther west. On the east side, the deep chasm of the North Fork Trinity River yawns in front of Backbone Ridge and beyond that are the highest Alps around Papoose and Grizzly lakes. Sawtooth Mountain and the high ridge above Canyon Creek are on the skyline farther east.

Although Whites Creek Lake and Rattlesnake Lake are only muddy ponds and have no fish, fishing is surprisingly good for feisty native rainbow trout in lower Whites Creek, and for steelhead fry and an occasional good-sized rainbow in the North Fork. The North Fork is also the only place you will be able to swim.

Trip 19
New River Divide Loop

Evidence of deer and black bear is everywhere along the divide, but these animals are wild and wary, so you won't see as many of them as you might in other places. Magnificent forests, ranging from big-leaf maples, alders and madrones in the bottoms of the canyons to stunted Jeffrey and western white pines on the crests, shelter a large number and variety of songbirds and raptors.

Trails on this loop are surprisingly good and well maintained despite (or possibly because of) light use. Only one short stretch near Bear Wallow Meadow is hard to follow.

Starting Point

The trailhead is at Hobo Gulch. See Trip 17 for directions to the trailhead and a description of the trail from the trailhead to Backbone Creek. If you are making this trip early in the season, you would do well to take a good look at the North Fork Trinity River where you first cross it above Helena. If the river looks too high to ford there, chances are it is too high to ford at Keystone Flat, although the stream bed is wider and flatter at the latter point.

Description

A three-way trail junction is on the north side of Backbone Creek .6 mile from the Hobo Gulch trailhead. The left (west) fork, signed "PAPOOSE LAKE LOW WATER TRAIL—BEAR WALLOW MEADOW" is your trail. Beyond 200 yards of willows, alders and boulders on the east bank of the North Fork, you turn to ford the river to Keystone Flat on the west bank. This crossing can be very dangerous during high run-off. If there is any question about the crossing, you should either turn back or do a rope-belayed crossing as described in Thomas Winnett's *Backpacking Basics*. A 150-foot length of climbing rope is not something you would enjoy carrying 25.5 miles unless you are a rock climber. However, if you need it at Keystone Flat, you will need it again at Morrison Cabin on the way back. Of course, you can use it along the way for bear-bagging your food.

Beautiful mixed forest covers Keystone Flat. The level trail follows an old road trace north under huge Douglas firs, ponderosa pines, incense cedars, black oaks, big-leaf maples and a few white firs. It's a bit early in the trip to camp, but you may be tempted by the almost perfect sites along the trail. If you decide to take a dip in one of the deep pools in the river, be advised that the heavily traveled North Fork trail overlooks the river from the steep east slope, and that many fishermen get up here from Hobo Gulch campground, so skinny dipping may be equivalent to exhibitionism.

The Whites Creek trail junction is .4 mile north of the North Fork Trinity River crossing. You turn northwest across Keystone Flat from the junction, then west up Whites Creek canyon on a shelf above the creek. Narrowing canyon walls push the trail closer to the creek, and you boulder-hop to the north bank .5 mile from the Keystone Flat junction. Pools in the small creek above the crossing provide surprisingly good fishing for small native rainbow trout and an occasional 9–10 incher.

A good campsite is just beyond the crossing. Very lush forest fills the bottom of the canyon—alders and maples along the creek and large Douglas firs higher up the sides. Some poison oak grows beside the trail in dry, open places. The good trail rises gradually except where narrowing canyon walls force steep, short climbs. Beyond one of these narrows, 1.8 miles from Keystone Flat, you climb out into a flinty hillside overlooking a fork in the creek. Both forks fall from pool to foaming pool in deep channels cut into exposed metamorphosed rock, to meet in a large pool overhung by ferns. Unfortunately, a Venturi dredge was operating in the large pool when we went by.

East of the north fork of the creek, you climb steeply north up a rocky hillside over a knob of black rock and across a flat to re-enter forest. A fine little tributary creek flows across the trail 2 miles from Keystone Flat. Fill your water bottles for the steep hill ahead. Steep switchbacks rise to a rocky point covered with serpentine shards. Rougher trail, very steep in places, zigzags to another outcrop, up the nose of a ridge and around to longer switchbacks up the side of the canyon through open forest and brush. At the top of the switchbacks you contour west around a shoulder, then turn north again far up on an east wall of a side canyon. Canyon oaks, black oaks, scrub oaks and manzanita give way to large Douglas firs and sugar pines after you dip down to cross a stream course that is dry by midsummer. Ice-cold, running water surfaces 100 feet down from the trail.

Bear Wallow Camp appears on the *Thurston Peaks* quadrangle in the vicinity of two sloping benches one-quarter mile farther on. Apparently it is a historic site only; nothing is here now, and the two gullies you cross have no water in them. Around the next point you turn north into another side canyon, where you can hear a stream running. You cross the stream 3.5 miles from keystone Flat, then climb steeply west across a brushy hillside to a wide gully

View down East Fork New River from the New River Divide

choked with alders and willows. This, believe it or not, is Bear Wallow Meadows.

The trail turns north beside the "Meadows" and disappears before it reaches a treeline above. Don't worry about it. You will find it again where it crosses a patch of grass at the end of the gully, and passes a tree with a sign affirming that this is indeed Bear Wallow Meadows. Two small, fair campsites are in the edge of the trees west of a spring flowing out of a pond in the grass. This is one of the few places in the Trinity Alps where there is literally plenty of firewood. Please us it sparingly, and be sure to hang your food. Bear Wallow Meadows does have bears, even if it doesn't have much in the way of meadows.

The trail above Bear Wallow Meadows has been relocated slightly from the route shown on the *Helena* quadrangle. It now turns and switchbacks up the hill north of the meadow before turning west over a spur ridge. You next begin a long traverse, generally northwest on good tread with some ups and downs into side canyons and gullies, and around shoulders covered with huckleberry oak and manzanita. Wide views open up behind you, down to North Fork Trinity Creek. You climb steeply north beside a little stream in a gully 1.8 miles from Bear Wallow Meadows, cross the stream where it ceases to flow, and top out at a flat on the ridge between Whites Creek and Gas Creek.

North of the ridgecrest an old sign on a tree beside the trail marks Hunters Camp, in a pleasant glade at the head of Gas Creek. Several excellent campsites are in the glade, and a spring is down the hill in a patch of willows. Beyond the Hunters Camp sign, you rise moderately, and turn northwest through open, mature white-fir forest to a junction with the New River Divide trail on the roadcrest of Limestone Ridge, 6.1 miles from the trailhead. An old sign at the junction has fallen in pieces to the ground. The park-like forest covering the divide here is as pretty as you will see anywhere. It is almost entirely mature white firs, widely spaced on an open floor with patches of pinemat manzanita and low ceanothus.

Side Trip to Whites Creek Lake

Tiny Whites Creek Lake hangs in a basin at the head of a fork of Whites Creek northeast of Pony Mountain. The lake is not the reason for the trip. It has no fish and you wouldn't want to swim in it. However, its surroundings and the views from 1.7 miles of virtually level New River Divide trail along the way are outstanding.

You can see Hunters Camp below as the trail contours through magnificent open forest around the east side of a hump south of the Whites Creek trail junction. Beyond the trees you traverse south across a steep, brushy hillside, rising gradually to the crest of a spur ridge at 1.2 miles, then turn almost directly west toward a rugged peak on the divide north of Pony Mountain. Another half mile, almost level through manzanita and huckleberry oak, brings you around to a shelf below the two peaks. The trail turns south over more open ledges and comes to a trail junction just beyond a small stream. A trail forks west over the crest from the junction, and eventually goes down to Jakes Hunting Ground and New River.

A solid mass of alders and willows fills 10–15-acre flat west of the New River Divide trail. Whites Creek Lake is a half-acre pond buried in the brush at the northeast corner of the flat. Its placid surface is a good mirror for the rugged face of Pony Mountain to the south. Other than that, the kindest thing that can be said about the lake is that it is a good home for frogs. A good campsite is out of the brush beside a small grove of western white pines. It would be an excellent site if it weren't for the pile of rubbish beside the too-large fire ring.

The ledge at the east edge of the shelf is a marvelous place to watch the run rise from behind the vast panorama to the east. The rosy light first touches the tops of the central Alps, from Thompson Peak at the north end down to Monument Peak and Weaver Bally Mountain at the south end. Intervening ridgetops along both sides of Canyon Creek and North Fork Trinity River light up in turn as the burning orb of the sun clears the ridge on the eastern horizon. Details soon appear in the gloom of the forested canyons below, and songbirds welcome the new day—an unforgettable experience, well worth the trip.

As you head north on the New River Divide trail from the Whites Creek junction, the large firs give way to ceanothus, manzanita and huckleberry oak brush that crowds the tread. You get glimpses down into the East Fork New River as the trail crosses to the west side of the ridge. A stately row of Jeffrey pines crowns a knife-edge crest .7 mile from the Whites Creek junction. You get your first good view west across the New River drainage from a bald summit .6 mile farther north. A series of blue ridges steps up to the western horizon beyond New River.

You skirt the east side of a bald knob to the north, then climb moderately northeast before turning west up the side of the ridge below a chocolate-hued outcrop. The trail ascends to the top of a meadow above the outcrop before turning north again to the brink of a steep drop-off. You are near the top of a low mountain straddling the divide. The massive bulk of Cabin Peak rises beyond a deep saddle to the northeast, and you can see the trail contouring around the south side of the peak.

The trail once dived straight down the north side of the mountain into the saddle, but it has been relocated since the *Helena* quadrangle was published to make one long switchback west, then go back northeast to connect with the old track two-thirds of the way down. The last third of the hill is still steep and rough in loose rock and gravel. A trail forks west in the saddle to run down the side of the ridge one-quarter mile to water and campsites at Marble Spring. You may want to make the trip to fill your water containers. No drinking water is available on the New River Divide trail in the next 4 miles north.

Disintegrated rock, almost like volcanic ash, crunches underfoot as you cross the saddle and start climbing though brush and scattered trees on the slope to the north. The brush soon thins, and you continue to climb north up an open, gravelly slope on the nose of the ridge. The trail turns over to the east side of the ridge .3 mile from the Marble Spring junction, and begins a long traverse east through heavy brush across the south face of Cabin Peak.

The crest of a spur ridge buttressing the southeast corner of Cabin Peak is 3.5 miles from the Whites Creek trail junction. You turn north from this crest to contour almost on the level through cool, dense forest, a welcome relief from the mile-long traverse across the hot, brushy south face of the peak. A trail to the top of Cabin Peak branches left a quarter mile into the woods. The unsigned trail once led to a lookout. The tower is gone now, but the 360° view is still there if you want to make the effort to see it. Beyond the trail junction, you come out into the open again and turn northwest around a shoulder of the mountain on finely broken red-rock talus. On the north side of Cabin Peak, the trail turns to descend moderately steeply a little east of north on the crest of the divide.

The ridgetop is generally level beyond the descent from Cabin Peak, but outcrops and knobs on the crest force the trail to climb from one side to the other. A very narrow, brushy crest 4.4 miles from the Whites Creek junction offers an unrestricted view southeast down Morrison Gulch all the way to the North Fork Trinity River. The trail down to Morrison Cabin marks a trace on the ridge beyond the gulch. A south cut-off to this trail climbs northeast from a junction .4 mile farther on.

From the junction below rock outcrops west of the crest, the New River Divide trail continues north. The north leg of the Morrison Cabin trail is

**Whites Creek Lake mirrors
Pony Mountain**

**Park-like forest of white firs
on the New River divide**

reached .3 mile north in open forest. Beyond this junction you drop down to Rattlesnake Camp on a flat hanging above the canyons of Cabin Creek and East Fork New River. In addition to a sign pointing out that this is indeed Rattlesnake Camp, a very important sign with the topo-map symbol for a spring on it points southwest down the hill. A well-used trail leads to two forks of the spring 100 yards down the hill. One fork has dried up, but a short length of plastic pipe emplaced in the other fork runs a pencil-thin stream of clear, cold water into a large enameled basin that someone has hauled in.

Campsites on the flat are littered and overused, and the supply of firewood is limited, but there isn't much choice if you need to camp within 2–3 miles of this point on the divide. There simply isn't any water anywhere else. The small flat is an excellent place from which to watch the sun set behind the ridges beyond New River, however. Rattlesnake Lake is a murky pond in a brush-filled draw east of the trail 250 yards north. Its water isn't fit to drink under any circumstances. A quarter mile north of the lake a trail forks west down to East Fork New River. This trail and its connection with the trail east to Morrison Cabin on North Fork Trinity River account for most of the heavy use of Rattlesnake Camp.

From the junction above Rattlesnake Camp the trail to Morrison Cabin climbs south at a moderately steep rate around the west side of a knob on the divide. As you turn east around the south side of the knob, you come to a junction with the south leg of the trail .3 mile from the New River Divide trail. You follow the crest of a razorback ridge farther east, then circle a knob and zigzag down a wider ridgetop before dropping over the south side of the ridge 1.5 miles from Rattlesnake Camp. Rough, gravelly trail descends steeply—very steeply in places—through thick manzanita, scrub oak and huckleberry oak to turn around to the brow of the ridge again .5 mile farther down.

From this point you look straight across the North Fork Trinity canyon to the face of the ridge between Grizzly Creek and Rattlesnake Creek. Some switchbacks have been added to the next 1.5 miles of trail down the brow of the ridge since the *Helena* quadrangle was drawn, but it is still very steep in places before you turn back west in Douglas fir forest on the canyonside above Morrison Gulch Creek. You make another switchback on the canyonside, and follow the creek down east to a ford 3.5 miles from Rattlesnake Camp. From the ford, the trail rises to the top of a low ridge between Morrison Gulch Creek and North Fork Trinity River, then follows the ridgetop east 150 yards before turning down toward the river along the edge of a lush, sloping meadow.

Rustic Morrison Cabin nestles under tall Douglas firs and ponderosa pines at the top of the meadow. The cabin was occupied during summers until 1990 by a family who mined a claim on the river and the creek. The Forest Service negotiated abandonment of the claim, and the cabin is now U.S. property. Please treat it with respect. It has considerable historic value.

At a sign below the cabin you ford the river again, and then climb up the east bank to find the North Fork trail 100 yards up the side of the canyon. The 6 miles back to Hobo Gulch trailhead are described in reverse in Trip 17.

Trip 20

Big French Creek

Trip Type: Round trip of 2 to 3 days or day-hike

Distance: 11.8 miles round trip

Elevation Change: 1460 feet, average 247 feet per mile

Season: Early May to late October

Topo Map: *Del Loma* (provisional 1982) 7.5′ quadrangle

The first two miles of this trip are outside the Trinity Alps wilderness, but are still about as wild as anything can be. This is the trip for those who can't wait to go backpacking in the spring, and really get away from it all. A good facsimile of coastal rainforest grows in the bottom of the steep-sided, narrow canyon. Curtains of moss and staghorn lichens hang from Douglas firs, big-leaf maples and alders. Fields of boulders and the trunks of canyon oaks are completely covered with a green velvet blanket. Twinflowers, woodland stars, pipsissewas and pyrolas decorate the floor of the forest. In more open areas, lupines lilies, mints and several species of orchids bloom in profusion. Thickets of dogwoods show their ghostly fake blossoms on the sides of the canyon. Brilliant blossoms of Indian rhubarb thrust above the water of the creek before the umbrella-like leaves unfurl.

Beautiful campsites nestle under trees on ledges above the swiftly flowing creek, where steelhead and an occasional salmon leap the low falls. The fair-to-good trail stays on the west side of big French Creek for the full length of the trip, so you need not be concerned about crossing the creek. The chances of your seeing anyone else on the trail are practically zero.

If you have read this far, you probably suspect that some flaws in this paradise haven't been mentioned. You are right. Poison oak grows profusely throughout the canyon, overgrowing the trail in many places. You would be well-advised to wear gloves, long pants and log-sleeved shirts while traveling, and to carry a pair of long-handled pruners to clear the trail. Be especially careful not to burn poison oak in your campfire—it can cause serious respiratory poisoning. Rattlesnakes are not uncommon. watch for them especially along the creek and at crossing of tributaries. Be sure to check yourself often for ticks; they can be a problem here in the spring and early summer.

There are no lakes and you will get only a glimpse of snow-clad mountains (Thurston Peaks) from the upper end of the trail. Fishing is good wherever you can find an open spot along the arbored creek, but the catch will be mostly steelhead fry no more than 6 inches long.

Big French Creek is still a beautiful place early in the season, and well worth the effort and minor drawbacks.

Starting Point

Look for the Highway 299 bridge over Big French Creek 6 miles west of Big Bar Ranger Station. Unfortunately, no signs identify Big French Creek or the road turning north just beyond the bridge, but it is the only creek of any size near this distance from Big Bar Ranger Station. Big Bar is 23 miles west of Weaverville.

Forest Road 5N13, the road to the trailhead, is signed where it forks left .2 mile from Highway 299. A sign for the trailhead and a fairly wide turnout that will park three or four cars are 2.5 miles up the narrow gravel road from the number sign. You are well up on the canyonside at this point and, if you come to a hairpin turn with a road forking to the right out of it, you've gone too far. The trail, marked by a blue ribbon when we were there, starts at the north end of the turnout.

Description

A new piece of trail has been built in recent years to go around the private property from which the Big French Creek trail previously began. The first part of the trail from the new trailhead is not very easy to find. The trail running straight down the hill is not it. That trail connects with an old trail coming up the side of the canyon that apparently was there before the road was built. Your new trail starts from the north end of the parking area and parallels the road, not more than 20 feet below it, for the first 100 yards.

Then the trail contours around the side of the hill, dips to cross two small streams, and switchbacks up to the top of a hump .5 mile from the trailhead. A junction with the trail from the old trailhead on private property to the west is on the hump. You turn right at the junction, and continue north on good tread, descending moderately along the side of the canyon through open forest of Douglas firs and madrones, then turn back southeast to a flat where a faint track goes on south. Your trail turns back north from the flat and descends gradually through magnificent forest that now includes black oaks and dogwoods. Persistent poison oak crowds the tread above and below where a trail forks right, down the hill, .8 mile from the trailhead. At this junction a sign points the way on north to Big French Creek.

Trip 20
Big French Creek

The woods grow more dense as you turn into a side canyon and cross a rushing tributary 1.3 miles from the start. A good, small campsite is under alders and maples on the north bank of the stream. Beyond the side canyon, a short, moderately steep rise greets you, followed by a gradual descent along the side of the canyon to the west bank of Big French Creek and a trail forking east across the stream. The junction is signed "UPPER WALDORFF RANCH—4 MILES." Public access through Upper and Lower Waldorff ranches is discouraged, so you shouldn't plan a loop trip that way. If the creek isn't too high, it is open enough to fish for a short distance above and below the Waldorff trail crossing. Good campsites are on Oak Flat above the east bank.

Two mossy flats north of the junction have fair campsites, but are heavily infested with poison oak. The trail rises 100–150 feet above the creek again before dropping into a marshy flat overgrown with dogwoods, hazelnuts, vine maples and alders. Another moderate climb along the side of the canyon brings you to Buckhorn Creek at the south end. Big French Creek is fishable for a short distance above and below the confluence of the two creeks.

You come close to the creek again after descending from the north end of Cherry Flat, then cross another flat littered with moss-covered boulders. A moderate climb starts you up the canyonside, then two steep switchbacks lead to a rim 1 mile from Cherry Flat where you look straight down 150 feet to the creek. Almost level trail weaves along the side of the canyon .8 mile from this perch to Willow Gulch, where you cross a fair-sized creek on slippery boulders. Speckled heads of leopard lilies nod above the rushing water. Two rather poor campsites are on a shelf above the north bank.

Instead of ending at Willow Gulch, as indicated on the *Ironside Mountain* quadrangle, the trail now continues up big French Creek another 1.4 miles to a large, forested flat opposite the confluence of the East Fork. Another set of steep switchbacks takes you up the side of the canyon again, where you catch glimpses of rugged Thurston Peaks on the northeast skyline before a final gradual descent to the flat. A large lean-to frame indicates semipermanent habitation of the flat at one time, and is still a good place to camp.

Trip 21

New River and Virgin Creek to Salmon Summit and Devil's Backbone

---

Trip Type: Loop trip of 5 to 9 days

Distance: 40 miles

Elevation Change: 22,120 feet, 553 feet per mile

Season: Mid-July to early October

Topo Maps: *Jim Jam Ridge* (provisional 1982), *Dees Peak* 1978, *Trinity Mountain* 1979, *Salmon Mountain* 1978, and *Youngs Peak* 1979 7.5′ quadrangles

Solitude, magnificent forests and incomparable views are the primary reasons for making this trip. Besides, it's a good conversation piece. How many people do you know who have walked up Virgin Creek to Salmon Summit or the trail along Devil's Backbone—or who have driven to Denny, for that matter?

It is very unlikely that you will meet anyone on this trail once you start up Virgin Creek from the New River junction. Some gold miners may be working Virgin Creek at the end of the jeep road that invades the wilderness to the confluence of Soldier Creek. The miners, unfortunately, are working legitimate claims. Virgin Creek does live up to its name above Soldier Creek, and virtually no one travels the rest of the way up the steep, wooded canyon to Salmon Summit or out to Devil's Backbone.

Except for stretches along Devil's Backbone and a few open, dry hillsides where canyon and Oregon oaks grow, the entire trip is in thick forest. Live oaks, tanoaks, madrones, big-leaf maples and Douglas firs line the bottoms of the canyons. Magnificent, dense forests of ponderosa pine, sugar pine, Jeffrey pine, black oak and white fir cover the upper basin of Virgin Creek and the Salmon

Trip 21
New River and Virgin Creek

Summit. This is one of the few places in the Trinity Alps where you will have plenty of firewood. Please don't try to burn it up all at once, be very careful about where you build fires, and above all make sure they are dead out.

An amazing variety of wildflowers bloom in the many different habitats found along the way. Deer and bear signs are thick throughout the trip, but the animals are sometimes hunted and therefore wary, so you will seldom see them in the thick forests. Many species of birds soar through the skies above, but squirrels, chipmunks and other rodents are noticeably absent from the local ecosystem, possibly for two reasons: Bears find them very tasty, and few humans come to feed them. Snakes are scarce as well, probably due to the lack of rodents. On the other hand, the insect, lizard and amphibian populations are doing quite well.

Fishing is good in New River and Virgin Creek. The catch is mostly steelhead fry, but on occasion a good-sized native rainbow trout will surprise you. Rock Lake and Red Cap Lake have eastern brook trout.

You can shorten your trip by a wide variety of alternatives. Due to the low elevation, early-season hikers can travel a long way up Virgin Creek before encountering any of the lingering snow that keeps the upper mountains inaccessible until summer. The condition of the access road and the ability to successfully ford Virgin Creek, however, may be more limiting factors than the snow higher up in the mountains.

Starting Point

First you have to get to the little settlement of Denny, a long way up the New River canyon. The signed road to Denny turns off of Highway 299 at Hawkins Bar, 46 miles west of Weaverville, or 10 miles east of Willow Creek. Beyond a relatively new, high bridge over the Trinity River you go a quarter mile to an intersection, where you turn back west, then north beside Hawkins Creek and past several houses and a subdivision to another intersection. At this fork your road turns right, and begins a long, twisting climb generally east up the side of the Trinity River canyon.

6.3 miles from Hawkins Bar, beyond some unbelievable hairpin turns, a dirt road forks left to Happy Camp and points north, and 1.2 miles farther at the end of your climb you reach a point on a spur ridge between the Trinity River and New River. Narrow pavement snakes down the east side of the ridge, then turns northeast through a gap in a spur ridge to a group of houses among neat orchards on a plateau far above New River. You finally come close to the river at Panther Creek, 14.5 miles from Hawkins Bar.

Denny Campground straddles the road 3 miles farther up the canyon. Denny Forest Service Guard Station is out of sight above the upper part of the campground. Someone is usually at the guard station who can write a wilderness permit as well as give you current information about the trails. The no-fee campground is large and very pleasant, with piped water during the summer, but as usual, no garbage service.

162

The actual town of Denny begins .7 mile up the road from the campground, and is strung out along the road for the next half mile. Continue along the paved road past Denny and Quinby Creek, 3.2 miles from Denny Campground, to the signed junction with road 7N15 on your left. If you come to the New River bridge, you've gone 1.3 miles too far.

Good, gravelled road doubles back west from the paved Denny road, climbing away from the river. The road turns north, then east around the shoulder of a ridge, and north again on the west side of the New River canyon across from the East Fork. You take the right fork at a signed intersection 4.7 miles from the paved road. Three or four other tracks turn off before you get to this intersection, but the main road is obvious. At 5.4 miles from the road you reach another signed junction, where you turn left as the track turns from gravel to dirt that is impassable in wet weather. The trailhead is in open forest at the end of the road, and has parking space and a stock tie area.

Description

A new foot and horse trail descends moderately .4 mile to the signed wilderness boundary. Just beyond the boundary you follow the trace of an old road, then foot trail again on a short, steep pitch down to Barron Creek in an alder thicket .8 mile from the trailhead. A foot-log is below the ford for your use if the creek is high, but generally the crossing should not present any problems. As you climb moderately out of the creek bed, tall Douglas firs, madrones and a few tanoaks grow above an understory of vine maples, ceanothus, redbuds and dogwoods on the sidehill. A few black raspberry vines growing in slide areas provide a welcome treat in season. You can hear New River at the bottom of the canyon to the east.

A short distance beyond Barron Creek you come to the west bank of New River. A cable crossing to a mining claim on the east bank, now removed, has left its mark on the trunks of two large firs. After following the west bank for 250 yards, the trail rises moderately up the canyonside, and then stays away from the river across steep hillsides, flats and ledges. Good tread follows the contour route of old mining ditches in places. A good spring flows across the trail .7 mile from Barron Creek.

Beyond the spring, the trail rises more steeply to a rocky point, around which the river roars in a horseshoe curve at the base of a steep-sided gulch cut into dark metasedimentary rock. You descend north of the point through rock piles of an old mining site, and past a large campground on a flat between the trail and the river. A well used trail turning left on the side of an old mining ditch leads only to a mining claim on the south bank of Virgin Creek. Your trail north crosses the ditch and drops to a flat where the Virgin Creek Guard Station once stood, 2.8 miles from the trailhead. That building was burned to the ground several years ago. Virgin Creek is at the north side of a wide bed of boulders north of the flat. It joins Slide Creek 200 yards east to form New River.

You ford Virgin Creek, and climb up the north bank to a junction with the Virgin Creek and Slide Creek trails, 3 miles from the trailhead. The crossing of

Trip 21
New River and Virgin Creek

Virgin Creek shouldn't be a problem by early to mid-summer, but may be dangerous during high-water periods early in the season. Forest Service personnel at Big Bar may be able to update you concerning the condition of the river.

Several excellent campsites are on the flat north of Virgin Creek. You should purify the water, especially since mining activity is occurring upstream. The trail turning east from the junction runs up Slide Creek and Eagle Creek, but your trail up Virgin Creek climbs west from the junction, across the hillside above the flat. You won't be close to Virgin Creek again in the next 4 miles of trail, and the first water on the trail is at Fourmile Creek, 2.8 miles away.

When we walked here, a sign on a tree a short distance up the Virgin Creek trail listed destinations of Virgin Buttes, Trinity Summit and Soldier Creek. Trinity Summit is not to be confused with Salmon Summit; Trinity Summit is the crest to the west at the head of Soldier Creek.

After 300 yards of steep climbing from the junction, you round a shoulder and turn north with the canyon to ascend moderately on a contour across steep, bare slopes and through open forest. Beside a mining claim sign posted on a tree 1 mile from the New River junction, a good trail forks left down the side of the canyon. As you climb over a steep point .25 mile farther up, you can see that a two-story house, built of lumber, not logs, is the first destination of the branch trail. The house seems quite out of place perched on a shelf on the other side of Virgin Creek.

The newer trail on the other side of the canyon also leads up to Barritt Cabin beyond Twomile Creek. A sign marks the old, unused trail to Barritt Cabin, dropping straight down the side of the canyon from a traverse beyond three switchbacks up the crest of a spur ridge. You can see the low log cabin from the Virgin Creek trail near the sign. The cabin may be occupied, and looks quite at home in its surroundings.

Beyond the Barritt Cabin sign, a number of dry-area wildflowers bloom on open slopes, including clarkia, brodiaea and pennyroyal. Clumps of sparse Oregon oak don't provide much shade for the moderate ascent. Some small, dusty bowls in the narrow tread are wallows made by California quail; the birds dust themselves to reduce lice infestations. The trail is generally good across the steep, open slope except where some small slides have run across the tread in a few places.

A completely different plant community greets you as you round a shoulder and descend into the side canyon of Fourmile Creek, 2.8 miles from the New River junction. Big-leaf maples and Douglas firs form a canopy above the little creek cascading over moss-covered boulders. Elderberries and dogwoods form the understory, with pipsissewas and mahonias blooming at ground level. The cool shade and cold, clear water are especially welcome on a hot summer day. A good, small campsite is on a bench before you drop down to cross the creek.

About 1.2 miles farther up the canyon, Virgin Creek makes an oxbow turn around a narrow, rocky point, and Sixmile Creek flows into Virgin Creek directly across from the point. You climb moderately almost west before you get to the top of this point. The trail turns back northeast from the crest to traverse an almost sheer rock wall before descending to a small flat beside the creek, 4.2 miles from the Virgin Creek crossing above New River.

The trail follows along the east side of the canyon to a crossing at the confluence of Soldier Creek. At the lower end of a long flat before the crossing, you come to the end of the Soldier Creek jeep road, which has a locked gate at the wilderness boundary to the west that presumably blocks entry to all but legitimate claim holders. The area has been heavily mined in the past, but only a few miners still hold claims, and more stringent regulations have reduced the amount of mining considerably. You may not see any miners, and hopefully you won't see too much evidence of their work. Excellent campsites are on the flat.

The road turns to cross both Virgin Creek and Soldier Creek just about at their confluence, 5.4 miles from the New River junction. The Virgin Creek trail is on a road branching to the right between the two creeks. Keep left at a fork 100 yards farther on, just past a miner's camp, and look for the foot trail turning up the hill just beyond a blazed tree on the right. A sign 20 feet up the trail says "VIRGIN CREEK TRAIL" and has an arrow pointing to "TRINITY SUMMIT."

You ascend steeply northwest for .4 mile, with the aid of a couple of zigzags, then turn back east around the shoulder of the ridge between Soldier Creek and Virgin Creek. A few more zigzags north bring you to the top of a hump on the side of the ridge and a junction with your return trail from Devil's Backbone and Trinity Summit. This trail will bring you back to this intersection nearly 22 miles later. At this point a sign points north to "SALMON SUMMIT—7" and back south to "NEW RIVER—6."

Twinflowers in Douglas fir forest along Virgin Creek

Coast elderberries and alders at Fourmile Creek

Trip 21
New River and Virgin Creek

The next 1.7 miles contouring along the canyonside, and descending to Eightmile Creek, are through uniquely beautiful forest. Douglas firs are the dominant trees, but the forest also includes very large sugar pines, Jeffrey pines, incense cedars, madrones, big-leaf maples, tanoaks and canyon oaks. In open spaces Washington lilies nod their pale lavender, speckled heads. The trail ducks in and out of three lush little gullies that harbor fugitive flowers from the Cascade Mountains—pipsissewas, mahonias, twinflowers and saxifrages.

At the confluence, Eightmile Creek is larger than Virgin Creek. Both are beautiful streams with umbrella-like leaves of Indian rhubarb vibrating above the currents. Large boulders beside the streams are decorated with intricate patterns of mosses and ferns, and delicate fronds of goat's beard wave in the breeze in more open spots.

A good campsite with an elaborate rock fireplace is on a little flat between the two creeks. It would be an excellent site if it weren't for the trash left behind by previous occupants. Carry out as much as you can. Eager little steelhead fry pop up in every pool in Virgin Creek below the confluence—very good for breakfast.

From Eightmile Creek you climb up the west side of the canyon and continue north, with some ups and downs well away from the creek, for a mile before descending to a series of ledges beside the creek again. At one point the trail runs down to the creek and might appear to cross, but doesn't—look for it continuing up the west bank. A large bench 2 miles north of Eightmile Creek

Goldminers' camp at Soldier Creek

offers excellent campsites, although there is little evidence that anyone has camped here. Above the bench, the canyon narrows, forcing the trail up the hillside again.

Another .5 mile north, a two-room cabin, framed with poles and walled and roofed with hand-split shakes, sits on a narrow shelf below the trail overlooking a 10–15 foot waterfall. The roof is mostly intact, but you probably won't want to sleep in the cabin unless a cloudburst hits you—the interior is pretty messy. A better place to camp is beside the remains of another cabin on a site dug out of the hill above the trail. The standing cabin is named Tenmile Cabin.

Jumbo Mine, a large hardrock gold-mining operation, was in the canyon above the cabins, but little trace remains of it today. Only one prospect hole across the creek is visible from the trail. Rumor has it that the remains of a 40-foot waterwheel and extensive diggings are up a side canyon, but we didn't find them.

Three short, steep switchbacks above Tenmile Cabin lead to the brink of cliffs overlooking the creek. After skirting the tops of cliffs, the trail climbs again, then levels off through dense forest to a brushy slope where a small stream tumbles down the canyonside. Head back into lush forest again, and pass two falls in the creek .8 mile from Tenmile Cabin. In a grove of beautiful, tall alders you cross Virgin Creek and then turn up the creekbed 150 yards to recross to the west bank and begin a steep climb as the creek turns east.

The trail crosses back to the south side of the creek 1.6 miles from Tenmile Cabin, and makes a very steep ascent with a few minimal switchbacks through heavy brush. As you climb higher, the brush changes to dense forest, which now

Bunchberry blossoms

Mount Shasta from Salmon Summit

includes red firs, and the trail turns north, then west to cross Virgin Creek again. A last crossing of the tiny creek below a mass of willows and alders brings you to the final climb to the summit through magnificent red-fir forest with queen-cup lilies and bunchberries blooming on the open forest floor.

You follow two more switchbacks, round a shoulder, and suddenly you are on top of Salmon Summit, 16.25 miles from the trailhead. The Marble Mountains appear on the horizon north of the deep trench of the Salmon River. Off to the southeast the central Alps around Thompson Peak raise snow-tipped peaks against a cobalt sky. Much farther away, pristine Mount Shasta floats above a series of forested ridges. Closer up, a trail marks a red-dirt trace across the brush-covered face of Youngs Peak, directly east across the upper canyon of North Fork Eagle Creek.

As you follow the trail north around the east side of a mountain, forest gives way to tall ceanothus brush. Push on through tough going for 300 yards, and you will find a trail junction on a knob in open forest. The only sign at the junction is one for Virgin Creek, back the way you came.

The trail to the right heads downhill .3 mile to Salmon Summit Mine and then over to Slate Gap and eventually connects with the Eagle Creek trail. Your route turns left, climbing up the mountain, descending along the northern side of the summit and arriving at lovely little Rock Lake, .6 mile from the junction.

The almost perfectly round lake sits right under the precipitous north face of the granite mountain. Granite talus falls into the water on the south side, but metamorphic rock slopes up from the rest of the shoreline. It's hard to say how this cup was formed. It appears to be a glacial cirque, but there is no evidence of glaciation along this part of the Salmon River Divide.

One good campsite and a few fair ones are under scattered red firs and western white pines above the eastern shore. The top of a spur ridge east of the lake offers breathtaking views of sunrises and sunsets over the Salmon River canyon. Coastal fog often creeps up the canyon at sunrise to set a series of ridges adrift on a pink sea.

Late in the season the water drops below the level of the outlet and the lake loses some of its aesthetic appeal. Fishing is good for eastern brook trout to 10 inches. Red newts will surprise you by rising to the surface to breathe, but they won't take flies.

From the lake your trail crosses the willow-lined outlet stream and makes a descending traverse around the head of the valley to a gorgeous little meadow in a saddle just over the crest of the ridge, where a profusion of sulfur flowers and naked eriogonums bloom in midsummer. You continue to descend a quarter mile, first through brush and thickets of incense cedars and then through more meadows before the trail climbs steeply back to the top of the ridge. After climbing along the ridge, steeply at first, you eventually begin a gently descending traverse along the eastern side of peak 6305 amidst open fir forest floored with grass and low brush, and then drop down more abruptly to the High Point trail junction in an open grassy saddle, 1.5 miles from Rock Lake. The High Point trailhead is .7 mile to the northeast.

A through-trip from New River to the High Point trailhead, or vice versa, is certainly possible, however, the transportation logistics are horrendous. Driving just one way between the two trailheads would require more than half a day. A better alternative would be to have a group start from each trailhead and exchange car keys when you meet in the middle of the trip. Another alternative would be to start your trip from the High Point trailhead and turn around at any point you wish down Virgin Creek. This direction might be better early in the season, since you wouldn't have to ford lower Virgin Creek.

You may not clearly see the trail in the tall grass as it heads northwest from the saddle past the sign with an arrow saying "EIGHTMILE CAMP," but an old roadbed almost immediately heads down from the saddle around the upper edge of the Eightmile Creek basin through wide meadows dotted with clumps of ceanothus and willows, and carpeted with wildflowers.

The road is a washed-out gully farther down, then gets better as it levels out. A good campsite is beside a little stream that has cut through the road .5 mile from the summit. Raw, red dirt that looked like a mine dump from farther up the hill turns out to be a massive slide at the head of Eightmile Creek as you rise slightly and reach its edge. You have to climb very steeply up the east side of the slide to cross, then drop back down to the road again on the west side.

Continue a moderate rise northwest across the head of the basin above a mass of willows, then climb more steeply through red-fir forest to the ridgecrest and a junction 1.7 miles from the High Point trailhead. The old road along the top of the ridge runs north toward Salmon Mountain and in 200 yards reaches a junction with a trail heading down .3 mile to Red Cap Lake (see Trip 32). Turn left (south) along the ridge road in the direction of the arrow on the sign marked "DEVILS BACKBONE." As you head through fir forest the trail gently ascends to the top of a knoll, marked 6555 on the topo map, where the path opens up and levels off in a large, grassy meadow.

Just as you begin to descend off the top of the knoll, the trail becomes indistinct and hard to follow in the tall grass. Where 3 white firs are growing close together on a small hummock, the route veers to the left (southwest)—watch for cairns that lead through the meadow and into the trees, where the trail becomes more pronounced. Your descent steepens under white and red firs until you wind your way out to the ridgecrest once more, next to a metasedimentary rock knob that has a sheer north face overlooking the steep hillside below. A short downhill jaunt brings you to Eightmile Camp, adjacent to another large, flower-covered meadow, 1.2 miles from the trail junction and 20.5 miles from the trailhead.

Eightmile Camp is a remote site nestled under tall firs overlooking a grassy meadow that is filled with wildflowers in season. A short, beaten path leads approximately 25 feet to a spring surrounded by vegetation, where a small pool is just the right size for retrieving water. Many of the previous visitors, although few and far between, must have been hunters, as there are cables to hang meat, places to tie stock, and lots of log rounds upon which to sit. Firewood is plentiful, but may require a short trek to acquire. Partial views of the distant terrain, including Devil's Backbone, can be had through gaps in the trees.

The route away from Eightmile Camp can be somewhat confusing. Right below the camp, the trail makes a hairpin turn and then follows a faint track east across an overgrown meadow to the east side immediately above a thicket of alders. A blaze on a fir tree at the far end of the meadow marks the resumption of distinct trail. The trail from Eightmile Camp to Devil's Backbone is not accurately shown on the *Salmon Mountain* topo map. The actual trail heads farther east, steadily downhill through lush vegetation of ferns and wildflowers under a dense canopy of fir. Approximately .5 mile from Eightmile Camp you hear and then cross a gurgling tributary of Eightmile Creek. Follow the western bank for a short distance, and then climb up to a little-used campsite next to a series of deadfalls.

The trail appears to stop right in the middle of the campsite, but it proceeds on a straight line over the deadfalls for 50 to 75 to feet where the trail can be picked up again. You continue on downhill beneath predominantly white-fir forest until a bend in the trail brings you to an open traverse of a hillside, and a dramatically different botanical zone of ponderosa pines, incense cedars, firs and manzanita brush. At the conclusion of this traverse the trail reaches the ridgetop of Devil's Backbone, .75 mile from Eightmile Camp.

Devil's Backbone got its name from its lack of shade and water. Nothing has changed. The trail along the crest can best be described as an undulating, rollercoaster hike south along the top of the ridge, with unobstructed and incomparable views west to the coastal range and east to the central Alps. This is probably not the best place to be in the middle of a very hot summer day! You will most likely see more bear scat than boot prints, which could very well be deemed a positive aspect.

Ascending south the trail skirts just below the high point (5725) of the ridge and then makes a steep descent, briefly interrupted by a level stretch, to a saddle. Views east to the snow-tipped peaks of the central Trinity Alps and west to the wild, wooded ridges of the coastal mountains are nearly constant companions. From the saddle you make a steep climb to the summit of a knob and a short descent to a very small, but welcome, grove of Douglas firs and knobcone pines, where you can squeeze under some partial shade. A slight descent from the trees and then some level walking through a long saddle bring you to the base of a rounded peak, 2 miles from the beginning of the hike along Devil's Backbone. Instead of climbing up the rounded peak, the trail traverses below it on the western side in open forest.

A gently undulating traverse in and out of light shade brings you to a long stretch, below the crest, of forest shade and thick vegetation. A 25-foot section is actually overgrown with vine maple—a stark contrast to the sparse, dry vegetation along the ridgecrest. This nice, pleasant stroll through cool forest is abruptly interrupted by an extremely steep turn upward that quickly returns you to the top of the ridge. The first half of this ascent is mercifully in the shade, but the second half is fully exposed.

170

Another traverse along the ridge leads to some shrub-covered metasedimentary rock cliffs that you pass on the east side. From this vantage point you have a spectacular view of the central Alps. A steep descent to the next low spot along the ridge brings you to a short, shaded section of predominantly Douglas firs before climbing up along rocky trail through manzanita and ceanothus to the top of the crest once more. A long brushy descent is briefly suspended by a short climb up a little knob, and then resumes, eventually coming under cool Douglas-fir forest. Proceeding through the forest, the trail switchbacks twice and heads down the hillside to a large wooded flat and Onemile Camp, 5.2 miles from Eightmile Camp.

Onemile Camp is a reasonably large camping area with plenty of firewood, fire pits, and old artifacts scattered around the site. Water can be obtained quite a way down the hillside from a spring. A faint trail leads downhill from the south end of camp next to two large fir trees, where you will notice a large downed timber with a segment cut out of it for the trail. A long, fairly steep descent along the trail brings you eventually (approximately .1 mile from camp) to Onemile spring, the first water close to the trail for nearly 5 miles since crossing the upper tributary of Eightmile Creek.

The trail climbs steeply away from Onemile Camp through mixed forest, then levels off, traversing the hillside south before another steep, short climb leads to the ridgecrest. A general descent brings you to a broad, densely tree-covered saddle from where the trail down to Virgin Creek heads northeast, .75 mile from Onemile Camp. Nailed to a western yew tree is an old, small, metal sign covered with pitch drippings, saying Virgin Creek with an arrow pointing down the very faint trail. Two cairns marked this intersection in 1993, but it is not an easy junction to see. You must pay close attention or you could easily pass it.

The trail between this junction and Virgin Creek is probably the least traveled section of one of the least traveled trails in the Trinity Alps. This fact becomes evident as soon as you step off the Devil's Backbone trail onto the faded track. It probably would be wise to contact the wilderness ranger at Big Bar for the current condition of this stretch of trail. The first 3 miles of trail from the junction generally traverse the ridge east above Soldier Creek, and the next 1.5 miles are a steep winding descent 1500 vertical feet down to Virgin Creek. You arrive at the junction with the Virgin Creek trail 4.4 miles from the Devil's Backbone junction.

Take a cooling dip in Virgin Creek before retracing your steps 9.1 miles down the canyon to the New River trailhead.

Trip 22

New River and Slide Creek to Historic Mining District and Eagle Creek

---

Trip Type: Loop Trip of 3 to 6 Days

Distance: 24 miles

Elevation Change: 7740 feet, 323 feet per mile

Season: Mid-May to late October

Topo Maps: *Jim Jam Ridge* (provisional 1982) and *Dees Peak* 1978
    7.5′ quadrangles

Some would say that solitude is its own reward, but combine it with the opportunity to taste a bit of Trinity Alps mining history and you have a very rich experience indeed. The New River/Slide Creek trail offers just such an encounter and much more. As on many of the more remote trails in the western Alps, you can almost be assured of not seeing anyone else for the greater part of this route. Old mining towns and related sites abound in the Historic Mining District, including the community of Old Denny, which, around the turn of the century, was home to 500 residents. Rich with history, other town sites, such as White Rock City and Marysville, invite the explorer to come and discover the treasures of the past. Most of the mining that took place in the Trinity Alps was placer or hydraulic, but this trail passes near the Sherwood and Hunter Mines, two of the very few examples of hard-rock mining in the Wilderness. Fortunately, the hordes of miners who once inhabited this region have all departed long ago, leaving the backcountry to recreationists. The more modern-day "agricultural miners," who were using the western part of the wilderness to grow illegal crops back in the '70s and early '80s, also seem to have left for greener pastures. If you happen to see any strange activity, however, please report it to the rangers at Big Bar Ranger Station.

Along with solitude and history, you will have the chance to travel alongside the cascading streams and deep green pools of Slide and Eagle creeks. Most of the trail, with the exception of the 3 miles through the Historic Mining District, is below the 4000-foot level and, consequently, the vegetation is primarily mixed forest, consisting of live oak, canyon oak, madrone, big-leaf maple and Douglas fir. Higher up, near White Rock City and the upper Eagle Creek basin, pines and firs predominate and in places produce pockets of dense forest. Occasional displays of wildflowers will be encountered in season.

Summer temperatures can be quite hot at this elevation, which makes the early summer and fall perhaps the best times to enjoy this part of the Trinity Alps. Several connections can be made, however, to trails leading up to the crest of the Salmon Mountains and correspondingly cooler temperatures.

Fishing has been reported to be very good in Slide and Eagle creeks. The deep green pools along Eagle Creek look particularly inviting, and the lack of fishing pressure on these streams should work in the favor of the angler who doesn't mind the effort expended to reach such waters. Check with the Fish and Game Department for current regulations as the Trinity River and its tributaries are closely monitored. In 1994 the entire length of New River was closed to fishing.

Due to the low elevation of most of this trail, you should be aware of two potential dangers: You will travel past some poison oak, but it is easily avoided without consequence if you know how to identify the plants; and rattlesnakes do inhabit this type of environment. As is prudent in other parts of the Trinity Alps, hang your food away from uninvited dinner guests, even though bears in much of the Big Bar District seem to be fairly skittish about humans.

Even though the trail may be free from snow by sometime in May (or even earlier in some years), the amount of run-off rushing down Virgin Creek at the ford, 3 miles from the trailhead and just above the confluence with Slide Creek forming New River, will determine whether you can progress beyond this point. Check with the Forest Service about the condition of this crossing before arriving at the trailhead.

Starting Point

Directions to the New River trailhead are described in Trip 21.

Description

Follow the New River trail as described in Trip 21 to the junction with the Virgin Creek and Slide Creek trails 3.0 miles from the trailhead.

Just after the ford of Virgin Creek the trail junction is marked by a sign attached to a tan oak reading "SOLDIER CREEK" with an arrow to the left (west), and "OLD DENNY" with an arrow to the right (east). Your trail to Old Denny climbs east above the roar of the creek through mixed forest of big-leaf maple, Douglas fir, tan oak and canyon oak. As the trail rounds a curve northeast, the forest thickens. Then you ascend to the top of a shoulder of the ridge that separates Slide and Virgin creeks, and descend into the Slide Creek drainage. During the descent down to the creek you catch glimpses of the channel that the rushing waters of Slide Creek have cut over time through the metasedimentary rock of the area. The descent continues until the trail is only a few feet away from and directly above the creek.

Beyond a clearing you immediately switchback away from the creek up to a bench with a campsite. Apparently this spot was the site of some old structure from a bygone era, as the remains of a 20-foot rock wall clearly indicate. A hundred feet up the trail from this site a small creeklet drifts across the path. The trail is in excellent condition up to this point, despite its lack of use.

About 2 miles from the Virgin Creek/Slide Creek junction, the trail suddenly steepens, makes a couple of switchbacks and climbs over a hill to a gully containing a seasonal creek.

Traveling .75 mile farther brings you to the signed trail junction of the Eagle Creek and Slide Creek trails, .15 mile upstream on Eagle Creek from the actual confluence of the two streams. The next 12.25 miles will take you on a loop up the continuation of the Slide Creek drainage, across Carey Ridge through the Historic Mining District, and down the Eagle Creek drainage before returning to this same point. Follow the sign to the right (east) in the direction of "OLD DENNY" and "MARY BLAINE MEADOWS." Down the trail 25 feet is another sign posted on a large fir that reads "BATTLE CREEK" and "SALMON SUMMIT." A short switchback leads down to the water and a boulder hop of Slide Creek. In higher water a foot-log may be available 150 feet upstream. Fill your water bottles since the next 3 miles are dry. Campsites are on the east side of the creek, but it appears they haven't seen much use recently.

Your trail climbs steeply away from Eagle Creek, switchbacks and comes around the ridge dividing the two drainages to Slide Creek once again. Under cool, mixed forest the trail traverses high above the creek, at times almost out of earshot, until it ascends up to a flat where the remains of an old cabin are found. Debris is scattered everywhere. From the nature of the debris, it would appear that the cabin is not all that old. From the cabin the trail is well-graded, gently rolling up and down without gaining or losing much elevation, and is high above the creek.

About 2.4 miles from the Slide Creek/Eagle Creek junction, and 8.2 miles from the trailhead, your path drops down to a large flat next to the creek that contains several good, shaded campsites. Plenty of mining paraphernalia is scattered about the flat, including an intact wood and metal hand truck. Firewood is abundant. This camp makes an excellent destination for those who get a late start, or for hikers wanting a moderate first day-hike.

Making a moderate ascent from the camp, your route climbs past a seasonal creek, up a steep hillside to an open area, then winds down to a flowing stream bordered with lush vegetation. Step across the stream and follow the trail into a grassy meadow, where you come upon a somewhat confusing trail junction, .2 mile from the camp. The confusion is alleviated once you proceed on the left-hand trail that trends northeast, 40 feet to a sign posted on a pine informing you that the other trail leads east to Milk Camp and Pony Creek. From the sign you head up and away from the meadow, noticing a brief transition in the vegetation to a predominantly evergreen forest. The trail soon becomes steep and dry, and remains so for much of the distance to Old Denny. A clearing along the way allows for views up to the crest of the Salmon Mountains.

Before you reach the actual town site of Old Denny, trailside mining debris becomes more and more prevalent. Heading through a dry drainage ravine, you reach a trail junction at the old townsite in a grove of second-growth oaks and firs, 10.3 miles from the trailhead. You're immediately struck by how many mining artifacts still remain after so many years. The ground is littered with all types of debris, including cast-iron skillets, metal pots, mining equipment, rubber shoe parts, tin cans, bottles and pottery shards. The second aspect of Old Denny that grabs your imagination is the fact that 500 people once lived and worked here as permanent residents. Looking around, it is hard to conceive that this area could have supported that large a population. A bustling mining town did, in fact, exist here once, but time has erased much of the evidence. The miners left long ago, and their buildings, some as high as three stories, have been replaced by mature second-growth forest.

Tattered old signs pass on some facts about the town: Old Denny was established by the founder, Clive Clements, in 1883, and was originally called New River City. The New River received its name when all the surrounding country had been explored except the rugged terrain around the river. The quest for gold eventually coerced humans to search for every possible location where the precious ore might exist and led to the "discovery" of the last river in the area, hence the name "New River." The last inhabitants left Old Denny in 1920, and seven decades later only a small number of temporary visitors pass through where once so many lived. Modern-day explorers can spend hours, if not days, poking around the old townsite and uncovering the rich history.

A crude, hand-lettered sign saying "WATER," points off to the right (east) where near a meadow you can locate a spring. Since this area supported such a large number of people at one time, you will be able to find any number of places to camp that are spread around the width and breadth of the old town. Please respect the area and leave it as you found it for those who may come after. Oddly enough, there are still a few private inholdings upstream from Old Denny, where some modern-day residents attempt to maintain cabins on a seasonal basis. Please respect these sites as well if you happen to come across them.

Instead of continuing on the trail up Slide Creek canyon, your route turns north from the junction at Old Denny in the direction of a sign attached to a fir that reads "MARY BLAINE MOUNTAIN" and "CINNABAR MINE." The trail climbs steeply away from Old Denny on a well-defined, but little used, track carpeted with leaves. Two long switchbacks lead to the top of the divide that separates the Slide Creek and Eagle Creek drainages. At this divide, .35 miles from the junction, another trail heads east, signed "MARY BLAINE MEADOWS." Your trail, signed "MARYSVILLE," descends, as the vegetation changes to predominantly fir forest, .3 mile farther to the site of the old town of Marysville. Unlike Old Denny, Marysville has little left to show the modern-day traveler except for some scattered debris.

A short distance from the townsite you pass an even less-traveled trail on the left that leads west to the ruins of the old Hunter Mine and other abandoned mines. The main trail heads up, steeply at times, through mixed forest and breaks into the open just before gaining the top of the ridge. White Rock City is just a short distance farther, .4 mile from the Hunter Mine trail junction, 1.1 miles from Old Denny and 11.4 miles from the trailhead.

For the backpacker, White Rock City is a more aesthetically pleasing site than Old Denny. Set on the side of a ridge, it has views out to the west and up to the summit of the Salmon Mountains. This wide, level site is a pleasant setting under cedars and pines, graced by cool mountain breezes. Many species of birds seem to inhabit the immediate vicinity. Even fewer people get to White Rock City than Old Denny, which may account for artifacts of greater number and better quality. Some debris from the old buildings that once stood on this site is scattered about as well. An unusual 75-foot-diameter circular pit is just up from the trail, its use a mystery. Plenty of nice campsites are around the townsite, firewood is plentiful, and an abundant source of water, Sherwood Creek, is .2 mile down the trail.

Leaving White Rock City, you head down to Sherwood Creek, climb away from the water, and traverse the hillside .3 mile from the creek through firs and cedars to a spring. Above the spring on the far side next to a seep is a campsite with a fire pit and a few old relics. The trail begins to descend and you break out of the evergreen forest back into oaks. Poison oak, which hasn't been sighted between the slope above Old Denny and here, begins to reappear in sporadic clumps. As the descent steepens, views open up through the trees to the south and east, and you begin to hear the roar of Sherwood Creek in the canyon below. Alert eyes will spy a large, unnatural hump on the steep slope below signifying the closed-off entrance to Sherwood Mine. Downslope 50–75 feet is the buried opening of the abandoned mine, with an old ore cart, rails and timbers. Soon after the mine you come upon a sign attached to a tanoak identifying the northwestern junction with the Hunter Mine trail, 2 miles from Old Denny.

Leaving the Historic Mining District behind, the trail makes a gentle ascent that steepens just before rising to the top of a ridge beneath ponderosa pines and incense cedars. Descending from the ridge you pass under cool fir and pine forest before eventually returning to oak forest, which has dominated at the lower elevations along your route. Rounding a bend, the track narrows as it makes a somewhat tedious descending traverse of a rocky hillside. Returning to mixed forest, the path widens again, making travel a bit easier. As you approach Battle Creek, the trail enters a zone of much denser vegetation and at times threatens to become overgrown. Up to this point, the seldom-used path has been in good condition and easy to follow, but this particular section runs the risk of becoming lost to the forest understory if not maintained.

About 13.4 miles from the trailhead and 3.1 miles from Old Denny, you hop across Battle Creek, a cool and refreshing stream under dense cover of Douglas firs. Climbing away from the creek, you quickly encounter a side stream, where the vegetation thickens, opening up again when you reach a dry, rocky slope dotted with ponderosa pines and cedars. The track narrows across this slope and footing becomes a bit tricky, but the tread soon widens again under mixed forest.

Ascending to the top of a ridge, the trail reaches another junction, .75 mile from Battle Creek. Attached to a cedar tree a sign with an arrow pointing to the right (north) says "ROCK LAKE." Your trail continues straight ahead, downhill past another sign on a ponderosa pine saying "SLIDE CREEK." Immediately beyond this sign, however, the trail cuts sharply left (south) and heads down away from the ridge across a dry, rocky slope. Through a forest of Douglas firs, incense cedars, ponderosa and digger pines the trail heads down and then up again to the summit of another ridge, which separates the Eagle Creek and Battle Creek drainages. Crossing over the ridge, the route descends into the Eagle Creek drainage under a forest of mostly Douglas fir and incense cedar.

Descending, steeply at times, you reach a clearing where the trail angles to the right, basically making a sweeping horseshoe bend, switchbacking twice, and then heading west into the trees at the bottom of the slope. Watch for cairns through this clearing. Continuing, the trail heads toward a union with Eagle Creek and shortly becomes almost impossible to follow. Once you reach the dry, open hillside, though, you can descend to the creek and pick up the trail again where it parallels Eagle Creek. Along the creek the trail becomes distinct, and the grade is more gentle, as you travel under tanoaks, canyon oaks and Douglas firs.

Soon after passing an old campsite, you come to the crossing of Eagle Creek, 15.4 miles from the trailhead, which should be an easy boulder hop in most conditions. The creek itself is a delightful stream, with deep green pools suitable for swimming and fishing. The creek rushes downstream along a much steeper route than does the trail, which is a dirt path covered with pine needles, smoothly graded and quite pleasant to walk on, beneath primarily Douglas-fir forest with lush trailside vegetation. Eventually, the route becomes basically an up-and-down venture, coming almost to the creek, climbing away from it, and repeating the whole process over and over. Campsites are few and far between along Eagle Creek, which is too bad because the creek is very delightful. If the desire to camp along the creek becomes too great, you can find sites with a little effort. A short climb brings you to the Slide Creek/Eagle Creek trail junction, 18.0 miles from the trailhead.

Retrace your steps 5.75 miles to the New River trailhead.

Trip 23

Green Mountain Trail to North Fork Trinity River

Trip Type: Through-trip of 3 to 5 days requiring a car shuttle or pick up

Distance: 17.6 miles; plus .5-mile round trip to Brushy Mountain, and 1.7-mile round trip to Green Mountain

Elevation Change: 10,875 feet, average 550 feet per mile

Season: Mid-July to mid-October

Topo Maps: *Jim Jam Ridge* and *Thurston Peaks* (both provisional 1982) 7.5′ quadrangles

Solitude, high ridges with expansive views, and deep-green forests are a few of the many benefits awaiting the traveler on the Green Mountain trail. Even the Forest Service would appear to be so convinced of this trail's lack of use that there isn't space at the trailhead for more than one car to park at a time. If you're not the first person to hike this trail in any given year, you'll still feel you are in one of the least visited areas in the Trinity Alps Wilderness. This lack of attention is certainly not deserved from the standpoint of scenery, for you will gaze down into lush green canyons, and up to Limestone Ridge, Thurston Peaks and the central Trinity Alps peaks.

Only one lake is along this route, and it is really nothing more than a murky pond. Even so, plenty of water exists in creeks and streams along the way. Camping is somewhat limited to specific locations as well, but the camps that do exist are more than adequate. One, Pony Camp, is set in one of the most scenic basins you could hope to find.

Wildflowers abound in many of the areas during the peak of the season, including some less-seen varieties. Wildlife is very plentiful in this part of the Trinity Alps, but since human contact in this part of the Wilderness is minimal, you are more apt to see their droppings than the actual animals themselves.

Starting Point

Approximately 29 miles west of Weaverville (6 miles west of Big Bar Ranger Station), Forest Service Road 5N13 turns north from Highway 299 just past a sign for "BIG FRENCH BAR." If you are traveling from the east, the turnoff is just beyond the end of the guard rail, not at the wide shoulder just after the sign. Shortly after the turn onto Road 5N13 another sign reads "FRENCH CREEK TRAILHEAD 3 MILES, GREEN MOUNTAIN TRAILHEAD 13 MILES." Off to the right of the gravel road you will notice the old abandoned highway bridge that used to span Big French Creek.

At .5 mile, Road 5N20 veers to the right and heads down to the water. Your road, 5N13, continues straight ahead, slowly climbing above the western bank of the creek, and in 2.7 miles from Highway 299 reaches the French Creek Trailhead. Just beyond the trailhead the road switchbacks uphill and passes many well-marked side roads and some clearcuts on the way up Barnum Ridge. About 6.5 miles from the highway you reach a clearing where you catch the first glimpse of Limestone Ridge to the west.

A major three-way intersection occurs 9.2 miles from Highway 299 just past an old corral. Continue straight ahead, now on Road 6N04, following the sign marked "GREEN MOUNTAIN TRAILHEAD 4 MILES." At 12.4 miles from the highway, approximately .5 mile past a turnoff signed "BUCKHORN CAMP," turn right on little traveled Road 6N19. This junction should be signed, but when we were last there the sign was lying face down in the brush. Your immediate sensation after turning down this road may well be your unwavering certainty that this can't possibly be the right road. The track is very narrow, overgrown with car-thrashing brush, and appears to be unused with the possible exception of the local wildlife. Perseverance will pay off, however, and in .3 mile you come to a parking area large enough for half a dozen cars. The actual trailhead is another .5 miles down the road, but there is essentially no parking there. A little creativity might earn perhaps a single space squashed into the hillside along the road. The trail begins climbing north up the dry hillside away from the road.

Make sure that you bring plenty of water to start your trip. There is no source close to the trailhead and water is not available until after 3.5 miles of mostly uphill hiking. If lack of water at the beginning of the trip is a problem, too much water at the end could pose an even more formidable obstacle. Check at the Ranger Station when acquiring your wilderness permit about the crossing of the North Fork of the Trinity River near Keystone Flat, .75 mile from the Hobo Gulch trailhead at the end of your trip. Inability to make this ford could cause real logistical nightmares, although the only time it should be impassable would be during early season run-off.

Description

The trail begins by heading steeply uphill on an old roadbed, passing the trailhead sign marked "LADDER CAMP 6 MILES, MARBLE SPRINGS 14 MILES," and

Trip 23
Green Mountain Trail to North Fork Trinity River

"SALMON SUMMIT 21 MILES." The first 100 yards are in the open alongside canyon oaks until coming under the welcome cover of fir forest. Climbing steeply for a mile, you come to the top of a ridge, make a brief descent and at 1.25 miles reach a junction with an old road to the top of Brushy Mountain.

Side Trip to Brushy Mountain

Brushy Mountain is very well named. The trail up to the summit is short, not at all steep, but overgrown with a great quantity of brush. If few people hike the Green Mountain Trail, even fewer make the quarter-mile ascent up Brushy Mountain. You will have to beat back some of the shrubby vegetation, but the view from the top will compensate for the minor discomfort. A nearly uninterrupted 360° panorama awaits you at the summit: east to Limestone Ridge and the central Trinity Alps peaks; north to the Salmon Mountains; and west and south to the ridges and canyons of the western Trinity Alps. If you are fortunate you may catch a glimpse of one of the many species of raptors that frequent this area.

Back on the main trail, you make a short climb and then begin a long, moderate descent. An abundance of wildflowers appear along this part of the old roadbed, despite an apparent lack of surface water. As the trail bends north, you have periodic views out toward Green Mountain and the steep climb awaiting you along its exposed southern flank. In 2.5 miles from the trailhead the saddle separating Brushy and Green mountains is reached as the predominantly fir forest gives way to oak and manzanita.

The crest of the Salmon Mountains from the Green Mountain trail near Limestone Ridge

The half mile ascent up the side of Green Mountain is steep and rocky, and if it is a warm day it will be hot as well. Once this obstacle has been surmounted, the trail re-enters dense fir forest, hops over a couple of rivulets and then crosses the primary creek that flows down into Willow Gulch, the first source of water in nearly 3.5 miles. (The topo map side trail down to a waterfall has become overgrown with lush vegetation and is no longer discernible.) The main trail makes a moderate ascent along the east bank of the creek, crosses over again .5 mile farther up in an array of wildflowers, and shortly passes Stove Camp on the opposite bank.

Stove Camp is the first flat spot big enough for a campsite within the first 4 miles. Only one established site exists, in a broad sloping area surrounded by towering firs. If you should encounter the rare possibility of a party already camped here, there are other potential areas available at Stove Camp, but please restore them to their natural condition upon your departure. An abundance of bear scat will make hanging your food a reasonable precaution, although bears in this part of the Wilderness are quite skittish around humans.

About one-quarter mile above Stove Camp, after crossing the diminishing creek a third time, you crest the ridge and come to a trail junction with an old road to the summit of Green Mountain to the west.

Side Trip to Green Mountain

The trail to the top begins by climbing moderately through a continuation of fir forest until about halfway up the mountain, where the grade of the trail levels out and the vegetation becomes predominantly manzanita. Unlike the trail to Brushy Mountain, this trail requires no bushwhacking and is quite easy to

Pony Mountain from the Green Mountain trail

follow. Continue up the road along the top of the ridge to reach the actual summit, .85 mile from the junction. The view from Green Mountain is somewhat occluded by trees to the north and south, but offers magnificent vistas of Limestone Ridge, Thurston Peaks and Jim Jam Ridge, plus a fairly comprehensive look at your route for the immediate future as it undulates over peaks and saddles to surmount the crest of Limestone Ridge.

From the Green Mountain junction your trail makes a series of rollercoaster trips northeast up to the tops of minor peaks and down into the saddles that separate them. In one of these minor saddles, 1.25 miles from the trail junction to Green Mountain, you encounter an interesting geologic formation in a large outcropping of darkish green rock. This rock is serpentinite; igneous in origin, but subducted, exposed to cool temperatures and metamorphosed to its current state. Views are often quite impressive along this part of the old road as you walk along the crest of the ridge connecting Green Mountain to Limestone Ridge.

In the next to last of the saddles, 5.9 miles from the trailhead, you see the first sign of civilization since the beginning of the trip, a wooden sign attached to a ponderosa pine, declaring "PONY CAMP" straight ahead and "LADDER CAMP" downhill to the left. The faint trail down to Ladder Camp quickly disappears, and the only more difficult task than finding the trail becomes finding Ladder Camp. If you intend to camp there I can only wish you good luck, since I never found the site.

Proceeding along the old road .3 mile from the junction your route actually becomes a bona-fide backpacking trail for the first time in 6.2 miles of hiking. The trail ascends the side of the last unnamed peak on the ridge and deposits you at the saddle that separates Green Mountain Ridge from Limestone Ridge. At this point the views are impressive, including the route of the trail north up to the crest of Limestone Ridge just below Pony Mountain. The more immediate path makes a level traverse around the head of a basin for .7 mile to the crossing of the delightful creek of Devils Canyon. Here you will find an idyllic stream cascading down narrow rock clefts, bordered by moss-covered rocks and lush foliage.

From the creek, the trail continues to traverse until it begins a continuous ascent up the side of Limestone Ridge. Well-graded trail crosses a barren slope, and just before you encounter some rocks, it climbs a series of switchbacks up to a notch in a satellite ridge, descends briefly, and then makes an ascending traverse up to the crest of Limestone Ridge. One odd geologic note is that the green rock found along this section of Limestone Ridge is not limestone at all, but a type of metamorphosed plutonic rock. This is the high point of your trail, with correspondingly spectacular views east to the highest Trinity Alps peaks. Below, one-quarter mile away, lies Pony Camp nestled in a cirque basin.

One switchback and a steady descent of 250 feet bring you to Pony Camp, tucked into a sloping meadow basin blanketed with wildflowers, below 7477-foot Pony Mountain. A spring meandering through the meadowlands assures the availability of water. The main campsite is beneath some old Douglas firs, and other sites are scattered around the basin. The view from camp plunges down the hillside to the lush green canyon below and rises up to the snow-clad granite spires of the central Trinity Alps above. For an even better view, you can fairly easily climb to the top of Pony Mountain. Considering all the attributes of Pony Camp, including the nearly guaranteed solitude, the one drawback the site is cursed with is hard to fathom—an inordinate amount of debris has been left behind by horse packers. Please plan on hauling some of it out, thereby helping to restore Pony Meadows to a pristine state.

Eventually you leave the pleasant environment of Pony Camp and begin the long descent to the North Fork Trinity River. Away from the camp your trail descends around a hillside into the cover of fir forest, switchbacks twice, and continues to descend along the top of a ridge. At the end of the ridge, the trail switchbacks sharply and descends moderately around the head of a minor basin and out to a crossing of Whites Creek, 1.3 miles from Pony Camp. Thirty yards prior to Whites Creek is an unsigned junction with a trail heading northwest to Jakes Upper Camp.

Whites Creek Lake can be found just off the trail, but it is little more than a shin-deep pond enclosed by alders and willows on all sides. There are no campsites around the lake, but a nice spot does exist next to the creek away from the trail under some western white pines.

Note: The remaining trail description, from Whites Creek Lake to Hobo Gulch, can be found in reverse order in Trip 19.

From the crossing of Whites Creek the trail is visible before you as it cuts across a manzanita-covered hillside on a level grade before heading downhill around a ridge. Uninterrupted views of Whites Creek canyon and the central Trinity Alps are more spectacular with each step. Approximately one mile from the crossing of Whites Creek the trail re-enters the shade of mixed-fir forest, working its way downhill to an inauspicious trail junction, 1.6 miles from the creek and 11.5 miles from the Green Mountain trailhead. If you don't pay close attention it might be easy to miss this intersection and continue on the Limestone Ridge trail. About the only landmark you can find in this forested saddle is an old campsite just off the trail. Turn right (southeast) at this junction.

The route to Bear Wallow Meadows begins by making a wandering descent through mixed fir and cedar forest. About one-quarter mile from the junction is a part of the trail that has been covered with deadfall as a result of the heavy winter of '92–93. Carefully follow the path by line of sight and pick it up again on the other side of the debris. This particular trail has received little maintenance in recent years. As your descent continues you cross many small tributary creeks surrounded by lush vegetation until a short climb leads you to the top of a ridge above Bear Wallow Meadows, where you can gaze out past the sugar pines to views of the central Trinity Alps, and Limestone Ridge around Pony Camp.

A short, steep, winding descent brings you to Bear Wallow Meadows, or at least the spot that bears the name. This basin, choked with shrubs as high as your head, certainly doesn't fit the normal description of a meadow. Despite what the map indicates, the only reasonable place to camp is just as you come to the "meadows" next to a spring flowing beside two small campsites in the trees. The area on the map designated Bear Wallow Camp is historical in nature only and has no appeal as a campsite now.

The trail heads downhill away from Bear Wallow Camp, sometimes steeply and occasionally through overgrown shrub oaks. Two tributaries of Whites Creek are encountered in steep drainages covered with dense vegetation and downed timber. The trail is easy to lose in these drainages so pay close attention. One campsite does exist below a large incense cedar at the first creek. The trail keeps on heading downhill steeply and you can draw some contentment from the fact that you are headed downhill and don't have to climb up this steep section of trail. Eventually you come to a crossing of Whites Creek, which is an easy boulder hop, and then hike .3 mile farther to the intersection with the North Fork Trinity River trail.

A sign at the intersection reads "BEAR WALLOW MEADOWS" and "PAPOOSE LAKE." You hike right (south) on the low water trail .4 mile to a ford of the North Fork Trinity River, and another .1 mile after the ford to a junction with the high water trail and the Backbone Creek trail to Russell Cabin. Just after this intersection you cross Backbone Creek and come to Keystone Flat. If you are in need of a place to camp at this point in your trip, Keystone Flat offers plenty of nice sites in the grassy flat or back along the river. From this point our trail makes a .75 mile moderate climb up to the trailhead at Hobo Gulch.

Trip 24

Salmon Summit Trail to Red Cap Lake

Trip Type: Round trip of 2 to 3 days

Distance: 4.1 miles to Red Cap Lake, 8.2 miles round trip

Elevation Change: 3290 feet, 361 feet per mile

Season: Late June to mid-October

Topo Map: *Salmon Mountain* 1978 7.5′ quadrangle

The Salmon Summit National Scenic Trail provides the wilderness traveler with solitude, relatively gentle walking through cool forest, and occasional ridgetop views of the wild and remote northwestern Trinity Alps. The trailhead is a long way from most population centers, but avoids the tedious, serpentine drive to Forks of Salmon and the High Point trailhead, which provides the other access to Red Cap Lake, as described in Trip 32. For those few who live west of the Alps, this hike may be one of the closer trips to their point of origin.

Red Cap Lake is a serene body of water set below a forested ridge and bordered by meadows that are carpeted by wildflowers in early summer. Chances are fair that you will be the only ones to camp there at any particular time. The potential for day-hikes from the lake to other remote areas in the northwestern Trinity Alps does exist, although trails are sometimes rather faint due to lack of use.

The trail itself is mostly forested, providing escape from the hot summer sun, but once in a while the trail does open up to reveal panoramic views of the surrounding ridges and valleys as well as more distant peaks. In spite of the lack of boot travel this trail receives, the tread is in good condition, well-graded and easy to follow.

Make sure you bring water with you to the trailhead since you won't find any along the road, at the trailhead, or on the trail until you reach Red Cap Lake.

Trip 24
Salmon Summit Trail to Red Cap Lake

The more daring might be inclined to hike the Salmon Summit National Scenic Trail all the way east to Cecil Lake, but such a route requires some tremendous logistics for transportation between the two trailheads. We hope to describe just such an adventure in a later edition of this guide.

Starting Point

Follow Highway 299 to the town of Willow Creek and head north on Highway 96 forty miles to the town of Orleans. (From the north, Orleans is 102 miles on Highway 96 from Interstate 5). Cross the Klamath River on a suspension bridge immediately north of the town of Orleans, and turn right (east) onto Red Cap Road. Forest Service road markers occur at every mile, and often at half mile intervals as well. Travel on paved road along the east bank of the Klamath River, past private residences and ranchettes in the river valley. At 1.5 miles from the highway, the road narrows and begins a long, winding ascent all the way to the trailhead. You cross a one-lane bridge at 4 miles and leave the last of the private homes behind. Five miles from the highway you reach a signed junction where County Road 532 turns right, but you continue straight on Road 10N01 in the direction of "LEPERRON PEAK, SHELDON BUTTE" and "HOOPA." Remain on this road, which turns to gravel 15 miles from the highway, 18.4 miles to the wide trailhead at the top of a ridge. There is room for a large number of cars, and a horse corral is just up the hill.

Description

From the parking area the trail quickly descends into forest cover of white fir, incense cedar, and Douglas fir, and then maintains an almost level course on a well-graded, dirt and pine needle path. Minor ups and downs accompany your slightly ascending walk under cool forest canopy, past occasional wildflowers and underbrush. The trailside vegetation varies considerably, from sparse to lush, and represents a good example of how different factors, primarily the amount of light the forest canopy allows down to the forest floor, combine to enhance or inhibit the amount of understory growth.

Approximately .75 mile from the trailhead you enter the Trinity Alps Wilderness just prior to Baylor's Camp, a dry camp area that appears to be used primarily as a hunting camp. Tucked beneath dense forest, Baylor's Camp has places to tie stock and hang meat, plus log rounds to sit upon by the fire. At the far end of the camp the trail bends to the left, and 5 yards farther on, comes to a signed junction with an old roadbed that leads north along the crest of the Salmon Mountains to Orleans Mountain. Your trail bends to the right (southeast).

The trail climbs a bit more steeply past the junction and eventually tops out at the top of the divide 1.3 miles from the trailhead, where the vegetation switches from dense forest to manzanita, dotted with an occasional fir tree. The first view from the trail is suddenly interrupted by the realization that the area behind you was once logged in the distant past, and the area ahead fell victim to a somewhat more recent fire.

Following the top of the ridge, the trail proceeds with views to the east and west until encountering an old downed log with an almost equally aged sign attached to it which reads "RED CAP LAKE." From this point the trail descends south off the ridge through the burned area, where small white firs are staging a comeback on the otherwise brush-covered slope. Shortly, you find yourself back in dense forest as your trail levels off and returns to its minor ups and downs.

Breaking into the open once more, the trail, now an old roadbed, traverses a dry, grassy hillside sprinkled sporadically with incense cedars. A short, open ascent brings you to Indian Rocks, a weathered diorite outcrop of exposed rock straddling the divide, 1.9 miles from the trailhead. From Indian Rocks you get an imposing view of nearly 7000-foot Salmon Mountain only 1.25 miles southeast.

You leave Indian Rocks behind, head into the trees again, and ascend, sometimes steeply, toward the summit of the unnamed peak between Indian Rocks and Salmon Mountain. Just before reaching the top, the trail skirts below the summit and makes a traverse over to the saddle that separates the peak from Salmon Mountain. Mount Shasta can be seen just above the farthest ridge to the east.

A gentle ascent from the saddle through cover of forest leads to a trail junction, 2.75 miles from the trailhead. Thirty feet past the junction a rustic sign says "SSNRT-6E03" with an arrow pointing uphill to the left, and "RED CAP LAKE" with an arrow pointing downhill to the right. Your trail down to Red Cap Lake leaves the Salmon Summit trail at this point and makes a steady, moderate descent through alternating open and closed forest to the basin below.

The trail descends for almost a mile before leveling off and making an almost imperceptible climb up through the trees and then across the meadows of the basin. Red Cap Lake soon appears, sitting peacefully at the head of the basin. The trail terminates on the east shore of the lake at the junction with the High Point trail near a large campsite.

Red Cap Lake is a shallow pond with a mud bottom and is crisscrossed with dead snags. Therefore, it does not lend itself very well to swimming. Even though there have been reports of large eastern brook trout inhabiting this lake, there was no indication of any fish in the lake the two separate times I was there in 1993. It was late in the season and perhaps the fish were well fed by then. The lake does, however, provide a wonderful setting in which to relax and enjoy the environment.

Meadows, carpeted with wildflowers in season, caress a good part of the shoreline around Red Cap Lake, occasionally attracting the wary wildlife of the area. Along the southern shore rugged slopes and cliffs rise up to the ridge above. The rest of the terrain around the lake is lightly forested, providing good campsites. Perhaps the best site is in a grove of trees at the southeastern edge of the lake just beyond the meadows. Almost any time you visit Red Cap Lake you probably will have your pick of campsites.

Trip 25

Big, Little and Wee
Bear Lakes

Trip Type: Day-hike or round trip of 2 to 4 days

Distance: 4.7 miles one way to Big Bear Lake, plus .75 mile off-trail to Little
Bear Lake

Elevation Change: 3200 feet, average 561 feet per mile

Season: Late June to early October

Topo Map: *Tangle Blue Lake* (provisional 1986) 7.5′ quadrangle

Big Bear Lake and its trailless companions, Little Bear Lake and Wee Bear
Lake, are the easternmost of all the Trinity Alps lakes. Along with Log Lake
they are in the Trinity Alps Wilderness courtesy of a 4-mile jog of the east
boundary. The Wilderness would have been greatly diminished had these
gorgeous lakes been excluded.

Big Bear and Little Bear are outstanding examples of Trinity Alps lakes, set
in granite cirques on the north side of rugged peaks visible from Highway 3
north of Eagle Creek. Wee Bear Lake is a diminutive, forested pond which
shares Little Bear's cirque but not its stature. Although the lakes are not at
very high elevations (5800 feet and 6240 feet, respectively), the steep-sided
cirques face north, and may retain some snow until midsummer. Their deep
waters are correspondingly cold.

This is a popular trip, and campsites at Big Bear Lake are very limited, so
you should ask at the Weaverville and Coffee Creek Ranger Stations, while
acquiring your wilderness permit, to see how many others are planning to camp
there during your stay. It is not unreasonable, by the way, to ask the Forest
Service employee you are dealing with at one ranger station to phone another
station to find out how many permits have been issued for a particular trail. In
fact, he or she will probably appreciate your interest since Forest Service

personnel want to avoid overcrowding whenever possible. You can still day-hike to Big Bear Lake if campsites are going to be full; and strong hikers with cross-country experience could make the journey all the way to Little Bear Lake as well, where people will be more scarce.

Fishing is good in both lakes for eastern brook trout up to 12 inches, and a lot of vertical granite offers excellent climbing and scrambling opportunities.

Starting Point

The Bear Lake Road veers left off Highway 3, where a sign states "BEAR LAKE TRAIL 3/4 MILE," below a bridge to the east bank of the upper Trinity River 8 miles north of the Coffee Creek junction, which is approximately 40 miles north of Weaverville.

Limited parking exists on the right just before a bridge over Bear Creek 1.2 miles from Highway 3. The trail starts up the hill on the other side of the road 200 yards south of the bridge. A sign reading "BEAR LAKE TRAIL" is partly obscured by vegetation.

Big Bear Lake in late June

Trip 25
Big, Little and Wee Bear Lakes

Description

Two trail signs greet you as you begin your hike up the hill from the road. One proclaims your route as "BEAR LAKE TRAIL 7W03" and the other informs you that the bridge crossing Bear Creek .9 mile up the trail is closed. The trail climbs steeply away from the road on three short switchbacks, then contours northwest along the side of the canyon above Bear Creek to a flat where the climb moderates through an open forest of Douglas firs, incense cedars and a few canyon oaks. Otherwise good tread is washed out and rocky in steeper places as the narrowing canyon pushes the trail closer to the creek.

A short distance above a sign, reading "STOCK CROSSING," posted on a tree along the right side of the trail you come to the remains of the old bridge that used to span Bear Creek. All that remains is a large, flat topped log that is now angled and slanted. Sure-footed, adventurous types may be tempted to cross here anyway, but the majority of travelers will be more content using the stock crossing below. To take the stock crossing route, follow the trail leading down from the sign to make the easy crossing of the creek. After the crossing, the trail climbs steeply away from the creek and around a ridge until the much smaller northern branch of Bear Creek is reached, and easily crossed. A brief climb south reunites you with the main trail coming up from the old bridge crossing.

Turning northwest you reach the crest of a razorback ridge that separates the main branch and the north branch of Bear Creek. From the upper end of the spur ridge three long switchbacks climb almost north again to a traverse northwest across the canyonside, through scattered western white pine, huckleberry oak and manzanita, which has overgrown the trail and needs to be cut back. According to a Forest Service wilderness ranger no maintenance was scheduled for 1993, so wear long pants through this section. A civic-minded backpacker with a pair of hedge clippers could do a real service at this spot.

Now you turn north away from the creek on steep, worn, washed-out, old trail to climb through mixed forest. The trail soon heads west among granite boulders, and then levels out headed southwest in a pleasant valley with patches of ferny meadow. A short climb through dense forest is interrupted briefly by a narrow avalanche swath, followed by more dense forest, and then another, wider avalanche swath inundates a part of the trail with debris. Both of these avalanches were triggered by the heavy, wet winter of 1992–93. The trail is covered by avalanche debris and then blocked by a very large downed incense cedar, making a detour imperative. Chances are, if the Forest Service does not clear the trail through this mess, repeated travel by backpackers will eventually create a distinct path. Until then, however, the trail can be picked up again by determining the point on the opposite side of the avalanche debris that represents the continuation of the trail along a straight line from where the trail disappeared. Through openings in the vegetation you can see the vertical granite walls at the head of Bear Creek canyon. The water streaming down the rocks to the southwest is the seasonal outlet stream from Little Bear and Wee Bear lakes in their cirque behind a massive, glaciated granite ridge.

Steep to very steep trail traverses the canyonside southwest through willow and alder thickets where rills sometimes run down the tread. Wildflowers and water-loving plants are in abundance here, and parts of the trail are overgrown with brush, creating mental images of nineteenth-century explorers thrashing through the African bush. Beyond a small flat, shaded by large mountain hemlocks and western white pines, 4 miles from the trailhead, you emerge onto tilted slabs of bare granite. Bear Creek cascades 200 yards away to the south as you follow cairns along the right edge of the slabs up toward the lake. The trail then continues through low brush, crossing the outlet stream just below the lake itself.

Big Bear Lake, at 28 acres, is one of the larger Trinity Alps lakes. The near-vertical walls of the granite cirque which holds it rise directly from the water on three sides. Snowbanks can linger under the north-facing wall until August in some years. Heavy brush grows to the water's edge on the open, northeast side, accented by scattered white firs, Jeffrey pines, mountain hemlocks and western white pines. Campsites are jammed into the brush along the north shore close to the outlet and just above on a granite shoulder. Unless you are alone at the lake, privacy may be hard to come by. Fishing for eastern brook trout to 12 inches is best off the log jam at the outlet and off the steep, rocky shoreline around the east side.

Cross-Country Route to Wee Bear and Little Bear Lake

When contemplating the route to Wee Bear and Little Bear Lakes, the first temptation might be to travel around the eastern shore and ascend the broad gap up to the ridge. While you can get to the lakes this way, it is certainly not the easiest way.

The most direct route is to ascend the northeast ridge a short distance back down the canyon from the lake. Ascend granite benches east above the lakeshore campsites to game trails that crisscross through brush and lead to granite shelves above. The goal is to bisect the top of the ridge at approximately its midpoint near some dead trees. From the ridge you can see a notch about .5 mile away from which flows the outlet stream of Wee Bear Lake. The traverse to the notch is straightforward, although it may require some minor ups and downs along the way. Cairns periodically mark the route, but the route-finding is easy enough that you shouldn't depend on them. Views down Bear Creek canyon are quite nice along the length of your traverse. At the notch, you have arrived at Wee Bear Lake, which in contrast to Big and Little Bear lakes is not very dramatic. If you choose to camp here, rather than by the more spectacular lake above, there are certainly places to do so.

The route to Little Bear Lake requires little time or effort. Follow the lakeshore to the southeast end of Wee Bear Lake, where you cross the multibraided marshy area and an obvious trail ascends the west side of the creek flowing from Little Bear Lake. In no time at all you will reach the north shore.

Little Bear Lake seems to be just a smaller version of Big Bear Lake. The clear, cold waters are ringed on three sides by impressive granite cliffs, snowbanks linger here into late summer as well, and the trees are of the same type and arrangement. There are, however, two important differences between the two lakes: Little Bear Lake's eastern shore has fine campsites without the shrubby vegetation, and is populated by far fewer campers. The cross-country route necessary to reach Little Bear Lake will require an expenditure of time, but is not difficult, and has some great rewards. Fishing is claimed to be much better here than at Big Bear as well, probably due to less pressure.

On your return trip back down to the trail you'll get views of Mount Shasta capping the skyline directly above the long reach of the canyon below.

Cross-Country Route to Log Lake

The off-trail route north 1 mile to Log Lake is easy to see, but difficult to travel for one reason: The battle with brush is continuous and unrelenting! Before you give up on the prospect, you should realize that while we were camped at Big Bear Lake a group of junior-high kids from Camp Unalayee made the descent from Log Lake without incident. If there is a best way to Log Lake, it must be one that avoids the greatest amount of brush. Descend down the trail approximately one-quarter to one-half mile and then begin an angling ascent up to the obvious (although not always visible from below) saddle directly southeast of Log Lake. From the saddle, pick your way down to the lake, nestled in a delightful cirque. Camping is limited.

Trip 26

Tangle Blue Lake
(Tangle Blue Creek and Scott Summit Trailheads)

Trip Type: Day-hike or round trip of 2 to 3 days

Distance: 3.3 miles one way from Tangle Blue Creek trailhead or 6.5 miles from Scott Summit trailhead

Elevation Change: 940 feet from Tangle Blue Creek, 2310 feet from Scott Summit; average 285 and 355 feet per mile respectively

Season: Mid-June to mid-October

Topo Map: *Tangle Blue Lake* (provisional 1986) 7.5′ quadrangle

Who could resist a moderate 3.3 mile hike to a lake with such a charming name? Rumor has it that Tangle Blue Lake and Creek were named by an early resident who started his trip into the wilderness after a long night of celebrating, and found his feet tangled and the air blue. Whatever legend prompted the name, the lake is, if possible, even more charming than its name. The final approach is through a large, lush meadow leading up to the top of a dike above the lake's north shore where nearly ideal campsites nestle under large firs.

A lovely inlet creek tumbles down the rocks above the south shore, and then meanders through a riot of wildflowers in a wet meadow before running into the lake. Other smaller meadows alternate with rock ledges and brush around the rest of the shoreline. One can walk around the entire lake with comparative ease, and fish most of the shoreline. Fair-sized eastern brook trout and rainbows will test your skills.

Rugged pinnacles top the crests on the west, south and east sides of Tangle Blue Lake's basin where rock climbers and scramblers will find the views from the ridgetops quite rewarding. The lake itself offers excellent swimming for cooling off after the descent. As might be suspected, Tangle Blue Lake may not be the place to find large amounts of solitude, but with the recent relocation of the trailhead back down the road 1.5 miles some visitors may not find the hike quite as attractive as it once was. Groups of youths from nearby Camp Unalayee, located at Mosquito Lake, hike to Tangle Blue Lake with some regularity, but otherwise the lake gets less visitation than one might expect. Part of the reason is the difficulty in getting to the trailhead, as will be evident from the directions that follow. The other approach from Scott Summit is easy to find, and is a very pleasant walk, but is almost twice as long.

Starting Point

The place to begin the trip is the ranger station at Coffee Creek, where personnel should be able to give you updates on the condition of the road, and whether or not the sign along Highway 3 is in place. Unfortunately, vandals seem to covet the Tangle Blue Lake trailhead sign, making it somewhat difficult for first-time visitors to make the proper turn off the highway. Highway 3 turns northwest away from the upper Trinity River at a junction approximately 51 miles north of Weaverville, and begins to climb toward Scott Summit at the northeast corner of the Trinity Alps. A mile up the hill you cross Scott Mountain Creek on a steel-culvert-and-concrete bridge in the middle of a hairpin curve. The wide, dirt haul road that leads to the Tangle Blue Lake trailhead forks left from the next curve above the bridge. The sign, if it hasn't been stolen, reads "TANGLE BLUE LAKE, TRAILERS NOT ADVISED." Even if the sign is missing, the two support posts should still be there. If you come to a second bridge along Highway 3 across Scott Mountain Creek, you've gone .25 mile too far up the hill.

A steel gate 100 yards from the highway should be open, but once again vandals have been periodically closing the gate (although closed, the gate won't be locked). Report any missing signs or closed gates to the Forest Service at Coffee Creek. The road to the trailhead does pass over some private land. However, access to the trailhead is guaranteed, but please respect the rights of these private landholders.

The road, designated as Forest Service Road 39N20, climbs very steeply north beyond the gate for 200 yards before turning west across the side of Tangle Blue Creek canyon. If it has rained recently, you may not be able to make it up this hill, even in four-wheel drive. The road comes close to Tangle Blue Creek creek 1.2 miles from the highway, where you cross a seasonal creek, then turns north up the hill again. At 2.0 miles, Road 39N20A takes off to the right as we continue left on Road 39N20 as it traverses the side of the canyon far above Tangle Blue Creek. At about the high point of this traverse, 2.8 miles from Highway 3, road 39N59 forks to the right (north) up the hill. Staying to the left at this junction, you travel another .75 mile to the trailhead at a broad sweeping intersection 3.6 miles from Highway 3. The trailhead begins just beyond the ample parking area at a locked gate across the continuation of the roadway. A sign says "GRAND NATIONAL TRAIL, WILDERNESS BOUNDARY 1-1/2 MILES, TANGLE BLUE LAKE 4 MILES, MARSHY LAKES 4-1/2 MILES."

To get to Scott Summit trailhead, continue up Highway 3 to the summit, 56 miles from Weaverville, then look for Forest Service Road 40N63 turning west just over the summit and north of Scott Mountain campground. On 40N63 turn right at the first road fork below the top of the ridge, then left at the next fork to contour along the side of the ridge and up to a locked gate 3 miles from the highway.

Hikers at the crossing of Tangle Blue Creek just below Messner Cabin

Trip 26
Tangle Blue Lake

Description

From the Tangle Blue Lake trailhead your trail descends along the continuation of the roadbed one-eighth mile to the crossing of Tangle Blue Creek on a single-track steel-and-wood bridge. Beyond the creek, the roadbed switchbacks sharply uphill and after a short stretch switchbacks again. At this switchback a dirt road, not shown on the topo map, takes off along the creek, but the main road continues uphill to the right as proclaimed by a Forest Service road marker with an arrow and the word "TRAIL" on it. You continue along the old roadbed as it climbs alongside the creek, never straying more than a stone's throw away from the cascading waters. Continue northwest on the main road past a lesser road heading up Horse Creek that forks behind and to the left .5 mile from the trailhead.

At 1.5 miles you reach what used to be the trailhead. The Forest Service has wisely chosen to add this distance to the hike, possibly averting some of the pressure that a beautiful lake such as Tangle Blue would receive otherwise. Here you will find another locked gate, as well as a sign designating the wilderness boundary. Just 100 feet up the road yet another sign reads "TANGLE BLUE LAKE TRAIL, TANGLE BLUE LAKE 2-1/2 MILES, MARSHY LAKE 3 MILES," and "EAGLE CREEK DIVIDE 6 MILES." Another one-eighth mile brings you to a grassy flat where late starters could find some spots to camp next to the creek.

Farther up the sometimes dirt and sometimes rocky road, an old and overgrown roadbed leads up to what was once the Grand National Mine. As your trail continues on up the canyon, watch for a sign on a large incense cedar which reads "TRAIL." The road gradually leads to a crossing of Tangle Blue Creek, which shouldn't present any problems, with the possible exception of peak run-off during the height of snowmelt.

Beyond the crossing, the road trace disappears as a path follows the bank of the creek for awhile and then heads into mixed forest, made up of Douglas Firs, Incense Cedars and Sugar Pines. Where your path makes a switchback, you pick up the road once more and journey another .25 mile to where the road brings you to a path again, and then shortly leads to a wide wash full of large boulders and the crossing of the double channeled outlet stream from Marshy Lake. A steeply slanted foot-log can be used during high water to make this crossing.

The old road reappears on the opposite side of the creek and rises west for 250 yards to a junction and a set of signs, one which reads "TANGLE BLUE LAKE TRAIL 8W01, TANGLE BLUE LAKES" with an arrow pointing left, and "MARSHY LAKE" with an arrow pointing right. The other sign designates the road as "GRAND NATIONAL TRAIL 8W23." Your trail to Tangle Blue Lake runs south across a beautiful meadow, then turns east to cross Tangle Blue Creek. You climb past the ruins of Messner Cabin on the east bank, and begin a moderately steep climb to the south. Several small streams run across, and sometimes down, the rough tread as you climb through mixed forest and willow thickets. At .5 mile from Messner Cabin the trail enters the pleasant meadow below the lake, where you catch the first glimpse of the impressive cliffs that ring the lake basin. The ascent moderates as you approach the line of trees at the top of the meadow.

Excellent campsites with mortared rock fireplaces are under large white firs on the rim at the top of the meadow overlooking the lake. More campsites are located around a much smaller meadow west of the outlet. For those in search of more solitude, the south end of the lake offers some limited camping. Fishing is fair to good, and a path leads around the entire lake, but is muddy in spots and overgrown in others.

Scott Mountain Trailhead to Tangle Blue Lake

The description of the first 4 miles, from the trailhead to the Pacific Crest Trail crossing of Marshy Lakes road, is in Trip 27.

Continuing toward Marshy Lakes, the road circles a wet meadow, then winds southwest down to an unsigned junction beside Marshy Lakes outlet creek .8 mile from the PCT crossing. The little used road turning left to ford the creek is your route to Tangle Blue. The road to the right leads to a private inholding. A signed trail to Marshy Lakes and East Boulder Lake turns right, beyond the ford. The first sign marking "TANGLE BLUE TRAIL 8W01" is beside the Telephone Lake trail junction 150 yards further along this road.

You continue another .25 mile generally east and almost level through open forest, then turn north and drop to ford the creek again in a steep-sided gulch. Ignore a trail turning right to an old cabin before the road descends to the creek. Rough, narrow track snakes east down the north side of the gully, then makes a wide loop around a flat before recrossing the creek on an old log bridge 1.5 miles from the PCT. Another .5 mile of rough, unused road, steep in places, runs south around the point of a ridge, and down to the Tangle Blue Lake trail junction at the bottom of the meadow below Messner Cabin.

Trip 27

Pacific Crest Trail (Scott Mountain Summit to Carter Meadows Summit)

Trip Type: Through-trip of 3 to 5 days requiring a car-shuttle or pick-up

Distance: 18.4 miles; plus 1.6-mile side trip to Telephone Lake, and 1.3-mile trip to Upper South Fork Lake

Elevation Change: 6785 feet, average 369 feet per mile

Season: Early July to early October

Topo Maps: *Scott Mountain, Tangle Blue Lake, Billys Peak* and *Deadman Peak* (all provisional 1986) 7.5′ quadrangles

The 18 miles of the Pacific Crest Trail (PCT) within the Trinity Alps Wilderness are without question the newest and best 18 miles of trail in the area. Paradoxically, this stretch of trail gets less use than many of the other trails, despite being very scenic, easy hiking and close to a whole string of lakes.

One reason for the lack of traffic is that this section of trail is near the midpoint of the PCT, and only very serious PCT walkers, starting from either Canada or Mexico, get this far. Another reason is that this part of the PCT is a long drive from just about anywhere. Whatever the reasons, the lack of attention is wonderful for those who do choose to hike this section. It is a marvelous way to see the eastern part of the Trinity Alps.

The PCT comes within a mile of each of a beautiful series of lakes north of the Scott River crest. In order from east to west, they are: East Boulder, Middle Boulder, Telephone, West Boulder, Mavis, Fox Creek, Section Line, Virginia, and upper and lower South Fork lakes. Although many of these lakes are not described in this particular trip, they can all be easily reached from the PCT, along with Marshy and Mosquito lakes, located south of the Scott River crest.

Along with the potential for solitude, the PCT offers ridgecrest walking abounding in spectacular vistas including Mount Shasta, Lassen Peak and the central Trinity Alps peaks. Much of the trail is constructed to a relatively level grade through a variety of vegetative zones including meadows, chaparral and evergreen forests. You will have to descend into the various drainages to find decent campsites, but because of the individual attractions that the lakes have to offer, this can hardly be considered to be a drawback. Solitude, panoramic vistas and diversity make the PCT a very worthwhile undertaking.

Starting Point

You have a choice of trailheads from which to start. The recommended route begins at the Scott Mountain Campground just off Highway 3 at Scott Mountain Summit. This route is 4 miles longer than the alternative, but it is all on the well-graded Pacific Crest Trail. The other choice is to begin at the Mosquito Lake/Marshy Lake road and hike one-and-a-half miles from the Wilderness boundary along the dusty road to an intersection with the PCT. The terminus of your trip as described is at Carter Meadows Summit on Forest Highway 93.

There are only two reasons for walking down the Mosquito Lake/Marshy Lakes road from the saddle where the PCT crosses the road 2.1 miles down the southeast side of the ridge. The first is a spring running into a pool just below the road .6 mile from the saddle. An excellent campsite is beside the pool where a cabin once stood. The second reason for walking down the road would be to go to Mosquito Lake and Camp Unalayee. The camp is .4 mile up a moderately steep road that forks right from the main road 1.8 miles below the saddle. Mosquito Lake is .2 mile above the camp. Backpackers are welcome to visit Camp Unalayee, but overnight camping is discouraged since 75–80 young people and a staff of 25 adults are in the area. Mosquito is a gorgeous little lake, surrounded by meadows, but hardly worth fishing while camp is in session, June through August.

A good reason for not walking the road, in addition to most people's natural preference for good trail over dusty road, is that you might miss the PCT where it crosses the road .3 mile beyond the Mosquito Lake junction. Although the trail is signed where it crosses the road, it is not very obvious. If you cross the Mosquito Lake outlet creek on the road, you have gone past the PCT junction.

Scott Mountain Campground Trailhead: The Pacific Crest Trail crosses Highway 3 at the very top of Scott Summit, and continues west just north of Scott Mountain Campground. Park well off the highway, but not in the campground, and look for signs and emblems marking the trail where it crosses old roads between the campground and Forest Road 40N63 on the north side of the summit.

Mosquito Lake/Marshy Lakes Road Trailhead: Turn left (west) from Highway 3 immediately north of Scott Summit on Forest Road 40N63 and travel a locked gate, which presumably stops all vehicular traffic at the Wilderness boundary except for Forest Service vehicles, those of Camp Unalayee and a few private inholders. Park along the side of the road as space allows.

Carter Meadows Summit Trailhead: To locate the trailhead for the end of Trip 27 drive north from Scott Mountain Summit on Highway 3 to the small town of Callahan. Just beyond the town turn left onto Forest Highway 93, which heads toward Cecilville, Forks of Salmon and Somes Bar, leading 11.7 miles to Carter Meadows Summit. A sign as you approach the summit reads "PACIFIC CREST TRAIL, 1/4 MILE." As the highway curves, an unsigned dirt road on the left quickly leads to a parking area large enough for about 10 cars. The trailhead is obvious at the far edge of the parking area.

Description

From Mosquito Lake/Marshy Lakes Road: A pleasant 1.4 mile walk takes you from the gate up to a saddle on the ridge east of Black Rock. Along the way you look across a verdant upper valley of one of the forks of Mill Creek to the dark east face of 7486-foot Black Rock.

A sign on the right side of the road in the saddle indicates an old trail that runs down the north side of the ridge to Big Mill Creek. The PCT is just below a sign to the left of the road.

From Scott Mountain Campground: Beyond a flat the excellent trail makes two long switchbacks and one short one to the top of the first hump west on the ridge. You are apt to see more cow tracks than boot prints on the trail as you continue west through manzanita and open woods on the crest of the ridge. An unusual combination of sugar pines and lodgepole pines appears before you enter a sparse forest of red firs with a lot of windfalls in a saddle farther west.

Mountain mahogany, usually thought of as an eastern Sierra and Great Basin tree, grows on a rocky hump beyond more switchbacks. You cross over to the north side of the ridge in fir forest 2.7 miles from the trailhead, and come out into a near-clearcut that appears to have been logged 15–20 years ago. The wilderness boundary at the southwest edge of the logged area very effectively points up the difference between multiple use and wilderness as you enter red-fir forest again.

From the boundary you circle around the side of a mountain to turn southwest into a saddle 4 miles from the trailhead, where the PCT crosses the crest right beside, but not on, the Mosquito Lake/Marshy Lakes road.

Whichever way you get to the saddle, the Pacific Crest trail drops away from the road immediately after it touches it in the saddle. You won't see the road above the trail again until you cross it 2.1 miles farther on.

As you traverse an open, brushy slope southwest of the saddle, you have an excellent view across Tangle Blue Creek canyon to the jumble of peaks beyond, and Grand National Mine hanging on the side of a ridge. Lassen Peak juts above the horizon far to the east, and the "back" side of Castle Crags can be seen nearer and a little farther north.

Two little streams, crossing the trail .6 mile from the saddle, probably come from the spring up by the road, but grazing cattle have made them unappealing. Another, slightly larger rill a short distance farther on doesn't look any better where it crosses the trail, but it does water a large garden of California pitcher plants on the hillside above.

After rounding the shoulder of a ridge, you turn west to a crossing of the Marshy Lakes road, 2.1 miles from the saddle. A tiny stream, lined with pitcher plants, runs across a flat west of the road. Again, it doesn't look like very good drinking water. A much larger stream in a ravine 250 yards from the road does look like good drinking water, but you should keep in mind that it is the outlet of Mosquito Lake, where all the people are.

You continue on a level contour from Mosquito Lake creek to the shoulder of a ridge overlooking the upper end of Tangle Blue Creek canyon and the lower end of Marshy Lakes basin. The Marshy Lakes are not yet in sight. The Marshy Lakes road is directly below (see Trip 26), and you can see Tangle Blue Lake shimmering in its cirque farther south. Mount Shasta crowns the horizon back to the northeast.

The PCT rises gradually from the shoulder, heading generally west along the north side of the Marshy Lakes basin. A trail connecting Camp Unalayee and Marshy Lakes, marked only by cairns above and below the tread, crosses the PCT 1 mile from the road crossing, and runs straight on up the hillside.

First-class tread on the Pacific Crest Trail above Marshy Lakes

Another .5 mile along the side of the basin brings both Marshy Lakes into view below. Upper Marshy Lake is indeed surrounded by marshes.

A large amount of effort was expended in building the PCT along this steep sidehill. Large rocks have been moved to avoid steep detours. Brush has been cut back 3 feet on both sides of the tread. Where the trail crosses talus slides, the tread has been blasted, dug out and leveled, and dirt has been hauled in to cover the broken rock. It is a first-class trail. Time will tell whether it will be maintained as well as it was built.

Metasedimentary rock here is rosy red to rust-colored on the surface, but when broken is dark blue-gray to indigo, mixed with pieces of light blue and white.

As you turn southwest around the head of a basin, a trail from Marshy Lakes, marked by signs on a large tree, crosses the PCT on its way across the crest to East Boulder Lake. The crest is only 200 yards up the little-used trail, and East Boulder Lake is .6 mile down the north side. Even if you don't want to make a side trip all the way to the lake, going up to the crest to look at the wide open basin in which the lake sits is well worth your time. Three little ponds, surrounded by meadows as green as billiard-table felt, sit on a wide shelf one-quarter mile below the crest, and a long strip of grass runs up through red-rock strata almost to the crest farther west. Bordered by more meadows, 32-acre East Boulder Lake fills the lower end of the basin below a drop-off.

East Boulder Lake gets quite a lot of traffic from the north side because a road comes within 2 miles, but it still harbors some very large eastern brook, rainbow and brown trout. The only drawback to this otherwise delightful basin can be the large number of cattle that sometimes graze in it.

The central Trinity Alps from the Pacific Crest Trail

The PCT continues its contour around the head of the Marshy Lakes basin through rough terrain behind some knobs and across the face of the cliffs where the tread has been blasted out of the rock. A beautiful little spring trickles down the rocks beside the trail .3 mile from the East Boulder Lake trail, the first water that looks safe since leaving the trailhead.

At the end of the contour around the basin, you are headed almost east, and then you climb moderately south to the top of the spur ridge between Marshy Lakes and Eagle Creek canyon, 7 miles from the trailhead at the locked gate. The trail turns west from this crest to ascend moderately across another spur ridge and along the side of the main ridge through brush, open forest and talus slides. Several small ponds are on a wide bench .25 mile below the trail, offering a good place to camp if you want to stop now.

After rounding the shoulder of another spur ridge, you come to a trail junction right on top of the Scott River divide, 2.4 miles from the East Boulder Lake trail junction. The trail north from here goes down the divide slope to Middle Boulder Lake, and the PCT now follows most of the course of an old trail that ran southwest down to the divide between Eagle Creek and Granite Creek. A trace of the old trail drops below the PCT as it turns southwest from the Scott River summit, but it doesn't go anywhere.

Middle Boulder Lake is a repeat of East Boulder Lake on a smaller scale. Two little ponds are on a bench just below the summit, and Middle Boulder Lake is almost a mile below them. The basin isn't as big, nor is it as verdant. Middle Boulder Lake, despite what the Forest Service Trinity Alps Wilderness map indicates, is inside the boundaries of Trinity Alps Wilderness.

You descend from this divide through a forest of foxtail pines that changes to red firs as you go farther down the side of the ridge. The trail skirts the edges of two meadows, then rises slightly and runs straight across a third meadow where you look up at 7790-foot Eagle Peak. The trail to Telephone Lake is in the trees along the upper, southwest edge of this meadow. The junction with it .4 mile from the Middle Boulder trail is not obvious, but it is signed.

Side Trip to Telephone Lake

The Telephone Lake trail northwest from the PCT is not hard to follow, once you've found it. A cairn in the edge of the meadow and blazed trees mark where it turns west to zigzag up the hill away from the meadow. Look for blazes on large foxtail pines at the upper edge of a small meadow higher up the hill, and they will lead you to the crest of the divide .25 mile above the PCT. West of the crest the trail drops very steeply to a heavily grazed meadow, then turns more northwestward to descend steeply again not far from the little stream that drains the meadow.

As you come out on top of a low ridge running north and south .4 mile from the crest, look for the lake off to the east. Telephone Lake is an irregularly shaped, 3.5 acre pothole lake with no outlet and no permanent inlet. The water level fluctuates 3–4 feet during the summer. A little bay at the north end, separated from the rest of the lake, gets warm enough for good swimming by late summer, and large rainbow trout rise occasionally.

Just beyond the Telephone Lake junction, the PCT passes a junction with a trail heading down to Eagle Creek and then descends around the southeast side of Eagle Peak, mostly in thick fir forest. A fair-sized creek flows across the trail in a mass of alders .5 mile from the junction. No cattle graze on this hillside, and the stream may look good enough to drink, but just beyond it a fine spring that looks even better flows from an iron pipe just above the trail. A fair campsite is below the trail beyond the spring, where a miner's cabin once stood.

Another spring, a quarter mile farther on, is piped through a piece of old, riveted, sheet-iron mining pipe. You climb a little from this spring to a very obvious trail junction, where the old trail, signed "BLOODY RUN TRAIL, EAGLE PEAK DIVIDE," turns left away from the PCT down to the divide at the head of Eagle Creek. A major trail crossing with signs is 100 yards down this old trail from the PCT. Trail 7W05 down Eagle Creek (Trip 28) turns left (east), and Wolford Cabin and Granite Creek are to the right (west).

The PCT continues making an ascending traverse along the south ridge of Eagle Peak to an open saddle on the top of the divide. A small rock knob east of the saddle presents a perfect opportunity to quickly climb to its summit and take in the magnificent views, north down the West Boulder Creek drainage, south across to the central Trinity Alps peaks, and west to Lassen Peak. For the more adventurous, it is possible to make the 475-foot climb, through low open brush, up the ridge to the top of Eagle Peak, where the views are even better.

A short descent culminates at another saddle on the ridgetop above the West Boulder Creek canyon. Campsites and water are available down in the pastoral canyon, but since there are no trails you will have to go cross-country to get there and back. Another mountainside traverse, beginning in open vegetation, then entering fir forest, crosses a lush creek and comes to the trail junction to Mavis Lake and Wolford Cabin in yet another saddle along the top of the ridge, 1.2 miles from the previous saddle.

The PCT contours around another unnamed peak, breaks out of the forest briefly into manzanita as the trail rounds a spur ridge, and then makes a long descending traverse to a three-channeled tributary branch of Granite Creek, 1.7 miles from the Mavis Lake/Wolford Cabin trail junction. Then 1.2 miles of traverse take you around another ridge and over to an open saddle where you encounter the junction for the trail down Saloon Creek to the North Fork Coffee Creek trail.

The PCT crosses over the crest to the north side of the Scott Divide, heading downhill and following an old roadbed as you bid farewell to the last of the views toward the central Trinity Alps peaks. In .2 mile you reach a junction with the Noland Gulch trail, where the old roadbed continues on toward the site of the abandoned Loftus Mine, as your trail, the newer, better-defined, PCT trends slightly uphill through the head of a meadow basin strewn with wildflowers and rimmed with rock cliffs. Cresting a ridge, you begin to round the head of the next basin and descend to the crossing of the east branch of the South Fork Scott River, 1.1 miles from the junction with the trail to Noland Gulch. A spring just a short distance upstream, gives birth to this lovely watercourse, which should be a reliable source of water for the thirsty hiker.

From the crossing you descend along and then away from the water .8 mile to a trail junction in a lush green meadow filled with wildflowers. To the right (north) is the trail to South Fork Meadows and to the left (south) is the trail to the two South Fork Lakes.

Side Trip to South Fork Lakes

The route to the lakes is short but quite steep. You begin the ascent amidst lush underbrush and below tall firs, and in .2 mile you reach a small basin with a steep rock headwall that rises straight up from the basin floor. A single campsite is at the near edge of this basin, quite suitable for those not interested in continuing the arduous ascent up to the lakes. For those who do go on, the trail proceeds through some tall grass, winds along the stream and quickly crosses over it. The route bends sharply uphill and then abruptly traverses to the right (northwest) through tall, dense vegetation past many seeps and creeklets flowing down from the springs above. A series of switchbacks face you now, and a last long switchback deposits you at the top of a rise where the trail mercifully levels out. From this point it is just a short distance to lower South Fork Lake.

Lower South Fork Lake is a pleasant but uninspiring little lake. Plenty of the necessities for camping exist here in abundance, but the extra effort required to reach the upper lake is well worth it. To reach the upper lake, travel around the lower lake to the inlet stream. Follow the trail along the right (west) side of the inlet stream .1 mile to the north shore of the upper lake.

Upper South Fork Lake is more picturesque than its lower neighbor with a steep slope that rises up out of the opposite shore leading to rock cliffs above. The abundant vegetation along the shoreline may slightly hinder your ability to enjoy the views or to fish the waters, but it is certainly possible to do both of those with a little effort. Rainbows up to 15 inches and smaller eastern brook trout test your skills. Camping is limited to the excellent sites along the northeast shore near the outlet. The fir-and-hemlock forest surrounding the lake provide adequate firewood.

From the trail junction to South Fork Lakes your descent on the PCT continues west until you cross the west branch of the South Fork of the Scott River. As the trail climbs away from the creek, you cross another smaller stream with wildflowers lining its banks, and the last long ascent continues to the trailhead. The PCT climbs almost a mile northwest from the west branch of the South Fork to a junction with the trail to Hidden Lake right below the Carter Meadows Summit parking area.

Trip 28

Eagle Creek

Trip Type: One way trip of 1 to 2 days

Distance: 8.5 miles

Elevation Change: 3430 feet, 404 feet per mile

Season: Early July to late September

Topo Maps: *Tangle Blue Lake* and *Billys Peak* (both provisional 1986) 7.5′
quadrangles

Upper Eagle Creek is one of the more remote areas in the eastern Trinity Alps. Chances are you will see many more cows than people along this route as cows do graze in a number of the beautiful meadows on the floor of the upper canyon and on Eagle Creek Benches south of the upper canyon. In spite of the grazing, which certainly isn't as heavy as in some other areas of the Alps, the meadows show a marvelous display of wildflowers in midsummer. Although you may see cows periodically, they shouldn't be present in large enough numbers to severely detract from your wilderness experience.

Farther down Eagle Creek, you will see effects of the big fire of 1987. A large part of the burn was in heavy brush, and revegetation has been rapid. Beyond the burn, you walk through a magnificent climax forest of firs, sugar pines and Jeffrey pines. Fishing in lower Eagle Creek is good for native rainbow trout.

If solitude, beautiful meadows, climax forest and good fishing sound attractive, you should take this hike—if you can reach the trailhead. Due to the heavy winter of '92–93 myriad trees blew down like scattered toothpicks across the Horse Flat campground and access road, making vehicular traffic too dangerous to allow. Physically, the removal of downed timber presents a minor problem. Bureaucratically, however, it becomes a much bigger obstacle. While the Forest Service waits for a ruling from a judge as to whether they can sell the fallen timber, the trailhead remains out of reach. If they can't sell the downed trees, some other solution (money) will have to be found. One season has already gone by without access to the campground or the trailhead, but hopefully, yet another season won't pass before this situation is resolved. Nonetheless, check with the Forest Service at Coffee Creek or Weaverville on the status of the trailhead before heading out on this trip.

The first decision you will need to make regarding this trip is from which route you will approach the trail, since this particular trail description begins not at a trailhead parking lot but out in the wilderness. A wide array of alternatives, each with its own appeal, are available for reaching (by foot) the head of the trail in upper Eagle Creek canyon.

Starting Point

The Eagle Creek trailhead (at the end of this trail description) is located at the Horse Flat Campground on Eagle Creek. To get there, start from the Coffee Creek junction 40 miles north of Weaverville and drive another 4.7 miles north on Highway 3 to a road turning left at a sign that says "CAMPGROUND." A sign for "EAGLE CREEK CAMPGROUND" is beside the road as soon as you turn off, but it can't be seen from the highway. Do not turn at the "EAGLE CREEK LODGE" sign, 2 miles south on Highway 3.

Your narrow, paved road crosses the Trinity River on a one lane bridge, then turns north not far from the river. You come to a bridge over Eagle Creek 1.2 miles from the highway. Keep left past the Eagle Creek Campground just beyond the bridge, and you will find a sign for the Eagle Creek trail near the upper end of the campground. Another sign identifies the road as 38N27.

A rough, narrow road climbs west up the north side of Eagle Creek canyon. At a fork 3.3 miles from Highway 3 you turn right up the hill through delightful Horse Flat campground in a climax forest of Douglas firs, Jeffrey pines and incense cedars. The trailhead is on the west side of a turnaround above the campground. Plenty of parking is available on the sides of the loop.

Eagle Creek and Horse Flat campgrounds are by far the best National Forest campgrounds (as distinguished from Recreation Area fee camps) on the east side of the Trinity Alps Wilderness. Eagle Creek Campground has piped water and garbage pickup, and charges a fee. Horse Flat campground provides no services, and is free.

Description

There are many different options for arriving at the upper end of the Eagle Creek trail. The original trail description from previous editions of this guidebook was a through-trip beginning at Scott Mountain Summit, following the Pacific Crest Trail to the intersection with the Eagle Creek trail (Trip 27). Another viable route is the trail from Tangle Blue and Marshy Lakes (Trip 26). The shortest car shuttle, providing the access road is open, would be to begin your hike from the Stoddard Lake trailhead, passing through Stoddard Meadows and Doe Flat to the Eagle Creek trail. Careful examination of the maps will reveal even more possibilities. Perhaps the easiest, although least interesting, way would be to hike the Eagle Creek trail to its end and then retrace your steps, following this description, to the trailhead.

Whichever route you choose to reach the Eagle Creek trail 7W05, the description begins 100 yards south of the Pacific Crest Trail, (.4 mile directly south of Eagle Peak on the *Billys Peak* quadrangle) at the four-way signed intersection with trails running west to Wolford Cabin, south to Doe Flat and north back to the PCT. The beginning of the trail as it heads east is not very propitious. After diving down the side of the ridge in thick woods, it disappears in a meadow. You can find it again by heading directly toward Mount Shasta on the distant northeast horizon. Infrequent blazes and a few ducks guide you down a steeper meadow below as you turn north toward the beginnings of Eagle Creek. Do not cross the creek here. The trail you see leading up to the forest on the other side of the creek goes over the ridge to the northeast and down to the Marshy Lakes/Tangle Blue Lake trail.

The Eagle Creek trail disappears in a maze of cattle tracks, but you should stay on the south side of the creek for another .5 mile. Pick out the best track you can find, staying away from the creek and heading generally east across a small spur ridge and through three heavily grazed meadows before turning north to cross Eagle Creek. If you are lucky, your crossing will be at the bottom of a large, wet meadow on the north side of the creek, and a semideveloped campsite will be above the creek to your right. If your crossing turns out to be above or below the campsite, you will have to reconnoiter until you find it or the Eagle Creek trail, which is fairly obvious in the meadows below the campsite on the north side of the creek. The trail runs among large firs 100 feet north of the campsite.

If you want to do some off-trail exploring, try Eagle Creek Benches, an area of forests, wildflower-filled meadows and ponds above the south side of the creek.

The next 1.5 miles of trail down the canyon wander through meadows and open forest north of Eagle Creek. Many excellent campsites are between the trail and the creek. Few people visit this part of the canyon, but a lot of cows graze here for two or three months each summer. As you enter the dense white-fir forest 2.5 miles from the junction, the canyon closes in and turns directly south. Another .5 mile brings you onto a step slope far above the creek. This area, formerly covered with thick, tall brush, was completely burned off by the forest fire of 1987. Very hot fire ran almost to the top of the ridge to the east, completely burning patches of forest as well as the brush, until it was slowed in the bare rock near the crest. You will be amazed, however, by how rapidly the vegetation has recovered.

Unless some work has been done since the summer of 1989, this steep piece of trail is in very bad shape. Some of the trail was dug out as a fire line, and the steeper pitches are severely washed out. The tread improves after you work your way down .7 mile of boulders and ruts, and the effects of the fire are not as obvious as you get closer to the creek. Lightning strikes started the fire on the ridge to the west. As you descend moderately on the east side of the creek, you can easily see the course of the fire down Bloody Run Gulch across the way. Only patches of forest burned here on the east side, and most of the mature trees survived. Within a few more years, to tell that this area had ever been burned will be nearly impossible.

A number of good campsites are on the benches beside Eagle Creek as the floor of the canyon levels a bit. Careful fishing will reward you with a panful of native trout to 8 or 9 inches long.

You soon leave signs of the fire behind as the canyon turns more southeast. Douglas fir dominates the mature forest, and head-high ferns crowd the good trail in moist spots as you descend moderately, well away from the creek again. Just beyond a stand of black oaks on a steep hillside 100 yards above the creek, you come to the Wilderness boundary 5.4 miles from the PCT junction. Even without the signs posted here, you know almost immediately that you're leaving the Wilderness. You step out of virgin forest into a logged-over flat and, directed by "TRAIL" signs on steel posts, soon find yourself on a graded and graveled haul road. A parallel road runs to the boundary line on the other side of the canyon. Besides providing easy walking, the only good thing to be said about this road is that it doesn't seem to be open to public vehicle traffic.

At a junction 1.5 miles down the road, keep right for another quarter-mile to a log-loading flat where the trail, marked by a steel-stake trail sign, turns up the hill to the left. You climb steeply for 50 yards, then turn to contour southeast again through beautiful mixed forest that now includes ponderosa and sugar pines. After detouring into two deep ravines to cross little creeks shaded by dogwoods and big-leaf maples, you descend moderately steeply across a dry hillside where canyon oaks appear for the first time on the way down the canyon.

About 8 miles from the PCT junction you come close to the creek pouring through a wide bed of boulders, then climb up the side of the canyon again to where a creek falls over a concrete wall just above the trail. This was part of the water system (no longer functioning) for Horse Flat campground. The trailhead is .2 mile ahead and 8.5 miles from the PCT junction at the upper end of Eagle Creek canyon.

Trip 29

Mavis, Fox Creek and Virginia Lakes

Trip Type: Day-hike or round trip of 2 or 3 days

Distance: 4.7 miles one way to Virginia Lake

Elevation Change: 1460 feet, average 311 per mile

Season: Early July to mid-October

Topo Map: *Billys Peak* (provisional 1986) 7.5' quadrangle

You spend more time driving than walking to get to this gorgeous trio of lakes (see the description of access to the north-side trailheads in Chapter 2). That's not all bad, however—it tends to prevent overcrowding. Even Mavis Lake, the easiest to reach from both north and south sides, isn't usually overpopulated if you don't count cows. The cows don't often get up to Virginia Lake, and neither do most of the people.

All three lakes have meadows around at least part of their shorelines, and are in wider, more open basins than many of the Trinity Alps lakes. All three have excellent campsites, but the number of cattle in the area should persuade you to purify the water before drinking it.

Fishing is good-to-excellent in all three lakes. The catch will probably be pan-sized eastern brook trout, but an occasional lunker brown, left over from a long-ago planting, may thrill you in Mavis or Fox Creek Lake. Mavis Lake warms up first, but even Virginia Lake is usually warm enough for a dip by mid-August.

A solid stand of mountain hemlock cloaks the north side of the Scott River divide above Mavis Lake.

Starting Point

You first have to get to Callahan. Consult your road map, Klamath National Forest map and Chapter 2 of this book to find out how best to do that.

Once you've gotten to Callahan, look for a road turning south just west of the East Fork Scott River bridge. It turns off before you get to the general store on the north side of the main street. This road, or street, becomes Forest Road 40N16 as you drive through the upper part of town, and you will find signs for McKeen Divide and Bolivar Lookout at the first junction above the town. You continue toward McKeen Divide.

If you can't find Forest Road 40N16, or if you are coming from Cecilville, look for forest Road 40N17 turning east off the Cecilville road 1 mile south of Callahan. It crosses the South Fork Scott River, and angles up the hill to meet 40N16 at a four-way intersection where you keep right toward McKeen Divide. The road turning east from the intersection goes to Bolivar Lookout.

You keep left on 40N17 at a signed junction on McKeen Divide 2 miles farther up. A number of side roads branch off below and above McKeen Divide, but the main road is obvious. It is a good, graveled road with only a few one-way stretches. Forest Road 39N10, signed "EAST BOULDER LAKE," turns left up the hill 3 miles above McKeen Divide. A sign for Mavis Lake points the way right on 40N17. A corral beside Boulder Creek .2 mile farther on marks the trailhead for Middle Boulder Lake, Telephone Lake and Eagle Creek.

You cross Wolf Creek 7 miles from Callahan, and climb steeply .5 mile to the signed Mavis Lake/Fox Creek Lake trailhead on the point of a spur ridge. Parking is off the road to the right where it turns left around the point toward Fox Creek.

Description

A steep pitch of 50 yards takes you from the south side of the road to the top of the ridge, where the trail ascends south at a moderate to moderately steep rate on the ridgecrest. You cross the Wilderness boundary .6 mile from the trailhead. The forest of Douglas fir, white fir, sugar pine and Jeffrey pine has been

Traffic is not a big problem in Callahan

selectively logged up to the old Primitive Area boundary 1.2 miles from the trailhead. The post for the sign that once marked the boundary now holds only a small, battered, bullet-ridden, metal sign proclaiming "CLOSED TO MOTOR VEHICLES." A small stream trickles down a gully east of the trail.

The orange metal markers with a black diagonal between two dots that you see nailed 12 feet up trees beside the trail mark a snow-gauging course.

At 1.5 miles the spur ridge you have been climbing merges into a large mountain. The trail makes a jog west, then continues to climb south across a west-facing slope. About 2 miles from the trailhead you come out of forest into a sloping meadow full of angelica and other flowers. An alder patch in the meadow has two small springs in it, but they may be dried up by late summer.

Beyond the meadow, the trail levels off through open white-fir forest for .5 mile to a little alder-lined creek. Delphiniums bloom beside the crossing, and a good campsite is in a grove of firs on the north side. Now you climb again to a trail junction 2.8 miles from the trailhead. Old signs here are confusing. The left fork actually goes to the top of the divide and a junction with the Pacific Crest Trail (see Trip 9); the right fork goes to Mavis and Fox Creek lakes.

The junction of the trails to the two lakes is marked by a sign on the ground 300 yards west—Mavis Lake to the left, Fox Creek Lake to the right. You climb a short pitch on the left fork, then level out past the east shore of a lily pond. Beyond a tiny stream you climb southwest over a moraine ridge, then drop down to the northeast shore of 3.5-acre Mavis Lake .4 mile from the last junction. The 3 miles of trail to Mavis Lake are in good condition despite moderately heavy horse and cattle use.

Mavis Lake is surrounded by a thick forest of firs, mountain hemlocks and lodgepole pines behind a narrow border of boulders and grass, except where meadows run down to the south shore. Good campsites are beside the trail as it approaches the northeast shore. A campsite with a built-up fireplace and sawed blocks for seating is by a tiny inlet stream too close to the southeast shore. Excellent campsites are on a ledge above the west shore. Enough firewood is

Fox Creek Lake is surrounded by meadows

available for years to come if we all use it conservatively. Trees around the shoreline make fly-fishing difficult, but there are plenty of fish.

From the junction below Mavis Lake, the trail to Fox Creek Lake contours west. You stay above an alder thicket and a wet meadow, then cross two alder-choked stream courses. The second one has a larger and cleaner stream of water than the first. Good trail turns northwest around a large hump of granite, then descends the side of a wide valley before turning southwest. A quarter-mile of moderate ascent along the side of the valley ends at the southeast shore of Fox Creek Lake, .8 mile from the Mavis Lake junction. The old trail shown on the *Coffee Creek* quadrangle coming up Fox Creek crosses the outlet creek (Fox Creek) 200 yards northwest. If you can find it, you can make a loop back that way, but it is not as good a trail as the ridge trail you came up. The trail from Fox Creek Lake up to the divide, also shown on the *Coffee Creek* quadrangle, does not exist on the ground. Careful study of the topo map will show you a 1-mile off-trail route to Section Line Lake if you want to explore.

More than twice as big as Mavis Lake, 9.5-acre Fox Creek Lake has wet meadows that are, unfortunately, subject to heavy cattle grazing around the entire shoreline. Thick forest covers the sides of the wide basin above the meadows except on the west side, where a rock face rises to a ridge. A ring of lily pads 25–50 feet offshore makes fishing difficult around the east and south shores. Better fishing is off rocks at the west end, but be careful not to hook a cow with your backcast.

Good-to-excellent campsites are above the north shore west of the outlet. A number of campsites near the end of the trail and around the south shore are much too close to the lake. Water obviously should be purified.

Although no trail is shown on the *Coffee Creek* quadrangle between Fox Creek Lake and Virginia Lake, a use trail of sorts, probably developed more by deer and cattle than by humans, does connect the two lakes. The .9-mile route begins above a path of alders at the north west corner of the lake, and runs up a gully to a saddle in the ridge west of the lake. You follow another gully from the top of the saddle, southwest up the other side of the ridge to a granite shelf where ducks mark the way to the floor of a wide, heavily forested valley. Continue to climb moderately southwest, then south, between dense forest and a steep slope littered with large granite boulders. You keep to the east of an alder thicket, a wet meadow and another alder thicket farther up the valley, then look for ducks marking the final, steep, quarter-mile climb almost southeast through big boulders to the shore of the lake just east of its outlet.

Although Virginia Lake is in a deep cirque close to the top or the divide, it has grass and meadows around its shoreline, backed up by dense forest of red firs, mountain hemlocks, lodgepole pines and western white pines. Labrador tea grows at the edge of the trees. It is a beautiful little 3-acre lake, more nearly pristine than the other two lakes, since cattle seldom get to it.

Only a few poor-to-fair campsites are up in the rocks east of the lake, but you can find plenty of good sites in the valley below if you decide to stay for a day or two. Fishing is excellent for pan-sized eastern brook trout.

Trip 30

Trail Gulch,
Long Gulch Loop

Trip Type: Loop trip of 2 to 4 days or day-hike to either lake

Distance: 9.3 miles for the complete loop if you stay on trail and include .9 mile on the road between trailheads

Elevation Change: 5410 feet, average 582 feet per mile

Season: Early June to early October

Topo Map: *Deadman Peak* (provisional 1986) 7.5′ quadrangle

There are two good reasons for making this trip—Long Gulch Lake and Trail Gulch Lake at the heads of their respective gulches. Those "gulches" are actually very pleasant valleys. The lakes are virtual twins, nestled in spectacular cirques beneath crenelated peaks that rise more than 1200 feet from lake level. The south shorelines of both lakes are bare rock and talus, but forests of red firs and mountain hemlocks interrupted here and there by meadows and willows, surround the rest of the shorelines.

These two beautiful lakes were just outside of the old Salmon-Trinity Alps Primitive Area. They were, happily, included in the Trinity Alps Wilderness when it was created.

Extensive meadows offer forage near both lakes and help to make them popular with equestrians as well as hikers, but they still get far fewer visitors than, for example, Caribou Basin. Many campsites, spread over a large area north of each lake, can accommodate a fairly large number of people without undue crowding.

Fishing is fair to good for rainbow trout in both lakes, and swimming is delightful by mid-August.

The names of the two "gulches" are a bit misleading—Long Gulch Lake is actually 1.4 miles closer to its trailhead than is Trail Gulch Lake. You can cut a little off the distance between the two lakes on the loop trip by making an off-trail traverse along the crest of the divide above North Fork Coffee Creek instead of following the trails down south of the crest and back up, but you will find the off-trail traverse very rough going.

Starting Point

As in Trip 26, you start from Callahan, but that's only the start. Take the Cecilville road, paved Forest Highway 93, south from Callahan approximately 11.5 miles to Carter Meadows Summit. This is the divide between the Scott River and Salmon River drainages, and also the point where the Pacific Crest Trail crosses the highway.

Forest Road 39N08 turns sharply left from the highway .7 mile toward Cecilville from the summit. The junction is not signed on the highway, but you will see a sign soon after you turn off. The good, gravel road circles the head of upper Carter Meadow, then turns west and south to cross Long Gulch Creek 1.7 miles from the highway. The Long Gulch trailhead is just west of the bridge. An undesignated car camp is in a grove of trees beside the creek.

To get to the Trail Gulch trailhead, continue west on Forest Road 39N08 around the shoulder of a ridge .9 mile to a fork in the road on the east side of Trail Gulch Creek. The trailhead is on the south side of the left road fork, 50

Hikers' gentians grow in this meadow in Long Gulch

yards west of the junction, and still east of the creek. A sign for Trail Gulch is at the junction. The trailhead has no trail sign.

If you are coming up Forest Highway 93 east from Cecilville, you can find the west end of Forest Road 39N08 at the entrance to Trail Creek campground, approximately 14 miles from Cecilville. A sign for Fish Lake, Trail Gulch and Long Gulch trailheads is at the junction beside the campground.

You keep left at a junction .3 mile above the campground, and continue east beside a creek and through Carter Meadows 2.9 miles to the junction beside the Trail Gulch trailhead. The Long Gulch trailhead is .9 mile east.

Description

You follow an old road trace south from the Long Gulch trailhead up the west side of a wide valley. Keep right past two forks and into a grove of mature Douglas firs .6 mile from the trailhead. We hope no one is getting up this far with a vehicle now, but an old sign at the edge of a 4–5-acre meadow beyond the trees pleads "PLEASE DO NOT DRIVE OR CAMP ON MEADOWS." Whatever, the road trace disappears here and you follow a foot trail southeast across the meadow, then up through alders beside a creek before you cross it to the east side.

More alders and a flower-decked meadow are beyond the crossing. Hiker's gentian is one of the many flowers beside the trail. You cross the Wilderness Area boundary and climb more steeply as you enter red-fir forest 1 mile from the trailhead, then cross another creek flowing from the east side of the valley at 1.3 miles. Turn right at a junction a quarter mile farther on, from where the left fork climbs to the divide. You climb more gradually past a large alder thicket to meadows beside the outlet creek from Long Gulch Lake, then turn west across the creek 1.8 miles from the trailhead and rise slightly into the large camping area on a flat above the lake's north shore.

Descriptions of Long Gulch Lake, Trail Gulch Lake and the trails between the two lakes are in Trip 11 in the reverse direction.

From the outlet of Trail Gulch Lake, a fair trail leads west .3 mile through forest an broken rock to a junction with a trail that comes over the divide from South Fork Coffee Creek (see Trip 11), and goes north down Trail Gulch. Good trail descends north from the junction, in thick forest, then turns northwest to go around a large alder patch at the head of a heavily grazed meadow. At the lower end of the meadow the trail continues north on an old road trace, now badly washed out. The descent through open forest and small meadows is moderate, with some steeper pitches.

A grove of quaking aspen appears on the other (east) side of Trail Gulch Creek 1.5 miles from the South Fork Coffee Creek junction. Some apparent junctions along this part of the trail are really splits in the trail that come back together farther along. Just beyond the Wilderness boundary, 2 miles from the South Fork Coffee Creek junction, you cross to the east bank of the creek. Another .8 mile north, descending moderately through ferns and young firs, brings you to the Trail Gulch trailhead, 3.1 miles from Trail Gulch Lake.

Trip 31

China Creek to Grizzly Lake

Trip Type: Round trip of 2 to 5 days

Distance: 7 miles one way

Elevation Change: 5540 feet, average 791 feet per mile

Season: Mid-July to late September

Topo Map: *Thompson Peak* 1979 7.5′ quadrangle

This is the short way to Grizzly Lake. To come up with any other reason for beginning a pack trip with the grueling, dry climb over the Salmon River divide from China Creek is difficult. The only good thing you can say about the climb is that there is shade on the north side of the divide. Coming back is something else—you should get an early start to avoid climbing the brushy south slope under the afternoon sun.

The popularity of this route seems to have grown exponentially in recent years. During an August weekend in 1993 there were over 30 vehicles and 2 horse trailers strung out along the shoulder of the gravel road for quite a distance. Apparently, there are many backcountry travelers who don't mind a tough climb or a long drive. Don't expect to be alone during weekends in peak season. Unfortunately, there is no guarantee of solitude in the middle of the week either.

Grizzly Lake, Grizzly Meadows and the high country around the highest summit in the Trinity Alps, Thompson Peak, are good enough reasons for a little torture in order to get there sooner, but if you have the time, the North Fork Trinity River approach to Grizzly Lake is much more pleasant. Also, unless you're coming from Oregon, the driving time to the Hobo Gulch trailhead is considerably less than to China Creek.

The descriptions of upper Grizzly Creek, Grizzly Meadows, Grizzly Lake and beyond are in Trip 17.

Trip 31
China Creek to Grizzly Lake

Starting Point

Travel west on Forest Highway 93 (Callahan/Cecilville Road) for 1.4 miles northeast of the small town of Cecilville and turn left (south) on the unsigned South Fork road that serves the East Fork Campground. This junction is 4.5 miles west of the Shadow Creek Campground. The East Fork Campground is beside the road just before you cross the East Fork Salmon River bridge.

The paved South Fork road wanders south through old dredge piles and brush 3.7 miles before turning to cross to the west bank of the South Fork. A four-way intersection is 100 yards from the bridge. The left fork goes to ranches and trailheads on up the South Fork Salmon River. The middle road is your road, Forest Service Road 37N07 to China Creek. The right fork heads back to Cecilville. A half mile farther up, another road forks to the right leading only to a log deck. Forest Road 37N07 winds around a ridge and up a canyon generally southwest to a junction, 2.3 miles from the intersection.

Turn right from the junction on the continuation of Forest Road 37N07 across the ridge through a cut. You pass two more road forks as you wind up the hill. Follow the 37N07 sign straight ahead at the first one, and keep left at the next fork, where signs will guide your way. As you come around the east side of a ridge, spectacular views of the South Fork Canyon, Packers Peak and Caribou Mountain open up ahead.

Forest Road 37N07 has good gravel surface all the way up the hill, but some of it is one-lane with turnouts. Cross China Creek 5.6 miles from the South Fork road, and .3 mile farther on, signs mark the trailhead. Park along the outside shoulder of the road, and fill your water bottles back at the creek. A hard, dry climb is ahead.

Description

The trail starts by climbing straight up the bank on the uphill side of the road. Steep and very steep tread zigzags up through madrones and ponderosa pines to a thick stand of Douglas firs farther west. The climb moderates a bit as you double back over the nose of the ridge you are climbing, then becomes steep and very steep again, headed south. The forest changes to predominantly white fir, still very dense, in the next mile as you switch from one side of the ridge to the other three more times. You may notice evidence of the 1987 fire that burned some areas of the canyon.

On a long switchback leg west, then one southeast, you climb to the top of a knob approximately 1 mile from the trailhead, and then the ascent eases again, headed south. More switchbacks take you to the flat summit of the divide 1.2 miles from the trailhead. The trail has been rebuilt, and relocated slightly from the route shown on the *Thompson Peak* 7.5' quadrangle. Although the trail is heavily used, and may be quite dusty, it is in good condition up to the summit. A few dry campsites are on the summit.

Old, deeply worn trail leads southwest off the summit. Then newer trail continues southwest, instead of turning south down the hill past Hunters Camp and China Spring as shown on the *Thompson Peak* quadrangle. Hunters Camp and China Spring are 100 yards down the hill from the crest and 50 yards east of the trail.

Some giant ponderosa pines are beside the trail one-quarter mile below the summit. You have good views from the more open hillside across to Thompson Peak and the snowfield on its north side. Rougher trail soon turns more southward and zigzags steeply and very steeply down through thick brush and sparse forest to a junction with the Grizzly Creek trail, 2.5 miles from the China Creek trailhead. A most welcome, clear, cold little creek rushes down the side of the canyon a short distance west down the Grizzly Creek trail.

Descriptions of the trail up to Grizzly Meadows, the climb to Grizzly Lake, the lake itself and the spectacular waterfall are in Trip 17.

Trip 32

High Point Trail to
Rock Lake and Red Cap Lake

Trip Type: Round trip of 2 or 3 days, or day-hike to each of the lakes

Distance: 7.6 miles round trip to both lakes; 4.2 miles round trip to Rock
Lake; 4.4 miles round trip to Red Cap Lake

Elevation Change: 5560 feet, 732 feet per mile; or 2320 feet, 552 feet per
mile (Rock Lake); or 3940 feet, 895 feet per mile (Red Cap Lake)

Season: Late June to early October

Topo Maps: *Salmon Mountain* 1978 and *Youngs Peak* 1979 7.5′ quadrangles

The elevation-change figure for this trip may be misleading since 1300 feet
occur in the .6 mile from the top of the ridge above Red Cap Lake to its shore
and back. Of course, you could skip Red Cap Lake and climb Salmon Mountain
instead, or go out along the ridge to Eightmile Camp, one of the most remote
places you would ever find. If you do skip Red Cap Lake, however, you will miss
the chance to fish for some large eastern brook trout. (Note the key words in
that statement are "fish for," not necessarily "catch.") Contrary to what the
1978 *Salmon Mountain* topo map indicates, Red Cap Lake is indeed within the
Trinity Alps Wilderness, and rightfully so.

    The abundant meadows and open hillsides along this isolated section of the
Salmon River divide and the ridge south of Salmon Mountain are covered, normally
toward the end of June, with a solid carpet of wildflowers. If you are a botanist
or wildflower enthusiast, you can find many unusual and interesting species.
Virgin, climax forest, predominantly red fir, covers the remainder of the crest.

    You most likely won't find many other people in this area, except during
hunting season and possibly at Red Cap Lake. What you will find here in large
numbers are black bears and black-tailed deer, or at least bountiful amounts of

their tracks and scats. Be sure you keep a clean camp and hang your food appropriately.

Difficult access and lack of publicity account for the paucity of visitors to this remote and beautiful corner of Trinity Alps Wilderness. From the south side a long and strenuous trip up the New River and Virgin Creek to the divide awaits you (Trip 21); and from the north side a whole day's drive from virtually any population center is required just to reach the High Point trailhead. Just making it to the town of Forks of Salmon from any direction is a tedious driving experience.

In spite of little use and low maintenance priority, trails along the top of the divide are for the most part, in surprisingly good condition.

This trip doubles back from Rock Lake past the High Point trail junction in order to reach Red Cap Lake at the other end of the trip, then doubles back again to the trailhead. A number of other routes and destinations can be planned by careful study of the topo maps, but be aware that some trails shown on the maps cannot be found on the ground. For example, the trail shown on the Forest Service Wilderness Map to Knownothing Lake absolutely does not exist. To further complicate matters, information from the Forest Service regarding the current condition of these trails is awfully hard to come by, since, depending on the trail, it may pass through two national forests and three different ranger districts. You definitely need something akin to a pioneering spirit to venture into this remote corner of the Trinity Alps.

Starting Point

Forest Highway 93 from Cecilville down the South Fork Salmon River canyon to Forks of Salmon is just about the most thrilling, and slowest, 18.5 miles of paved road you will ever see. One-lane, blind hairpin curves, hung on the sides of steep cliffs, are at least five to the mile. The same "highway" coming up the main Salmon River to Forks of Salmon from Somes Bar at the confluence of the Salmon and Klamath rivers is just as crooked, if not more so. If you're tempted to circumvent Highway 93 by traveling southwest from Etna and Sawyers Bar, guess again—that road is the worst of all. Unfortunately, an easy way to reach Forks of Salmon by automobile simply does not exist.

If you haven't been totally dissuaded from taking this trip by the description of the roads to Forks of Salmon, from the town head south upriver and cross the South Fork bridge to a three-way junction. Turn onto the road farthest to the left, signed "10N04." The road starts south up a canyon, then crosses a creek and switchbacks up the nose of a ridge before turning south again far up on the side of the canyon. Several little-used roads branch off on the way up, but the main road is obvious at all forks. Climb another set of switchbacks and enter a large burned area, the result of a fire in 1977. Renewal is slow here—gaunt skeletons of trees reach for the sky poking up through new brush, dwarfing the younger pines and firs. Some of this area burned again in 1987.

Trip 32
High Point Trail to Rock Lake and Red Cap Lake

At a junction 6.4 miles from the highway, continue straight on Road 10N04. In the middle of the burned area at 7.6 miles from the highway you round a curve and pass road 10N05 on the right. A three-way junction is reached at 8.7 miles, where all roads are identified by number and are signed "NOT MAINTAINED FOR PUBLIC USE." However, the condition of your road, 10N04 turning to the left, is fine. After passing a couple of lesser roads along the way, at 12.5 miles you re-enter live forest, which is very beautiful in contrast to the burned area.

The next junction, 14.7 miles from the highway, is just beyond the knob called High Point. You reach it as you traverse the southeast side of a long ridge overlooking the upper basin of East Fork Knownothing Creek. The highest hump you see on the summit directly south is just above Rock Lake. Road 10N04 turns left down into the valley, but you turn up road 10N07 along the side of the ridge for .8 mile to an old log landing, where some vehicles will have to stop. The road diminishes to a narrow, one-lane track at this point, and the shrubby vegetation hems in even the narrowest of vehicles. A rough, steep track, passable to most vehicles, climbs straight up the side of the ridge west from the landing, then turns up the crest to an almost level area overgrown with tall grass with plenty of room to park, 14.9 miles from the three-way junction back at Forks of Salmon. This is the trailhead, right at the Wilderness boundary.

Description

An old jeep track climbs moderately on the east side of the ridge .5 mile to a trail junction in the saddle at the top of the Salmon River Divide. Just above the junction, nailed to a dead fir tree is a trail sign with an arrow pointing to the right saying "EIGHTMILE CAMP" and an arrow to the left saying "ROCK LAKE."

The trail south along the summit to Rock Lake is well-defined as it climbs away from the saddle through open fir forest floored with grass and low brush. The ascent is steep at first, then eases as you turn southeast across the face of the ridge. Beyond another steep pitch, you head south again and descend moderately on the ridgecrest before turning over the crest to drop down more steeply across the southwest side. A mile from the jeep road you come out in the open above steeply sloping meadows and begin to climb back toward the summit through brush and thickets of young incense cedars. A moderately steep pitch east through red firs brings you to a gorgeous little meadow in a saddle where a profusion of sulfur flowers and naked eriogonums bloom in midsummer.

Considering the low maintenance priority in this area, the trail from the jeep road to this saddle is in very good shape. Before you start the moderately steep ascent southeast up the ridge again, take a moment in the meadow to look up at the ledge below Rock Lake and the steep-sided mountain behind the lake. Many wildflowers, including paintbrush, lupine, valerian mint and wallflower, bloom beside rougher tread as you turn more east across a north-facing slope.

As you climb higher, little Knownothing Lake comes into view, surrounded by brush at the lower end of the valley below. There is no trail, but if you don't mind battling some brush, you can cross-country to Knownothing Lake from the saddle. A half mile of moderate to moderately steep climbing around the head of the valley brings you to the metamorphosed rock ledge that is the north lip of the cup containing 2-acre Rock Lake. You soon step across the tiny, willow-lined outlet stream, and all of the lake comes into view as you climb a short distance on the trail that runs over the shoulder of the mountain and down to a junction with the Virgin Creek trail (see Trip 21).

The almost perfectly round lake is right under the precipitous north side of a granite mountain that sits on the divide. Granite talus falls into the water on the south side, but metamorphic rock slopes up from the rest of the shoreline. How this cup was formed is hard to say. It appears to be a glacial cirque, but there is no other evidence of glaciation along this part of the Salmon River Divide.

One good campsite and a few fair ones are under scattered red firs and western white pines above the eastern shore. The top of a spur ridge east of the lake offers breathtaking views of sunrises and sunsets over the Salmon River

Morning fog fills the Salmon River canyon north of Rock Lake

canyon. Coastal fog often creeps up the canyon at sunrise to set a series of ridges adrift on a pink sea.

Late in the season the water drops below the level of the outlet and the lake loses some of its aesthetic appeal. Fishing is good for eastern brook trout to 10 inches. Red newts will surprise you by rising to the surface to breathe, but they won't take flies.

To get to Red Cap Lake, return 1.6 miles to the saddle and the High Point trail junction, then follow an old road northwest down the other side of the ridge along the upper edge of a wide meadow dotted with clumps of ceanothus and willows. Carpets of wildflowers cover the meadow and the sides of the old road trace. One of the more unusual varieties is skullcap, looking somewhat like a tiny white penstemon.

The road is a washed-out gully farther down, then gets better as it levels out. A fair campsite is beside a little stream that has cut through the road .5 mile from the summit. Raw, red dirt that looked like a mine dump from farther up the hill turns out to be a massive slide at the head of Eightmile Creek as you rise slightly and reach its edge. You have to climb very steeply up the east side of the slide to cross, then drop back down to the road again on the west side.

Continue a moderate rise northwest across the head of the basin above a mass of willows, then climb more steeply through red-fir forest to the ridgecrest and a junction 1.7 miles from the trailhead. The old road on the ridgecrest runs north .5 mile to High Spring at the foot of Salmon Mountain, and south 1.25 miles to Eightmile Camp and a series of beautiful meadows right along the ridgecrest. Travel north down the road approximately 200 yards to a signed junction with the spur trail that heads down to Red Cap Lake. The trail, made up of 13 switchbacks, does not appear on the 7.5 min. topo map, but in reality leads .3 mile to the lakeshore and an intersection with the trail from the northwest (Trip 24).

You can see the 2–3 acre lake as soon as you start zigzagging west down the very steep hillside. It looks gorgeous from up on the ridge, reflecting the sky among lush, green meadows except for red cliffs and talus slopes above the south shore. A long traverse north in the middle of the descent takes you across meadows and gullies to more switchbacks west through scattered firs. Eventually you reach the bottom of the basin and traverse across meadows to meet the north shore of the lake near a campsite sheltered by a grove of firs.

On close inspection, the lake is shallow and weedy, with a very soft mud bottom crisscrossed with large, water-logged trees that jut from the surface here and there. It is not a lake for swimming. It *is* a lake for fishing. "Catching" may be a different story, however. Large eastern brook trout inhabit the dark waters, but you may have difficulty hooking them, and because of the weeds and logs you may also have a tough time landing any fish you do hook.

Plenty of opportunities are available for further exploration. Salmon Mountain, back to the north, doesn't require any technical climbing ability to reach the 6956-foot summit. The route out to wild and lonely Eightmile Camp and the remote country beyond is fully described in Trip 21.

Index

Place names and other subjects that appear in the Table of Contents are not repeated in this index. Please look first in the Table of Contents for more-often-used names and subjects.

Index

Index